Party Polarization in Congress

The political parties in Congress are as polarized as they have been since the early 1900s. This book examines more than 30 years of congressional history to understand how it is that the Democrats and Republicans on Capitol Hill have become so divided. It finds that two steps were critical for this development. First, the respective parties' constituencies became more politically and ideologically aligned. Second, members, in turn, ceded more power to their party leaders, who implemented procedures more frequently and with greater consequence. In fact, almost the entire rise in party polarization can be accounted for in the increasing frequency of and polarization on procedures used during the legislative process.

Sean M. Theriault received his Ph.D. in political science from Stanford University in 2001. An Associate Professor at the University of Texas at Austin, he has received numerous teaching awards. His first book, *The Power of the People: Congressional Competition, Media Attention, and Public Retribution*, was published in 2005. He has published a number of articles on a variety of subjects including congressional retirement, the Louisiana Purchase, and redistricting commissions. Professor Theriault resides with his partner, Anthony Bristol, in Houston and Austin, Texas.

Party Polarization in Congress

SEAN M. THERIAULT
The University of Texas at Austin

CAMBRIDGE UNIVERSITY PRESS
Cambridge, New York, Melbourne, Madrid, Cape Town, Singapore, São Paulo, Delhi

Cambridge University Press
32 Avenue of the Americas, New York, NY 10013-2473, USA

www.cambridge.org
Information on this title: www.cambridge.org/9780521717687

First published 2008

Printed in the United States of America

A catalog record for this publication is available from the British Library.

Library of Congress Cataloging in Publication Data

Theriault, Sean M., 1972–
Party polarization in Congress / Sean M. Theriault.
p. cm.
Includes bibliographical references and index.
ISBN 978-0-521-88893-6 (hardback) – ISBN 978-0-521-71768-7 (pbk.)
1. United States. Congress. 2. Political parties – United States. 3. Opposition (Political science) – United States. I. Title.
JK1021.T32 2008
328.73'0769–dc22 2008002445

ISBN 978-0-521-88893-6 hardback
ISBN 978-0-521-71768-7 paperback

Contents

Acknowledgments

My fascination with party polarization began in 1993 when I was a staff assistant for the Legislative Counsel in the U.S. House of Representatives. Our office was an island in a sea of partisan discord. Stridently nonpartisan, yet under the auspices of the Speaker, the office is responsible for turning legislative ideas into legal language for both Democrats and Republicans. Frequently, the lawyers in the office would scribe a major legislative program with one side in the morning and the tools for its destruction with the other side in the afternoon. Having nonpartisan experts drafting the proposals that will work their way into the U.S. Code provides all Americans with uniformity that would be impossible if each party had its own set of drafters. Even though I left the office in September 1994, my friends in the office say that it is as nonpartisan as it was the day I left.

The office was the perfect place for me to land after my graduation from the University of Richmond. I have always been more comfortable in a family than I have been on a team. Families, much like the Legislative Counsel's Office, figure out a way to put their best face forward. Of course, disagreements occur, but they are hashed out behind closed doors and not in public. Teams, on the other hand, compete and fight in the light of day. While the teams on Capitol Hill embarrass themselves in a multitude of different episodes (some of which are recounted in this book), the Legislative Counsel's Office continues to perform its duties and responsibilities to both the warring teams and the American people. To be clear from the outset, polarized parties need not necessarily be warring parties. It so happens that in the current context, those terms are highly correlated, though we could certainly have responsible parties without the adolescent behavior that has accompanied the polarized parties of today.

This book, I am proud to say, has been a family effort (though I have formed teams – if but in my own mind – against some mean reviewers over the course of this project!). First, and foremost, I must thank my "kids." Since my last Ph.D. year at Stanford, I have come to benefit from hundreds of undergraduates who have been actively engaged in this research project. Listing the students, here, is perhaps my proudest professional accomplishment: Ginger Turner, Court Chillingworth, Anthony Lee, Michael Riemenschneider, Krista Anderson, Carolyn Liu, Nathan Hess, Jonathan Ma, Wesley Yeo, Joe Kanada, James Aldredge, Sean Haynes, Stephanie Portillo, Pam Britton, Corey Herrick, Keith Rainwater, Jeremy Brown, Chris Kilmer, Travis Ridgley, Renee Castillo, Chris Ledel, Kevin Robnet, Brent Chandler, Angie Long, Roxanna Rocha, Lars Clemensen, Leah Mayo, Trae Schultz, Daniela Diaz, Adam Miller, Mark Shanks, Amy Ehlert, Kevin Moczygemba, Chrissy Stegemoller, Liz Hanks, Anne Moore, Colleen Thompson, Hunter Harris, Sara Mueller, Aaron Wood, Nada Antoun, Katie King, Roxanna Rocha, James Aldredge, Chris Ledel, Jodie Rosello, Pam Britton, Chuck Miller, Jessica Rowland, Renee Castillo, Regina Moore, Micah Royer, Brian Chang, Stephanie Noboa, Jonathan Skates, Nikki Iles, Audra Tafoya, Graham Keefe, Andrea Eckelman, Jennifer Kirkham, Stephen McArthur, Lance Gooden, Karen Kolb, Brandon Oliver, Tracey Johnson, Enrique Marquez, Lisa Penn, Lauren Kincke, Jonathan Bartov, Ian Bates, Katie Clemens, Mamta Desai, Trent Engledow, Melody Fisher, Jon Kim, Lindsey McPheeters, Aaron Plumlee, Mark Sanchez, Ella Schwartz, Mark Wimmer, Josh Campbell, Chaille Jolink, Adam Rosenfeld, Nick Bacarisse, Matthew Bessman, Ana Bradshaw, Jordan Leu, Sandra Menjivar, Rachael Klopfenstein, Ross Ziev, Addie Bryant, Grace Garcia, Bret Schenewerk, Carolyn White, Dana Scott, Andrew Carls, Sean Kilkenny, Jeff Asher, Carl Holshouser, Joshua Huck, Katy Quinton, Angel Alfaro, Zac Evans, Brent Chaney, Patrick Luff, Megan Morrow, Matthew Allen, Stephen Myers, Jack Gumpert, Chris Jackson, Edward Cloutman, Ann Gore, R.D. Leyva, Kedron Touvell,

Taryn Dusek, Cody McGregor, Chuck Rossen, Rea Ferandez, Victoria Fowler, Ryan Giggs, Allison Steinberg, Brittany Sukiennik, Megha Salani, Brittany Webre, Drew Jacoby, Brad Janssen, Srujana Pattabathula, Sierra Smith, David Stanley, Vinay Vaz, Michelle Nguyen, Chris Baek, Parker Ramsdell, Stephen Gilstrap, Jessica Janak, Aaron Jaramillo, Natalie Ramirez, Brady Franks, Abbie Berger, Erica Pincus, Tristan Sierra, Alicia Stoll, Michael LaCour, Michael Austin, Patrick Sheets, April Kyle, Hayden Winkler, Wayne Mullanix, Kacy Shindler, Michael Windle, Cathy Patton, Zack Hall, Brianna Bishop, Renee Lattimore, Jeffrey King, Jonathan Shuffield, Eduardo Gardea, and Robin Rosales. I am proud to call each of them fellow researchers and friends. It saddens me that their colleague, Brendan Murray, did not get to see the publication of this book to which he so richly contributed.

This project is better because of the advice I have been given by my extended family in my own Government Department at the University of Texas at Austin and in political science departments throughout the United States. Departments at Texas A&M, Houston, Southern Methodist, Rice, Austin Community College, Nebraska, Michigan, Stanford, Wisconsin, Emory, and Oklahoma heard various parts or earlier versions of this manuscript. A weeklong seminar, under the direction of Dave Rohde and John Aldrich, at Duke University provided a thorough vetting of the manuscript. Numerous friends and mentors have read, reread, and rereread numerous versions of this manuscript, including Roger Davidson, Barbara Sinclair, Jon Bond, Sarah Binder, Dave Lewis, Dan Palazzolo, Randy Strahan, Andy Karch, John Sides, Kathryn Pearson, Jen Lawless, Wendy Schiller, Joe Copper, Frances Lee, Scott Adler, Jacob Hacker, Greg Koger, Dave Rohde, John Aldrich, Mike Brady, Brendan Nyhan, John Coleman, Tim Nokken, Liz Gerber, Barry Weingast, Eric Schickler, Kurt Weyland, John Hibbing, Marc Hetherington, Glen Krutz, Harold Stanley, and three classes of Texas undergraduates in my Party Polarization courses and one class of Montana undergraduates in Greg Koger's Political Parties class. Alas, I have benefited from a multitude of chairs, discussants, and fellow panelists at numerous conferences and a plethora of anonymous reviewers; even the reviewers on the other team helped to make the manuscript better when I begrudgingly followed their advice. Paul Sniderman once again helped me navigate the treacherous waters of book publishing. Eric Crahan, at Cambridge University

Press, made those waters feel like a calm afternoon on Austin's Town Lake. I graciously thank Richard Herrera, Gary Jacobson, Keith Poole, and George Edwards for being generous with their data.

My immediate families have given me the stability, support, and encouragement that I've needed to complete this book. My life with Anthony Bristol (and the "Booboos") is the best of what families offer. Each day with them is better than the one before. Last, but certainly not least, I dedicate this book to my parents, Barbara and Albert. My mother embodies compassion and my father decency. They have never once faltered in giving me the unconditional love that every child so richly deserves.

1

Party Polarization in the U.S. Congress

One year to the date after the Supreme Court's *Bush v. Gore* decision brought the 2000 presidential election to an end, the House of Representatives passed the Help America Vote Act (HAVA). By passing the bill, which authorized $2.65 billion to help localities both update antiquated voting equipment and recruit, hire, and train poll workers, House members hoped they had solved the problems that led to the fiasco in Florida. Three hundred and sixty-two legislators, which included substantial majorities of both parties, voted for the bill's final passage; only 20 Republicans and 43 Democrats voted against it.

Congressional observers and the American public may have been surprised to see the House, an institution criticized for being trapped in partisan warfare, find a bipartisan solution to one of the most highly partisan episodes in American history. Indeed, Democrats and Republicans alike praised House Administration Committee Chair Bob Ney and Ranking Member Steny Hoyer for working together to insure that future ballots are properly cast and appropriately counted. Congressman Chaka Fattah, a Democrat on the committee, offered the following assessment during floor debate: "I want to thank Chairman Ney, who I think has exhibited extraordinary leadership in moving this forward, and Ranking Member Hoyer, [for] bringing together a bipartisan group of people."[1]

[1] Congress, House of Representatives, 107th Congress, 1st session, *Congressional Record* (12 December 2001): H9290.

The overwhelming final passage vote belied procedural differences, which had substantive disagreements at their root, between Democrats and Republicans in the House. John Conyers, the ranking member on the Judiciary Committee, wanted to offer an amendment to the committee bill that would have required state and local governments to meet much more stringent federal voting standards. The Republican leadership prevented the House from voting on his amendment when the Rules Committee reported a closed rule, which the House adopted on a highly partisan 223–193 vote. All but 3 Republicans voted for the rule and all but 16 Democrats voted against it. Fattah's very next comment after praising the committee leaders described the Democrats' frustration with a closed rule: "I know there are some who are disappointed in the rule. I am disappointed in the rule. I would have preferred that we would have been able to have a more open process here on the floor in terms of the House fashioning its will."[2] Nonetheless, when given only a choice of the status quo and the Ney-Hoyer Bill, Fattah and many of his fellow Democrats voted for the latter. When the Republicans blocked Conyers from offering his amendment during floor consideration, the Democrats settled for including it in their motion to recommit the bill to the House Administration Committee with instructions to adopt the amendment and to report forthwith. The House rejected the motion to recommit, 197–226, when all but 1 Republican and 11 Democrats voted along party lines. Within 10 minutes of this rejection, the House passed the bill.

Substantive differences did not play out in the final passage of this bill; rather, substantive disagreements were fought over procedural questions. Rather than defeat Conyers's language in amendment form, which may have subjected their members to criticisms from future opponents, Republicans defeated it through two procedural votes: (1) adoption of a closed rule and (2) defeat of the motion to recommit. The Republican leadership reasoned that they could most easily accomplish their substantive goal (defeat of Conyers's language) in the least electorally damaging way through a sophisticated use of procedures. The Republican's procedural machinations frustrated Democrats, who resorted to using additional procedural machinations on a piece of legislation that enjoyed overwhelming bipartisan support.

[2] Congress, House of Representatives, 107th Congress, 1st session, *Congressional Record* (12 December 2001): H9290.

I. The Argument of the Book

The story behind the House passage of the election reform bill illustrates the argument of this book: the divide between the political parties in Congress can increasingly be characterized as a disagreement about procedures. Behind the simplicity of that statement lurks a complex process involving the voters, the representatives, and the legislative process over more than 30 years of congressional history.

Since the early 1970s, the voters throughout the United States have become increasingly balkanized. For a variety of speculated reasons, voters' decisions on election day are increasingly similar to their neighbors' decisions (Gimpel and Schuknecht 2004, Oppenheimer 2005). The electorates within particular geographic jurisdictions cast increasingly partisan votes. For example, in the 1976 presidential election, when Jimmy Carter beat Gerald Ford by about 2 percentage points in the popular vote, 26.8 percent of the American public lived in a county that gave one of the presidential candidates at least 60 percent of the vote (Bishop 2004). In other words, roughly three-quarters of the American public lived in a county where the presidential votes were distributed fairly evenly between the two candidates. Twenty-eight years later, when George Bush beat John Kerry by about 2.5 percentage points in the popular vote, 48.3 percent of the American public lived in a county where either candidate secured at least 60 percent of the votes. In less than three decades, 80 percent more Americans lived in a county filled disproportionately with either Democratic or Republican voters.

The geographic sorting of partisans throughout America has been exacerbated by at least three political processes. First, voters are increasingly likely to match their ideology with their voting record and partisan identification (Fiorina 2006). Liberal Republicans and conservative Democrats have increasingly been isolated by both their ideology and their party. As the electorate has sorted itself ideologically, jurisdictions have increasingly elected consistently ideological candidates within and between elections.

Second, the creation of safe Democratic and Republican districts through redistricting has created increasingly polarized constituencies (Carson et al. 2007). House districts, which are subject to political manipulations, have become even more partisan than counties, whose borders remain constant. Again comparing data from the 1976 and 2004 elections, 113 representatives in the House came from districts where Carter or Ford got at least 60 percent of the vote compared with 217 representatives who came from districts where Bush or Kerry got at least 60 percent of the vote. Although redistricting is the political punditry's favored explanation for party polarization, political scientists have uncovered relatively little systematic evidence that partisan gerrymandering has had any real effect on growing the partisan divide in Congress. Nonetheless, in particular states in particular redistricting cycles, enough evidence can be harnessed to at least provide the pundits with stories to substantiate their claims.

Third, the increasing importance of increasingly polarized party activists in the nomination process has resulted in the election of increasingly ideological congressional candidates who have increasingly ideological roll call voting records (McClosky, Hoffman, and O'Hara 1960, Herrera 1992, Layman and Carsey 2000, and Fiorina 2006). As the political party professionals have lost power to the hard-edged single-issue interest groups in the early stages of the electoral game, more moderate candidates either are choosing or are being forced to step aside in lieu of more ideologically pure candidates. When these ideologically purer candidates get elected, they are more accountable to and responsive to the ideologically extreme constituents that helped elect them.

The natural sorting of the American voter into purer partisan enclaves in combination with the ideological sorting, redistricting, and nomination manipulations comprises the electoral explanation for party polarization. Although this explanation is logically compelling, the systematic evidence is unconvincing. The electoral explanation suggests that the polarization of members should be differentiated according to the partisanship of their constituencies, and yet, member polarization is pervasive. Perhaps the simplest way to understand that there is more to the party polarization story than changes in the electorate is that even members from the surviving marginal districts – those districts that roughly divide their votes between the two presidential candidates – elect members who cast increasingly ideological votes. Democrats representing these moderate constituencies in the mid-2000s have roll call records that are almost 25 percent more liberal than the Democrats who represented moderate constituencies in the mid-1970s; Republicans in these districts vote 50 percent more conservatively than their 1970s counterparts.

This finding and others like it do not suggest that changes in the electorate are irrelevant to party polarization. The floor debate during the Help America Vote Act nicely illustrates the crucial link between these electoral changes and party polarization in the U.S. Congress. That link is the legislative process. Over the last half century, as the American electorate has sorted and has been sorted, the constituencies that have comprised the respective party caucuses have become more homogeneous. No longer is Speaker Nancy Pelosi trying to mollify two roughly equal ideological wings of the Democratic party as her counterpart, Speaker Sam Rayburn, had to do in the 1950s and 1960s. The dilemma that members used to face between doing what their parties wanted them to do and what their constituents wanted them to do has dissipated as the preferences of a member's party and her constituency have increasingly aligned.

When members stopped being pulled in two different directions, they ceded more power to their party leadership (Rohde and Aldrich 2001). In order to enact the party's agenda in the most efficient and most electorally pleasing way, the majority party leadership has increasingly worked its will procedurally. As John Dingell famously remarked, "If you let me write the procedures and I let you write the substance, I'll [beat] you every time."[3] In debating the Help America Vote Act, the Republican party leadership reduced the Democrats' legitimate substantive argument to a squabble about procedures. Furthermore, they spared their members from having to cast any truly substantive vote other than the one to make voting in federal elections more standardized. Under a less restrictive rule, Democrats would have forced Republicans to either abandon their party or vote against strengthening federal protections in the voting process – a choice Republicans were happy to avoid. As the minority party has been shut out of substantive debates, it has increasingly relied on procedures to make substantive arguments. When the Democrats could not offer the Conyers language as an amendment during floor debate, they offered it as a motion to recommit the bill to committee. Because of

[3] Quoted from Oleszek (1996, 12) – the original Dingell quote contained spicier language than the one reported in Davidson and Oleszek's Congress textbook. John Jackley (1992, 113) attributes a similar quote to Tony Coelho when he was Majority Whip: "Give me process and the other guy substance, and I'll win every time."

the Republican's use of procedures, the Democrats had to rely upon procedures to make their substantive point.

The HAVA debate is not atypical. In the 108th Congress (2003–4), members cast modestly fewer amendment and final passage roll call votes on their most important legislation than the 93rd Congress (1973–4) did. The number of procedural votes that they cast, however, doubled. In the 93rd Congress, there may have been a vote on the special rule of debate for the bill (but not always because most rules were uncontroversial); in the 108th Congress, there was a vote on the special rule as well as the motion to recommit, which would not have been offered in the 93rd Congress because the House would have already given the language a full hearing during the amending process. Furthermore, the increasing degree of party separation on the procedural votes dominates the modest increase in party polarization on amendment and final passage votes. When the procedural votes stopped establishing only the time and manner of debate and started dictating what they could debate, the roll call votes went from being largely unanimous to being almost completely divided along party lines.

Only when the changes within the constituency interact with the legislative process does the complete picture of party polarization in the U.S. Congress come into clearer focus. The Senate, whose constituencies and legislative processes are not as easily manipulated as those of the House, has not been immune to party polarization. In fact, the Senate is about 80 percent as polarized as the House. Although the constituency changes and legislative process changes have also been felt in the Senate, its party polarization has been driven largely by former Republican House members who took the strategies and practices from their House days with them when they moved to the Senate. It is not all former Republican House members who polarized the Senate; rather, it has been almost exclusively those former House members who came to the Senate after 1980.

II. Conclusions Reached in the Extant Literature

This comprehensive explanation for party polarization in the U.S. Congress overcomes the biggest weakness in the extant literature. The two existing families of explanations – those that examine electoral changes and those that examine institutional changes – are independently incomplete. Those scholars who endorse the electoral explanations, including redistricting, the sorting of constituents, and the takeover of party nominations by the extremists have not shown the direct effect that constituency changes have had on the members of Congress. Furthermore, they are unable to explain why even those members from marginal districts have become decidedly more polarized over the last 30 years.

The institutional explanation, by itself, is also incomplete. Those scholars who suggest that institutional changes brought about party polarization in Congress do not rigorously show what gave rise to those changes or why and how the party leadership went about passing and implementing the changes in the institution. It is unlikely that Speakers Jim Wright, Newt Gingrich, and Denny Hastert are simply smarter than their predecessors or that they understand the connection between procedures and the final substance of legislation in a more nuanced way. In this book, I show that as the party caucuses have become more homogeneous, the rank and file members have ceded more power to their party leadership (Aldrich and Rohde 2001). The modern speakers are not necessarily smarter: they are just managing a more cohesive caucus than Speakers James Lawrence Orr, Nicholas Longworth, and Sam Rayburn.

Although the extant literature remains divided as to *the cause* of party polarization, it largely agrees on four basic conclusions. I use these accepted findings as building blocks throughout the construction and testing of my argument.

First, the parties in Congress have been polarizing for around 35 years. For the better part of the 100 years following the end of the Reconstruction, the parties slowly converged to the point that George Wallace, in 1968, complained that there "was not a dime's worth of difference between the parties." Beginning in the years immediately after Wallace's observation, however, party voting in Congress began to increase. A decade and a half later, Poole and Rosenthal (1984) became the first political scientists to recognize and document the modern divergence in how political parties voted in Congress. Although Coleman (1997), Fleisher and Bond (2000, 2003), Rohde (1991), and Stonecash et al. (2003) begin their analysis in the years immediately after World War II, their findings, for the most part, show that most polarization has occurred since the late 1960s and early 1970s. This finding is coupled with another set of polarization studies that only begin rigorous data analysis with the late 1960s and early 1970s (Collie and Mason 2000, Roberts and Smith 2003, and Theriault 2006).[4]

Second, party polarization can be demonstrated with any number of interest group ratings, ideology scores, or roll call summary measures. Different scholars using different methods and different data all show the same basic divergence between Democrats and Republicans in the halls of Congress. Party votes (Coleman 1997 and Stonecash et al. 2003), Party Unity scores (Coleman 1997, Rohde 1991, and Stonecash et al. 2003), DW-NOMINATE scores (Jacobson 2000, Theriault 2006), Americans for Democratic Action (ADA) scores (Brewer et al. 2002, Stonecash et al. 2003), American Conservative Union (ACU) scores (Collie and Mason 2000), and a mixture of ADA and ACU scores (Fleisher and Bond 2000) all show that Democrats have become more liberal and Republicans have become more conservative since the 1970s. Shipan and Lowry (2001) even show how the parties have diverged in a particular policy area.

Third, in as much as the Senate is analyzed, a high degree of similarity is present in divergence between the parties in both the House and the Senate. Fleisher and Bond (2003) and Theriault (2006) are the only aforementioned studies that rigorously deal with the Senate. Both show that the Senate has polarized almost as much as the House over the exact same time period. In fact, the correlation between House and Senate polarization mirrors the correlation among the various scores used to demonstrate polarization within either chamber.

Fourth, as party polarization grows and consumes more column inches in newspapers and more time in party caucus meetings, its causes need to be better understood. Parties composed of ideological members in the extreme lead to policy stalemate and, at the very least, make lawmaking more difficult (McCarty, Poole, and Rosenthal 2006, Gilmour 1995, and Groseclose and McCarty 2001). Although an internally consistent majority party may have an easier time garnering bare majorities to pass legislative proposals, the supermajoritarian requirements of cloture and overriding presidential vetoes make the enactment of that bill into a law more difficult (Krehbiel 1998 and Brady and

[4] Jacobson (2000) conducts half of his analysis from the 1950s onward and the other half from the 1970s onward.

Volden 1998). In part as a consequence of this stalemate, but probably more so as a consequence of the bickering rampant throughout the media, the public reacts negatively to the venom that surrounds a Congress trapped in partisan warfare. As polarization erodes public approval of Congress, the democratic legitimacy of "the people's branch" is undermined (Hibbing and Theiss-Morse 1995, 2002; King 1997; and Hetherington 2005). To resurrect Congress from its low public regard, an increasing number of political pundits and politicians have advocated reforms of both our electoral rules and institutional procedures. Redistricting commissions, open primaries, filibuster-free judicial appointments, and independent blue ribbon commissions are four reforms that have caught on to retard the causes or to alleviate the consequences of party polarization.

III. The Plan of the Book

Whereas the scholars researching party polarization have reached consensus on a number of crucial issues, such as the timing of polarization, the ways to demonstrate polarization, and the importance of understanding polarization, they remain largely divided on the cause of polarization. By the end of the book, I will not satisfy the reader who is in search of *the* cause. Rather, I explore, investigate, and integrate the various causes of party polarization. I will satisfy the reader who is looking for a more thorough understanding of the divide between the parties on Capitol Hill. In doing so, I do not turn the lights out on any particular cause, though I do suggest that the light shining on particular explanations and features of party polarization ought to be adjusted. I explicate the increase in party polarization in ten chapters, which are grouped into three different parts.

The first part of the book lays the groundwork for the analysis, which is presented in the second two parts of the book. The second chapter describes party polarization in Congress, going back to the end of Reconstruction in the late 1800s. This historical background provides a context to understand the current rise in party polarization. Furthermore, this chapter shows how pervasive polarization is throughout the country. In short, polarization cannot be explained entirely by the transformation of southern conservative Democrats into conservative Republicans. The third chapter explicates my argument for party polarization, by first introducing and then building upon the existing polarization studies. Only when the constituency-based changes interact with the legislative process can the entirety of party polarization in the U.S. Congress be understood and explained.

The second part of the book examines the changes that have been taking place in members' constituencies since the 1970s. Chapter 4 examines the changes brought about by redistricting. Chapter 5 examines the ideological and geographic sorting of constituents into more politically homogeneous districts. At the end of the chapter, I show how even members in politically heterogeneous districts have cast increasingly ideologically purer votes. Chapter 6 examines the effect of party activist extremism on member voting in Congress.

While the second part of the book provides the reasons why the legislative process has changed, the third part of the book describes the mechanisms of how it has changed and the ramifications of its changes on party polarization. Chapter 7 examines the connection between politically homogeneous districts and member behavior inside the chambers of the U.S. Capitol. As the constituencies have become more politically slanted, so, too, have the members, the party leaderships, and the committee leaders of both parties in both chambers. Chapter 8 shows how the evolving floor procedures have affected party polarization. In short, almost the entire growth of party polarization in both the House and the Senate since the early 1970s can be accounted for by the increasing frequency of and the increasing polarization on procedural votes. Chapter 9 explicitly considers the link between polarization in the House and polarization in the Senate. Finally, chapter 10 concludes by recapping the lessons of this book and by suggesting future avenues of research for scholars interested in explicating the rise in party polarization in Congress.

PART I

BUILDING BLOCKS FOR EXPLAINING PARTY POLARIZATION

Part I of this book provides the base from which my polarization argument builds in parts II and III. Chapter 2 lays out a systematic description of party polarization and how it has varied over time. The twentieth century began with parties that were even more polarized than the parties today, but the ideological gap between them narrowed for much of the twentieth century. Beginning in the early 1970s, however, members of both parties in both chambers began casting more divisive votes. Chapter 3 places the existing explanations for this increased polarization over the past three decades into a comprehensive model that is then rigorously analyzed in the remainder of the book.

2

A Brief History of Party Polarization

Horrible images of plane crashes, collapsed buildings, and panic throughout New York and Washington, D.C., dominated the airwaves on September 11, 2001. As the president was shuffled from secure location to secure location, members of Congress attempted to restore calm and stability to the American government. On the evening of the attacks, more than 150 legislators – both Democrats and Republicans from both the House and the Senate – gathered on the steps of the U.S. Capitol to declare their solidarity. Speaker Dennis Hastert thundered, "When America suffers, and when people perpetrate acts against this country, we as a Congress and a government stand united and we stand together to fight this evil threat."[1] After a moment of silence, the legislators broke into a spontaneous a capella rendition of "God Bless America."

A day later, Senate Majority Leader Tom Daschle, a Democrat, articulated the same message on the Senate floor: "The world should know that the members of both parties, in both houses, stand united."[2] Hastert's and Daschle's actions followed their rhetoric: within a week, both chambers of Congress passed a Use of Force Resolution giving

[1] Quoted in John Lancaster and Helen Dewar, "Outraged Lawmakers Vow to Keep Hill Going: Briefly Evacuated, Congress Returns to Show Resolve," *The Washington Post*, September 12, 2001, p. A21.

[2] Quoted in Helen Dewar, "Congress Unites to Declare Outrage, Resolve: Casting Differences Aside, Members Back Bush's Intent to Punish People Behind Attacks," *The Washington Post*, September 13, 2001, p. A21.

the president wide latitude to retaliate against the perpetrators of the September 11 attacks and a $40 billion emergency appropriation to help the affected areas. Both pieces of legislation passed unanimously in both chambers but for Congresswoman Barbara Lee's lone dissenting vote on the Use of Force Resolution. Indeed, the entire atmosphere of the American government had been transformed:

> Congress is working in unity to erase the memories of partisan rancor that has been the natural order of Capitol Hill for so many years. The world is different now, they remind one another, so the dysfunctional battles and petty disputes between Republicans and Democrats are inappropriate. Instead, the lawmakers agree, their nation and the world must see that everyone in the United States government is on the same team – working to wipe out terrorism, making sure Americans never have to see such terrifying images of death and destruction in their homeland again.[3]

In the wake of the worst foreign attack ever on American soil, Congress was roundly praised for its unity, resolve, and courage:

> Amid what may be remembered as the single greatest tragedy in our nation's history, Congress stood fast. On the darkest of days, gestures matter, and the show of defiance orchestrated by House and Senate leaders Tuesday stood out as a beacon for millions of citizens groping for answers in the wake of the senseless barbarism perpetrated in New York City, rural Pennsylvania and at the Pentagon. The light inside the Capitol dome never flickered.[4]

This editorial in *Roll Call* was typical of newsrooms' praise for Congress in the days after the 9–11 tragedies.

The political parties, to a naïve congressional observer, may have appeared to enter a new era of cooperation in which the "us" versus "them" mentality was being transformed from Democrats versus Republicans to Americans versus al Qaeda. While Ground Zero continued to smolder, however, partisanship crept back into the Capitol. Before the week was out, Congressman Michael E. Capuano wanted to get back to "daily life." He warned that bipartisanship might last "a week, or it could be a month," but at some point there will be

[3] Karen Foerstel and David Nather, "Beneath Capitol's Harmony, Debate Simmers Patiently," *CQ Weekly*, September 22, 2001, p. 2186.
[4] "Standing Fast," *Roll Call*, September 13, 2001, p. 1.

a return to issues where "I don't think bipartisanship will last."[5] True to Capuano's warning, the upcoming election season jolted the parties back into their pre-September 11 bickering. Within a year of the terrorist attack, the bipartisan atmosphere on Capitol Hill and throughout the country was a faded memory.

In South Dakota and Georgia, Democratic senators were accused of aiding Osama Bin Laden by opposing Bush's design of the Department of Homeland Security – not the overall thrust of the legislation, but the minor details therein. In Montana, highly suggestive photographs from the 1980s forced a Republican challenger – who had been a hairdresser – out of the Senate race. In Arkansas, a conservative Republican senator was castigated for divorcing his wife of twenty-nine years and marrying a younger former staffer in his office. His challenger, after promising to leave the issue aside, spoke incessantly of family values and Christian principles.

President Bush, who had exercised strong bipartisan leadership in Congress a year earlier, raced around the country trying to defeat not only his liberal opponents, but also Democratic lawmakers who cast many votes for his most important legislative accomplishments. Indeed, 2002 was one of the most highly charged partisan elections in American history. "The last few election cycles have been tame compared to what we're seeing this year," commented Darrell West in 2002, "there are more negative ads and more misleading or exaggerated ones than in past years."[6]

The voters on Election Day did little to squash the overtly partisan and mean-spirited attacks. In Georgia and Arkansas, incumbent senators were defeated while most members, representing mostly partisan districts, were returned to Congress with increased vote margins. Bush and the Republicans successfully regained a majority in the Senate, embittering Democrats, who feared that Congress would simply rubber stamp Bush's conservative agenda rather than provide a thorough review and debate in Congress. More frustrating for Democrats

[5] Quoted in David S. Broder, "Lawmakers Standing on Same Side of Aisle, at Least for Now," *The Washington Post*, September 16, 2001, p. A21.

[6] Quoted in Howard Kurtz, "In Ads, It's a Campaign Smackdown: Spots Invoking Bin Laden, Corruption and Crime Termed a Growing Trend," *The Washington Post*, October 25, 2002, p. A3.

was that they did not have an institutional platform from which to pursue their own legislative agenda.

This was the immediate backdrop for the 108th Congress (2003–4), which is described in the first section of this chapter. The second section offers a broad sweep of history by summarizing more than 120 years of party polarization in the U.S. Congress from Reconstruction to the 108th Congress. The third section takes a closer look at the current polarizing period, which began in the late 1960s and early 1970s.

I. Party Polarization in the 108th Congress (2003–4)

With, at best, mixed economic news and a controversial war raging in Iraq, little on the congressional agenda in the 108th Congress did not get trapped in partisan warfare. Although several major pieces of legislation, primarily those with direct links to September 11, 2001, passed with strong bipartisan support, such as the $87 billion appropriation to finance military operations in Iraq and an intelligence overhaul, other issues were highly charged partisan affairs. For example, after having failed to override Clinton's veto in 1996, 1997, and 2000, the Republicans finally succeeded in enacting the partial birth abortion ban. Casualties of the partisan warfare included the importation of prescription drugs and a constitutional amendment "protecting" heterosexual marriage.

Various summary measures, which political scientists and political observers have come to rely on to characterize partisanship in Congress, all suggested that the bipartisan legislation linked to September 11 was an anomaly in the 108th Congress. On measure after measure, the parties were divided into separate camps, with an increasingly vacant zone between them where moderates were once plentiful. Throughout this book, I primarily analyze one of these measures, Poole and Rosenthal's DW-NOMINATE (1997).[7] Their algorithm for determining member ideology, DW-NOMINATE, not only takes account of all nonconsensual votes in one congress, but all nonconsensual votes over all congresses. In that way, the scores from one congress can be

[7] The algorithm for the scores is described in Poole and Rosenthal (1997); the scores, which were updated for the 108th Congress, were downloaded from http://voteview.com/dwnl.htm, accessed on May 17, 2005.

directly compared to the scores of a different congress, though they suggest that these comparisons should only be made "during one of the stable 2-party periods of American history."[8] The DW-NOMINATE scores exist, roughly, on a −1 (extreme liberal) to 1 (extreme conservative) scale.[9]

In the 108th Congress (2003–4), no Republican House member had a more liberal DW-NOMINATE than the most conservative Democratic House member (see panel A of figure 2.1).[10] Not only were the parties completely divided, but the most liberal Republican, Representative Jim Leach, had a 0.151 more conservative DW-NOMINATE than the most conservative Democrat, Representative Ken Lucas.[11] This gulf between the two is more than 7 percent of the entire DW-NOMINATE ideological continuum. Although the complete separation of the parties is unique to the House, party polarization is not. Panel B of figure 2.1 shows the spread of the Senate DW-NOMINATE scores for the 108th Congress. Only Democratic Senator Zell Miller was more conservative than the most liberal Republican, Senator Lincoln Chafee, and two other Republicans.[12]

DW-NOMINATE are not alone in showing the divergence between Democratic and Republican voting on Capitol Hill. Table 2.1 shows

[8] From Keith Poole's web page, http://voteview.com/page2a.htm, accessed on July 16, 2005. Undeniably, cross-congress comparisons can be subject to stringent, and perhaps appropriate, criticisms. Differences in membership, differences in party leadership, differences in legislative agenda, and differences in legislative procedures can all cast doubt on the reliability of cross-congress comparisons, especially considering that members are restricted to linear changes through their congressional careers. Even with their faults, these scores provide the most effective avenue for analyzing cross-congress ideological change. Additionally, the post-Reconstruction period is considered a stable two-party period.

[9] Poole and Rosenthal restrict individual members' scores to change linearly over the course of their careers. They maintain that "higher polynomials in time did not appreciably increase the fit" of the ideological score compositions. As a result of this parametric restriction, some DW-NOMINATE scores exceed −1 and 1.

[10] The one exception to this claim is Representative Ralph Hall, who started in Congress as a Democrat. He was barely more conservative than the most liberal Republican, Representative Jim Leach. Hall switched parties by the end of the 108th Congress.

[11] Incidentally, Ken Lucas and Jim Leach were no longer in the House as the 110th Congress commenced. Lucas honored a self-imposed term limits pledge and retired in 2005. Leach lost in the 2006 election to David Loebsack.

[12] Like their moderate House counterparts, neither Zell Miller nor Lincoln Chafee retained his seat in the 110th Congress. Miller retired at the conclusion of the 108th Congress and Chafee lost in the 2006 elections to Sheldon Whitehouse.

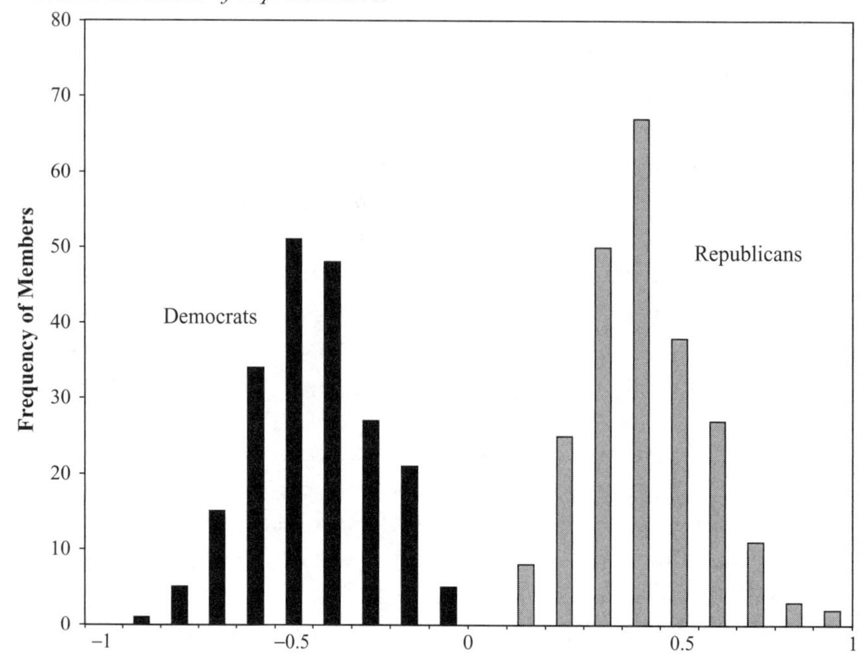

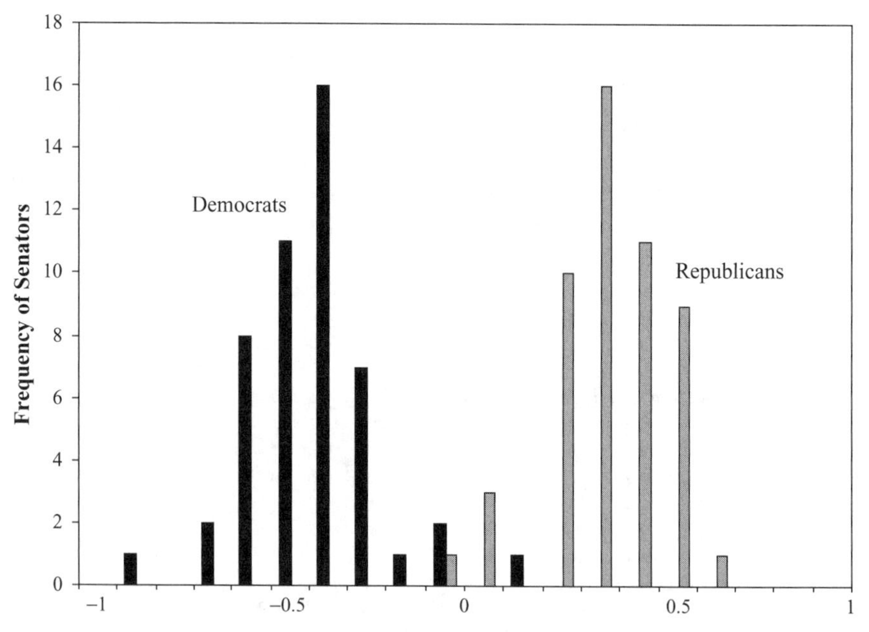

FIGURE 2.1. The Spread of DW-NOMINATE Scores for Democrats and Republicans in the 108th Congress (2003–4).

TABLE 2.1. *Summary of Party Polarization, 108th Congress (2003–4)*

	(A)	(B)	(C)	(D)	(E)
	Political Party Averages		Party Difference	Polarization Scores	Second Moment Separation
	Democrats	Republicans			
DW-NOMINATE	−0.40	0.46	0.86	0.43	5.27
Americans for Democratic Action	87.8	10.8	77.1	0.77	6.68
American Conservative Union	18.5	86.1	67.7	0.68	5.15
Christian Coalition	22.4	88.4	66.0	0.66	3.78
Party Unity[a]	9.2	93.6	84.4	0.84	13.13
Presidential Support	29.7	87.5	57.8	0.58	5.66
Party Disparity[b]	0.12	0.88	0.75	0.75	2.78
The Senate					
DW-NOMINATE	−0.38	0.37	0.76	0.38	4.83
Americans for Democratic Action	85.3	16.7	68.6	0.69	4.74
American Conservative Union	15.0	84.9	70.0	0.70	5.67
Christian Coalition	13.8	93.5	79.7	0.80	4.01
Party Unity[a]	11.0	93.6	82.6	0.83	8.85
Presidential Support	56.9	94.5	37.6	0.38	6.30
Party Disparity[a]	0.21	0.79	0.59	0.59	1.71

[a] Party Unity Scores for Democrats are converted to Republican Unity Scores to preserve the polarization format.

[b] Party averages for the party disparity scores are computed by taking the average percent of party members voting "aye"; for all 401 votes that were taken on the 37 most important pieces of legislation considered in the 108th Congress.

the averages for Democrats (column A), Republicans (column B), and the differences between the averages (column C) for six measures: DW-NOMINATE scores, Americans for Democratic Action (ADA) scores, American Conservative Union (ACU) scores, the Christian Coalition scores, and Congressional Quarterly's Party Unity and Presidential Support scores. The seventh measure, party difference, is computed by comparing Republican votes to Democratic votes on the 37 most important pieces of legislation considered in the 108th Congress.[13]

The Polarization Scores (column D) indicate, on a scale of 0 (no polarization) to 1 (total polarization), the extent to which the parties were polarized in the 108th Congress. For example, if the Democrats were only half as liberal and the Republicans were only half as conservative as they could have been the parties would have been 50 percent polarized. In the House, the parties were only 43.2 percent polarized on the DW-NOMINATE scale, but were 77.1 percent polarized on the ADA scale and 84.4 percent polarized on the Party Unity scores.

The Second Moment Separation (column E) takes into consideration not only the averages of the parties, but also their standard deviations. The values in this column are the average of how many standard deviations the average Democrat is from the average Republican and how many standard deviations the average Republican is from the average Democrat.[14] Given the number of standard deviations between the average Democrat and the average Republican, the Second Moment Separation values suggest that the party averages are quite distant and that the party spreads are quite small. The table shows that DW-NOMINATE scores offer a fairly conservative estimate for polarization. Nonetheless, no matter how the roll call positions are sliced or diced, Republicans on Capitol Hill in the 108th Congress were separated from Democrats.

II. Party Polarization since Reconstruction

Party positions first congealed in Congress when the supporters of the Jay Treaty coalesced into the Federalist party and the opponents

[13] These party difference scores are comprehensively explained and rigorously tested in chapter 6.

[14] It is necessary to take the average of these two numbers because, although the difference between the two parties is the same, the standard deviations for the two parties are different for each of these measures.

organized into the Democratic-Republican party (combs 1970). Ever since, the differences between the political parties comprising the U.S. Congress have waxed and waned. This section explores the divide between the Democratic and Republican parties going back to Reconstruction.

Party Polarization at the Turn of the Twentieth Century

Its splintering in the 1860 presidential race, secession from the Union, and southern defeat in the Civil War decimated the Democratic party throughout the nation. Within 20 years, though, the Democrats were making a comeback. Republicans were already divided from Democrats when Congress handed Rutherford B. Hayes the keys to the White House in 1876, upon his promise to end Reconstruction. As the Republican carpetbaggers were sent north, the South again elected Democrats. In the 45th Congress, the first one after Reconstruction had ended, the Democrats had an average DW-NOMINATE score of −0.40, whereas Republicans' averaged 0.41. The distribution of ideological scores broken down by party for the 45th Congress presented in panel A of figure 2.2 looks strikingly similar to that in figure 2.1.[15]

As the Democrats reasserted their dominance in the South, the parties continued to polarize. Nearly a quarter of a century later and a century before the beginning of the 108th Congress, the 58th Congress (1903–4) met. It shared several characteristics with its modern-day counterpart. First, both congresses were the first congresses following American tragedies. On September 14, 1901, President William McKinley died after being shot by an anarchist at the Pan-American Exposition in Buffalo, New York. Three days shy of the 100-year anniversary of his death, America and the world reeled from the terrorist attacks on the eastern seaboard of the United States. Second, the news from both congresses was dominated by foreign events. News during the 58th Congress was consumed with the Panama Canal, while news during the 108th Congress was dominated by the war in Iraq. Third, at the conclusion of both congresses, popular and controversial presidents, who were both accused of overstepping their constitutional prerogatives, were reelected. Teddy Roosevelt defeated Alton Parker in 1904 and George W. Bush defeated John Kerry in 2004. Fourth,

[15] Although figure 2.2 shows the data only for the House of Representatives, the Senate data are virtually identical.

Panel A: The 45th Congress (1877-9)

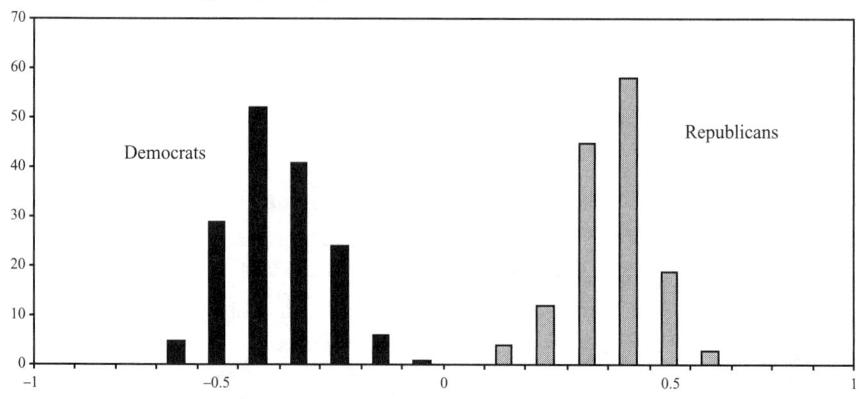

Panel B: The 58th Congress (1903-4)

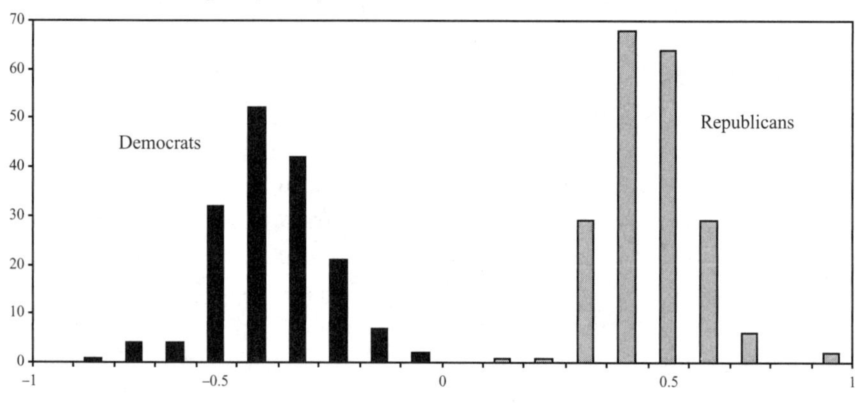

Panel C: The 93rd Congress (1973-4)

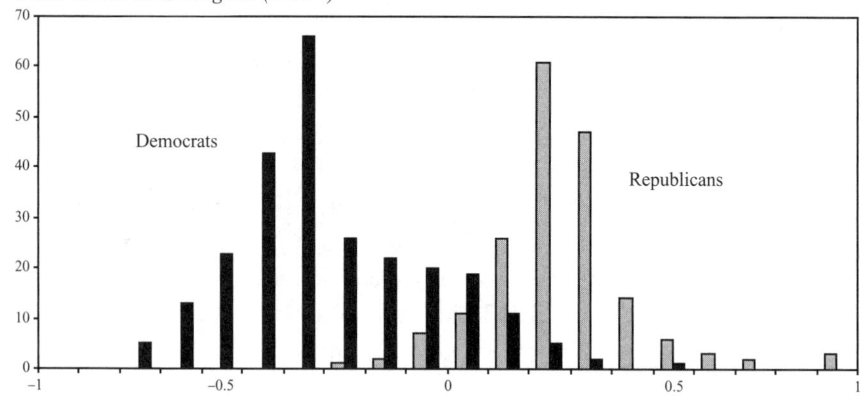

FIGURE 2.2. Party Polarization in the House of Representatives.

the congressional political parties of both congresses were internally homogenous and externally heterogeneous. In fact, the 58th Congress was even more polarized than its modern-day counterpart (see panel B of figure 2.2). Not only was there no ideological overlap in either chamber, but also the parties' means in both chambers were separated by more than 0.9 on the DW-NOMINATE scale. These scores are more polarized than either the 45th or the 108th Congresses. So, too, were the congresses before and after it. In fact, according to the DW-NOMINATE scores, the first decade of the twentieth century was the most polarized in post-Reconstruction American politics.

Party Dynamics in the Middle of the Twentieth Century

If the intervening 100 years between the 58th Congress and the 108th Congress showed pictures similar to figure 2.1 and panels A and B of figure 2.2, I could end this book in the second chapter by declaring that, in fact, the contemporary Congress was not polarized, at least not in comparison to its predecessors. The picture that does emerge from the past 100 in between these bookend congresses shows first a very gradual convergence followed by a more marked divergence between the political parties in Congress. Figures 2.3 and 2.4 show both the degree of heterogeneity between the parties and the degree of homogeneity within the parties in the House and Senate, respectively. The light (likewise, *dark*) gray area represents the spread of the Republican (*Democratic*) party one standard deviation above and below the mean. The lines running through the gray areas are the means of the respective parties' DW-NOMINATE scores.[16] The figure shows that the overall trend from 1877 until at least the mid-1930s is one of party convergence. This convergence, which continued through the Roaring Twenties, the Great Depression, and World War II, reached its zenith in both the House and Senate with President Dwight D. Eisenhower's election in 1952.

The parties remained converged throughout the middle third of the twentieth century. In fact, from the 73rd (1933–4) to the 92nd Congress (1971–2), the party averages were usually less than 0.60 apart (reaching a low of 0.52 percent in the 83rd Congress) of the

[16] Jacobson (2000, figure 2–2) shows that for this time period, the mean and the median are almost identical. Unlike the median, however, the mean's second moment can be calculated.

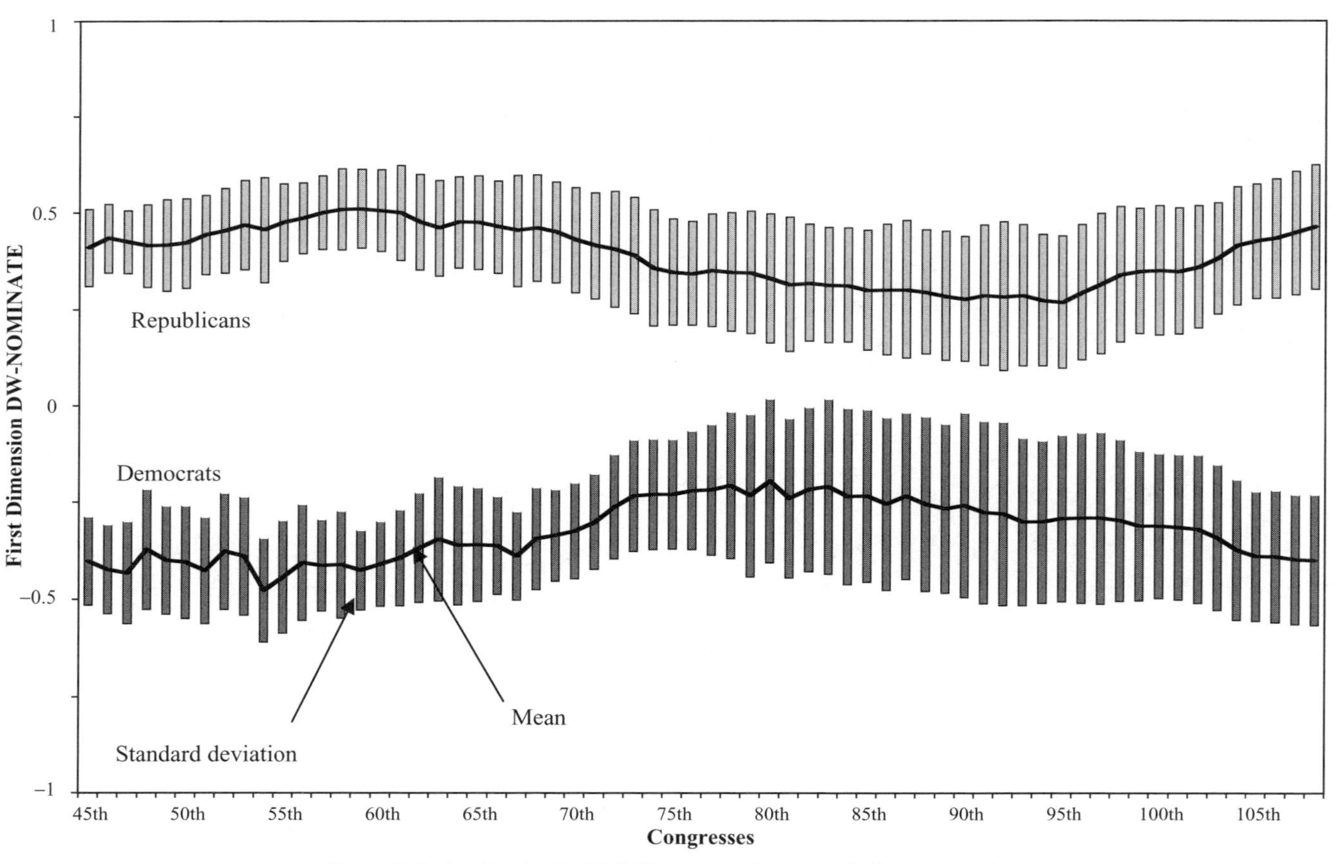

FIGURE 2.3. Party Polarization in the U.S. House, 45th to 108th Congresses (1877–2004).

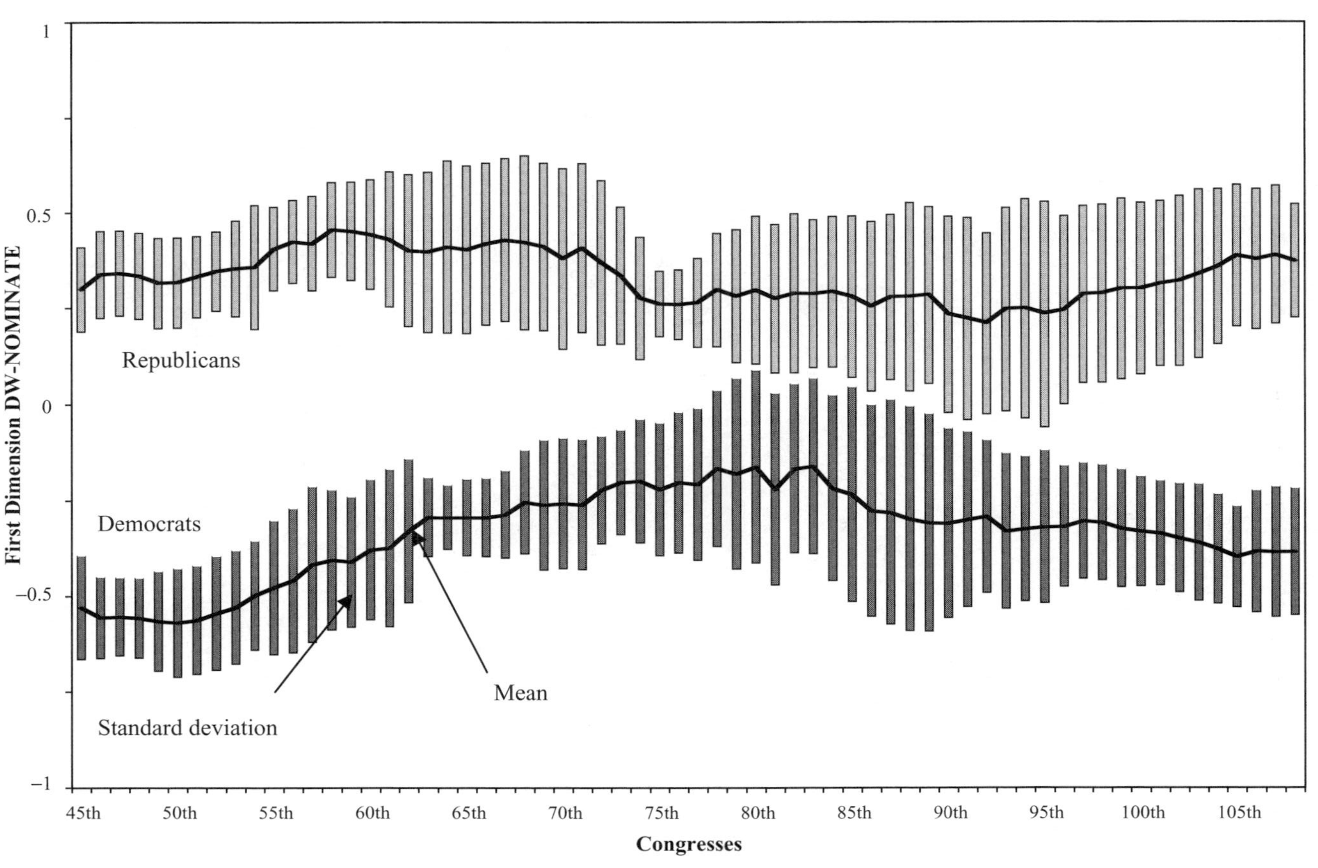

FIGURE 2.4. Party Polarization in the U.S. Senate 45th to 108th Congresses (1877–2004).

DW-NOMINATE scale. Over the 38 years, the Senate was even less polarized than the House (reaching a low of 0.45, also in the 83rd Congress). This period, characterized by comity and stability under the leadership of Speaker Sam Rayburn, has come to be known as the "Textbook Congress" (Shepsle 1989). In this era, the political party leadership was relatively weak vis-à-vis the committee system and most members stridently adhered to and vigorously enforced the House norms and Senate folkways (Asher 1973, Matthews 1960, Clapp 1963, and Fenno 1966).

Even though the issues – including those resulting from the Great Depression, World War II, the Korean War, the Civil Rights Movement, and the Vietnam War – that these congresses confronted were the biggest and most important of the century, they confronted them first as Americans, second as members of Congress, and only third as Democrats or Republicans. Although Civil Rights and the Vietnam War would become highly contentious partisan battles, the predominance of conservative southern committee chairs kept the Democratic party from employing overtly partisan strategies on the major issues until the Textbook Congress gave way to the post-reform Congress.

By the end of this 40-year period of stability, the parties were decidedly not polarized, giving rise to George Wallace's complaint that there was "not a dime's worth of difference" between the parties in the 1968 presidential election. Panel C of figure 2.2, showing the 93rd Congress, differs dramatically from figure 2.1 and the first two panels in figure 2.2. Not only were the party averages more than one-third closer (Democrats had a −0.28 average and Republicans had a 0.28), but also both parties, especially the Democrats, occupied more space on the continuum than in those congresses that either preceded or succeeded it. Furthermore, 95 percent of Republicans were more liberal than the most conservative Democrat, and 36 percent of Democrats were more conservative than the most liberal Republican. This trend was not lost on political observers, who, beginning with the Eisenhower Administration, declared "the end of ideology." This assessment reflected the cutting-edge work in academia. Anthony Downs (1957) predicted that as these electoral coalitions raced toward the political middle in hopes of capturing the pivotal "median voter," political parties would, under certain conditions, converge.

Political scientists lamented what they deemed the end of "responsible government." The American Political Science Association (1950, 17), in a rare attempt to influence politics, released a report entitled "Toward a More Responsible Two-Party System," in which it warned, "It is dangerous to drift without a party system that helps the nation to set a general course of policy for the government as a whole." Many political scientists joined in decrying what were described as "weak parties" and calling for a return to more ideologically based parties (Bailey 1959, Burns 1963, Broder 1972, and Sundquist 1988). Although the trend of convergence continued another 20 years, "responsible" parties returned with a vengence.

Party Polarization in the Post-Reform Congress

Perhaps out of deference to the learned professionals in political science, as a result of the political tumult caused by the Vietnam War and Watergate, or in the wake of various successful reform efforts, the political parties in Congress began separating in the mid-1970s. This book rigorously examines this period from 1973–2004. I begin with the 93rd Congress (1973–4) for several reasons. First, figures 2.2, 2.3, and 2.4 demonstrate that party polarization began in earnest in the early 1970s. Within 10 years of Watergate, the parties' mean DW-NOMINATE separated by 13 percent in the House and 19 percent in the Senate. By the end of the 108th Congress, the separation between the parties had increased to 44 percent in the House and 38 percent in the Senate. This monumental change dwarfs the changes occurring during the middle of the twentieth century. Beginning the analysis prior to the 93rd Congress would anchor the analysis in congresses in which little changed weakening the trends analyzed throughout the rest of the book. As such, beginning with the 93rd Congress provides the cleanest analysis by which to understand the current trend of polarization.

Second, in 1973, the House implemented electronic voting. Up until then, the clerk had to call the entire roll during a floor vote, which could take more than an hour. With electronic voting, roll-call votes now can take as little as five minutes (when the House takes a series of votes in succession). This transition to electronic voting certainly changed the leaderships' floor strategies for deciding which issues should be subject to roll-call votes (Smith 1989). Given that the analysis in this book depends so heavily upon the actual roll-call votes conducted on the House floor, the inclusion of both actual roll calls and electronic votes in the same analysis would be suspect.[17]

Third, by 1973, the tumult caused by the Supreme Court decisions of the 1960s had worked their way through the congressional redistricting process. A series of decisions mandated that states redraw their district lines a number of times during the 1960s.[18] Due to the ever-changing district boundaries in the 1960s, it is much more difficult to see if members' voting behavior is tied to their constituencies. By the time the 93rd Congress met, the members had to come from precisely equal population districts from across the state – the standard still in use today.

III. The Development of Polarization Scores

Most of the analysis up until now analyzes ideology as measured by DW-NOMINATE. The "liberalness" of the Democratic party was compared to the "conservativeness" of the Republican party to show the degree of ideological difference between the parties. From these scores, which necessarily entail a comparison between the parties, I develop a measure called "polarization scores." These polarization scores collapse the ideology of Democrats and the ideology of Republicans into one number – the separation between the parties. This transformation from ideology scores to polarization scores makes the analyses throughout the book easier. Instead of conducting parallel analyses to explain the growing conservativeness of Republicans and the growing liberalness of Democrats, the use of polarization scores simply requires an analysis of the growing divergence between Republicans and Democrats.

Polarization scores are the proportion of total possible polarization between the two political parties. As proportions, they vary between 0 (no polarization) and 1 (total polarization). If a legislature was equally divided between Democrats and Republicans and party affiliation had

[17] This concern, of course, does not affect Senate roll call votes, which even after 1973 are still done by the clerk calling the roll.

[18] See Cox and Katz (2002) for an excellent review of these Supreme Court opinions.

no effect on roll-call voting, the polarization score would be 0. If, on the other hand, party affiliation perfectly predicted roll call voting, the polarization score would be 1. If party affiliation perfectly predicted half of the votes and had no effect on the other half, or if the parties perfectly controlled half of the legislators and had no effect on the other half, the party polarization score would be 0.50.

To put more flesh on the bone, consider the following "Senate" made up of only four senators. Their actual DW-NOMINATE scores from the 93rd Congress (1973–4) are:

Church	Democrat	−0.38	Stevens	Republican	0.11
Hollings	Democrat	−0.21	Dole	Republican	0.27
Democratic	**Average**	−0.30	**Republican**	**Average**	0.19
		Polarization Score: 0.24			

In comparison to a totally polarized chamber where every Democrat scored −1 and every Republican scored 1, this four-person chamber has a polarization score of 0.24, which is the average of the Republican DW-NOMINATE average and negative one times the Democratic DW-NOMINATE average.[19] In other words, the chamber was only about 24 percent as polarized as it could have been. Now consider the following four senators' DW-NOMINATE from the 108th Congress:

Kennedy	Democrat	−0.57	McCain	Republican	0.25
Breaux	Democrat	−0.07	Lott	Republican	0.49
Democratic	**Average**	−0.32	**Republican**	**Average**	0.37

This four-person chamber has a polarization score of 0.35. In comparing the two chambers, we could say that the Senate in the 108th

[19] Polarization scores are weighted for the number of members from each party. The example in the text does not consider the weight because both parties in the fractious congress had two members. If the Democratic average of −0.30 were based on four senators instead of two, the polarization score of this six-senator congress would be 0.26.

Congress is 0.11 more polarized than the Senate in the 93rd Congress. A nice feature of this algorithm is that polarization scores can be computed using any of the roll call summary measures discussed in table 2.1.

This simplification of partisan ideological scores into polarization scores does not come without a cost. Once the members of both parties are combined into one score, the distinction between Democrats and Republicans is lost. In other words, by simplifying the partisan ideological scores, I am unable to draw distinctions between the growing liberalness of Democrats and the growing conservativeness of Republicans. For example, from the 93rd to the 108th Congress, the Democrats in the House (likewise, *Senate*) became 0.10 (*0.05*) more liberal on the DW-NOMINATE scale and Republicans became 0.18 (*0.13*) more conservative. When the data separated by party are analyzed together in the development of the polarization scores, the fact that Republicans were responsible for more than half the change in polarization is masked by a number that indicates that the House (*Senate*) is 0.14 (*0.09*) more polarized.[20] Throughout the analysis, when the data call for it, I revert to ideology scores to show distinctions between the polarization of Democrats and the polarization of Republicans. For most of the analyses, however, the polarization scores suffice because the parties polarized similarly.

The black bars in both panels of figure 2.5 show how the polarization scores in the House (panel A) and Senate (panel B) have changed since Reconstruction (the 45th Congress). The overall impression left by figure 2.5 is the same as that left by figures 2.3 and 2.4. The political parties were far more polarized at the end of the eighteenth century and at the beginning of the nineteenth century than they were at any other time since Reconstruction. Party polarization was lowest in the middle third of the twentieth century (from roughly 1932 to 1974). Since 1973, polarization has increased every congress, almost without exception.

As further evidence of the second claim from chapter 1, different measures yield very similar pictures. Party polarization, at least since the 1970s, can be demonstrated with a variety of roll call summary

[20] See Theriault (2006) and Hacker and Pierson (2005) for a more thorough analysis of how much more the Republicans have polarized than the Democrats.

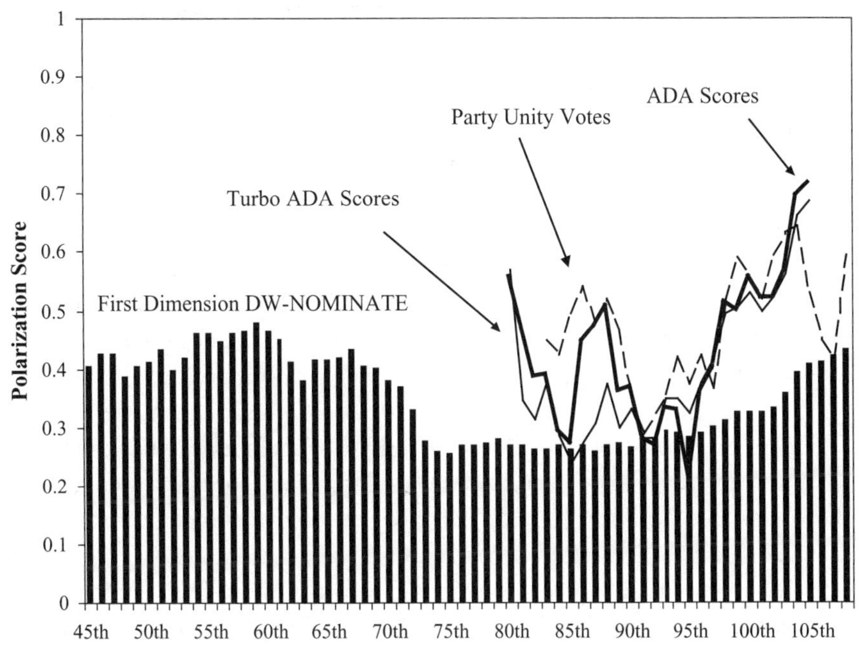

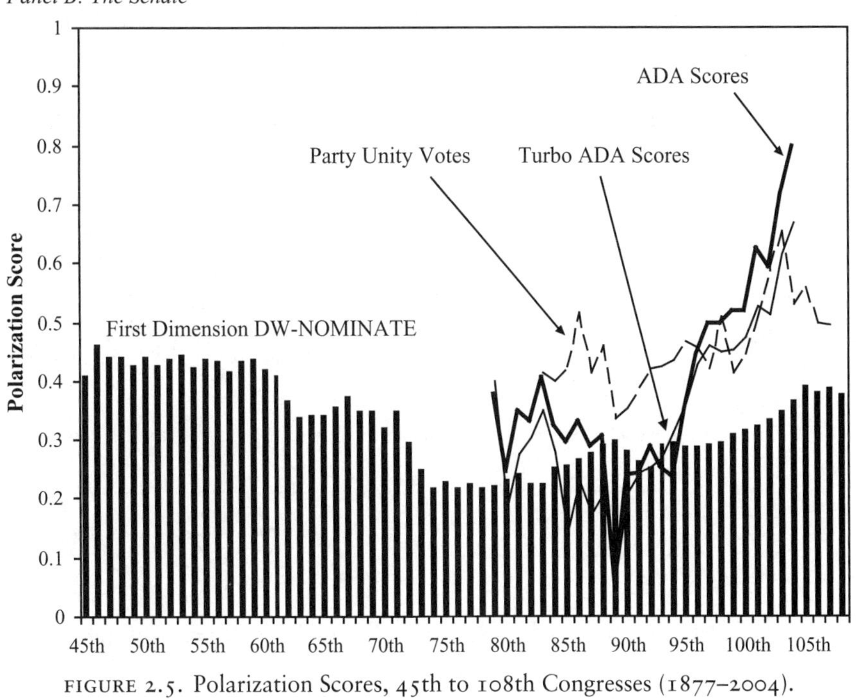

FIGURE 2.5. Polarization Scores, 45th to 108th Congresses (1877–2004).

measures. Party Unity voting in the U.S. House and the ADA measures suggest that the mid-twentieth century congresses were almost as polarized as the current congresses.[21] Nonetheless, all of the measures show that party polarization has increased since the mid-1970s. Between the 93rd Congress (1973–4) and the 105th Congress (1997–8) – the last congress for which the Turbo-ADA scores are available – the DW-NOMINATE polarization score increased 39 percent, the ADA polarization score increased 118 percent, the Turbo-ADA score increased 98 percent, and the percentage of Party Unity voting increased 49 percent.

Panel B of figure 2.5 shows that the Senate polarization scores closely mirror the House polarization scores.[22] Again, both ADA measures show less polarization in the mid-twentieth century, though from the 1970s onward, all the measures are closely aligned. From the 93rd Congress to the 105th Congress, the DW-NOMINATE polarization score increased 33 percent, the ADA polarization score increased 178 percent, the Turbo-ADA score increased 162 percent, and the percentage of Party Unity votes increased 26 percent.

Not only do all the measures show a pronounced increase in the polarization of the chambers since the early 1970s, but all of the measures are highly correlated within the chambers and also across chambers. Over the 22 congresses from the 84th Congress to the 105th Congress, where we have estimates for the four measures in both chambers, the correlation between any two is never less than 0.45 and is always statistically significant (the highest p-value is 0.02).[23] When

[21] DW-NOMINATE show that the mid-century congresses were less polarized than either the ADA-based scores or the Party Unity votes. Parts of the disparity among these scores arise from the use of only the first dimension of DW-NOMINATE. The second dimension of these scores shows more disparity in the mid-century and less disparity toward the end of the twentieth century. Also, according to Poole-Rosenthal (1997), the second dimension plays a much smaller role in member voting. When both dimensions are considered, the Poole-Rosenthal scores show a slightly different polarization trend (see Theriault 2005).

[22] Their correlation is 0.47 ($p = 0.07$).

[23] The correlation coefficients for the two chambers from the 84th to the 105th Congress are:

House of Representatives				Senate			
	DW-NOM.	ADA	T-ADA		DW-NOM.	ADA	T-ADA
ADA	0.73			ADA	0.74		
T-ADA	0.87	0.88		T-ADA	0.70	0.95	
P. Unity	0.45	0.80	0.68	P. Unity	0.74	0.77	0.71

the data are restricted to the current polarizing period, the series are even more highly correlated.[24]

The stark difference between how Democrats vote and how Republicans vote is also present at the individual roll call vote levels. The Congress has taken 7027 roll call votes on the 609 most important pieces of legislation, as designated by Mayhew (1991) and Edwards et al. (1997, 2000), from 1973 to 2004.[25] For each roll call vote, I compute a party difference score, which is simply the absolute difference between the percentage of Republicans and the percentage of Democrats who vote the same way on the roll-call vote.[26] For example, if all members vote together, the party difference measure would be 0. If every Democrat voted against every Republican, the measure would be 1. If 60 percent of Democrats sided with 90 percent of Republicans, the party difference measure would be 30 percent (90 percent – 60 percent). In both the House and the Senate, the party difference scores in the 108th Congress are more than twice as much as they were in the 93rd Congress (see figure 2.6). Given this increase over time, it is not surprising that the party difference trends are highly correlated to the trends of the DW-NOMINATE scores.[27]

The polarization score analysis based on DW-NOMINATE, ADA, Turbo-ADA, Party Unity votes, and party difference scores verify three findings from chapter 1. First, the parties are polarized (and have

[24] The correlation coefficients for the two chambers from the 93rd to the 105th Congress are:

House of Representatives				**Senate**			
	DW-NOM.	ADA	T-ADA		DW-NOM.	ADA	T-ADA
ADA	0.93			ADA	0.91		
T-ADA	0.97	0.99		T-ADA	0.89	0.98	
P. Unity	0.44	0.82	0.82	P. Unity	0.64	0.70	0.70

[25] Mayhew updates his list every Congress. The most important legislative enactments can be found at: http://pantheon.yale.edu/~dmayhew/data3.html. Using Edwards' methodology, I updated his list of major failures. The list can be downloaded at: http://web.austin.utexas.edu/seant/failed.pdf

[26] The computation of the party difference measure is the same as Turner's (1970, 42) "index of likeness," except that he subtracts the difference measure from 100 to arrive at his likeness score.

[27] They are highly correlated with one another (0.86; $p = 0.00$) and DW-NOMINATE scores (0.88 for the House and 0.95 for the Senate; both $p = 0.00$).

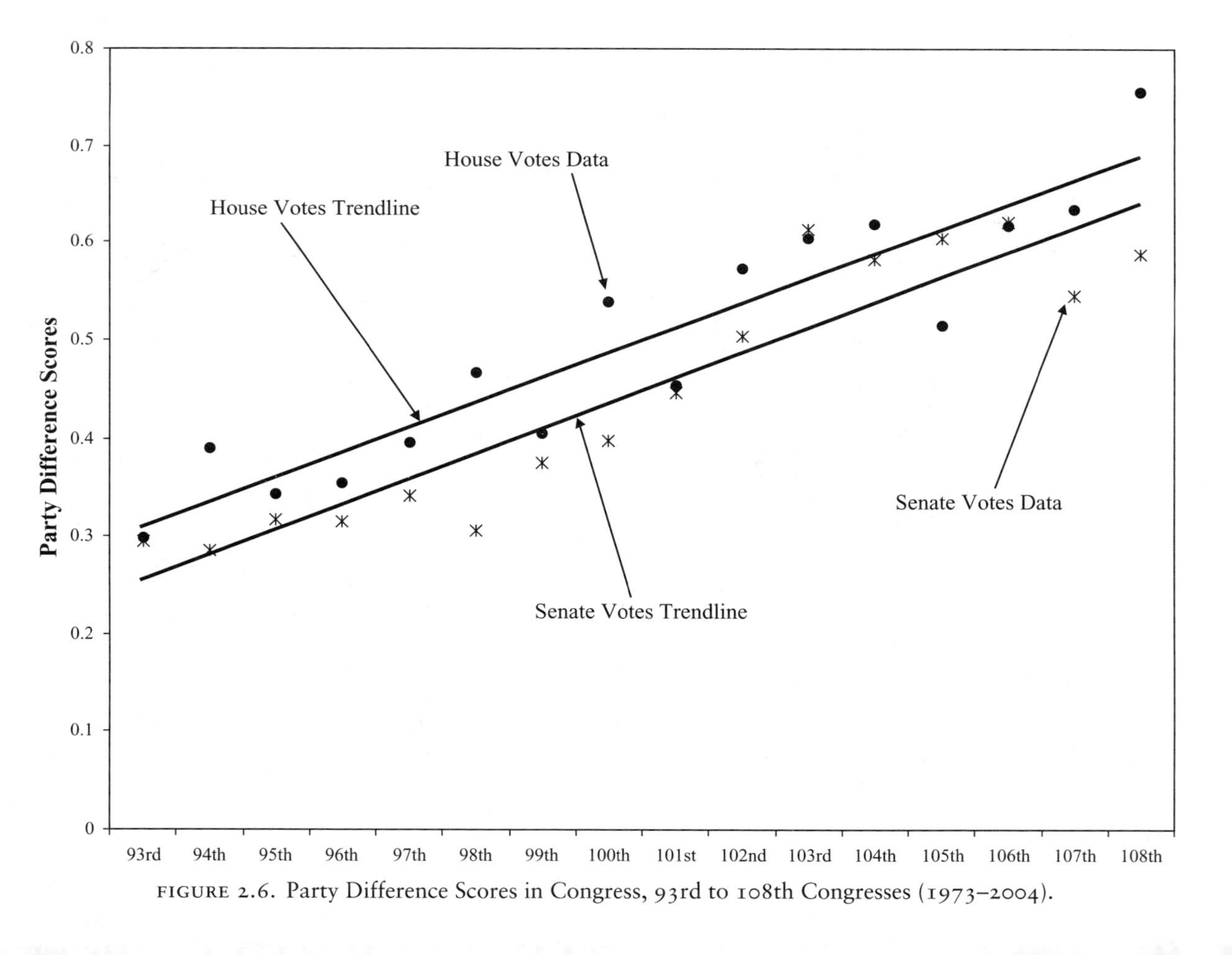

FIGURE 2.6. Party Difference Scores in Congress, 93rd to 108th Congresses (1973–2004).

TABLE 2.2. *Kansas's Polarization Score*

District	Party	Member	PR Score	Polarzation Score
Panel A: Polarization Score in the 92nd Congress (1973–4)				
1	Republican	Keith Sebelius	0.33	0.33
2	Democrat	William Roy	−0.21	0.21
3	Republican	Larry Winnn	0.27	0.27
4	Republican	Garner Shriver	0.20	0.20
5	Republican	Joe Skubitz	0.21	0.21
		Kansas's Polarization Score		**0.24**
Panel B: Polarization Score in the 108th Congress (2003–4)				
1	Republican	Jerry Moran	0.45	0.45
2	Republican	Jim Ryun	0.59	0.59
3	Democrat	Dennis Moore	−0.26	0.26
4	Republican	Todd Tiahrt	0.48	0.48
		Kansas's Polarization Score		**0.45**

become more polarized over time, especially since the early 1970s). Second, the polarization is not dependent upon the measure analyzed – all the measures paint very similar pictures. Third, both the House and the Senate have polarized similarly over time.

What these analyses do not show is that the substantive difference between the parties' positions has similarly grown. The various roll-call-based measures show that on key votes (ADA scores), all non-consensual votes (DW-NOMINATE), and votes on major legislation (party difference scores), the parties are increasingly voting differently from one another. None of these measures considers the substance underlying the roll call votes. In this chapter and for the remainder of the book, the term polarization refers to the divide between how the parties vote and not necessarily the substantive difference between the parties. The latter of these trends is a worthwhile research project, but beyond the scope of this book.

IV. Polarization Scores within State Delegations

Just as party polarization scores can be computed for the entire House and Senate, so can they be computed for all state delegations within

TABLE 2.3. *Most and Least Polarized State Delegation in Congress*

State	Polarization Score	State	Polarization Scores 93rd Cong.	108th Cong.	Change
Panel A: The House of Representatives					
Most Polarized in the 108th		*Delegations with the Greatest Increase in Polarization*			
Arizona	0.63	South Carolina	0.14	0.51	0.37
Colorado	0.61	Colorado	0.26	0.61	0.35
Massachusetts	0.56	Georgia	0.13	0.45	0.32
Indiana	0.51	Massachusetts	0.24	0.56	0.32
South Carolina	0.51	Virginia	0.13	0.42	0.29
Wisconsin	0.50	Louisiana	0.04	0.33	0.29
California	0.49	Oklahoma	0.14	0.41	0.27
Minnesota	0.48	Oregon	0.19	0.45	0.26
Oregon	0.45	Mississippi	0.10	0.36	0.26
Georgia	0.45	North Carolina	0.19	0.44	0.25
Least Polarized in the 108th		*Delegations with the Least Increase in Polarization*			
West Virginia	0.25	Iowa	0.57	0.35	−0.22
Arkansas	0.28	West Virginia	0.29	0.25	−0.04
Connecticut	0.29	Nebraska	0.32	0.36	0.05
Kentucky	0.30	Tennessee	0.30	0.35	0.05
Louisiana	0.33	Arkansas	0.24	0.28	0.04
Tennessee	0.35	Pennsylvania	0.32	0.37	0.05
Iowa	0.35	New York	0.33	0.40	0.07
Nebraska	0.36	California	0.41	0.49	0.08
Mississippi	0.36	Washington	0.34	0.43	0.09
Alabama	0.37	Maryland	0.30	0.39	0.09
Panel B: The Senate					
Most Polarized in the 108th		*Delegations with the Greatest Increase in Polarization*			
Wisconsin	0.62	New Jersey	0.04	0.58	0.54
Oklahoma	0.61	Alabama	−0.03	0.48	0.51
New Jersey	0.58	Maryland	−0.01	0.50	0.51
Wyoming	0.57	Mississippi	−0.07	0.41	0.48
Kentucky	0.52	Massachusetts	0.15	0.51	0.36
Massachusetts	0.51	New York	0.13	0.46	0.33
Maryland	0.50	Kentucky	0.21	0.52	0.31
Alabama	0.48	Kansas	0.15	0.43	0.28
Michigan	0.48	Oregon	0.01	0.28	0.27
Idaho	0.48	Pennsylvania	0.01	0.25	0.24
Least Polarized in the 108th		*Delegations with the Least Increase in Polarization*			
Maine	0.07	Maine	0.49	0.07	−0.42
Georgia	0.13	Nebraska	0.52	0.21	−0.31
Louisiana	0.15	South Dakota	0.66	0.36	−0.30
Nebraska	0.21	Montana	0.52	0.29	−0.23
Arkansas	0.24	Arizona	0.64	0.42	−0.22
Pennsylvania	0.25	Indiana	0.46	0.26	−0.20
Indiana	0.26	Iowa	0.61	0.47	−0.14
Ohio	0.26	Virginia	0.43	0.31	−0.12
Alaska	0.26	Utah	0.44	0.34	−0.10
Rhode Island	0.26	Rhode Island	0.37	0.26	−0.11

both chambers.[28] These state polarization scores will be helpful in analyzing the geographic-based explanations for party polarization. To appreciate their derivation, consider the Kansas House delegation in the 93rd and 108th Congresses (see table 2.2). In both congresses, the lone Democrat was among the least polarized members (i.e., the most moderate) of the entire delegation. Kansas's state polarization score nearly doubled from 0.24 in the 93rd Congress to 0.45 in the 108th Congress.

A perusal of these scores for all states in both congresses shows that polarization has not occurred uniformly throughout the United States. Some states have experienced more polarization than other states. Over the polarizing period from the 93rd Congress (1973–4) to the 108th Congress (2003–4), a few states have even become more moderate. The states with the most and least polarized House and Senate delegations in the 108th Congress, as well as the states that have polarized the most and least in both chambers are listed in table 2.3.[29]

The table reveals four interesting facts. First, perhaps because the Senate has fewer members, state delegations are more variable in the Senate than they are in the House. The House (*Senate*) standard deviations of the state polarization scores in the 108th Congress are 0.10 (*0.12*). Second, these standard deviations are lower than they were in the 93rd Congress –0.11 (*0.18*) – indicating that polarization is currently happening more consistently throughout the United States than it was more than 30 years ago. Third, as witnessed by the inclusion of Massachusetts on both most polarized lists and Nebraska on both least polarized lists, the scores between chambers are correlated (0.521, $p = 0.001$).[30] Fourth, polarization seems to be partly, but not

[28] States that are uniformly liberal or uniformly conservative will have polarization scores similar to states that have some liberal and some conservative members. For example, if a state has two liberal Democratic members that both have ideology scores of -1, its polarization score is 1, which is the same as a state with one liberal Democrat (with a -1 score) and one conservative Republican (with a score of 1). As such, these scores should be interpreted in light of how they polarize the chambers and not as a degree of contentiousness within state delegations.

[29] Because the results for House delegations with two or fewer members are so idiosyncratic, they are not listed in table 2.3. For the record, Delaware, Hawaii, Maine, Montana, and Rhode Island had less polarization than Maryland and Nevada and Vermont had more polarization than North Carolina.

[30] Although the polarization scores are correlated across chambers, they are not necessarily correlated over time. For example, in comparing the 93rd Congress to the

totally, a southern phenomenon (see Brewer, Mariani, and Stonecash 2002). Seven House and three Senate state delegations that have polarized most are southern; however, two southern House delegations and one southern Senate delegation are among the states that have polarized the least.[31] Although the House (*Senate*) state delegations in the South polarized 2.5 (4) times more than the northern delegations, North and South in both the House and Senate have polarized (see figure 2.7).[32] These state polarization scores are helpful in putting some flesh on the bone of party polarization. Additionally, they are helpful in analyzing the role of redistricting in party polarization. In chapter 4, I test to see if states with radical redistricting changes polarize more rapidly than states with little or no redistricting changes.

V. The Mechanisms Underlying Polarization

This section analyzes the divergence between the parties by exploring the underlying dynamics that have led to the increased polarization. Although the parties in Congress and state delegations to both the House and the Senate have certainly polarized, it is the seat-by-seat changes from one congress to the next that provide the micro-building blocks producing the trends captured in figures 2.3 and 2.4. Over the past 30-plus years, long-serving members have become more ideological over the course of their careers, and new, more ideological members are replacing their more moderate predecessors.

Two vignettes illustrate the micro-level mechanisms of polarization. First, in 1976, Gale McGee, Chairman of the Post Office and Civil Service Committee, sought a fourth term for his Wyoming Senate seat. McGee, a Democrat, was legendary in using his committee power to send money back to Wyoming. His opponent, Malcolm Wallop,

108th Congress, the state polarization scores were significantly lower in both the House (0.28, $p = 0.05$) and Senate (-0.01, $p = 0.97$).

[31] McCarty, Poole, and Rosenthal (2005, 32) analyze polarization including and excluding the South (see their figure 2.18). They show a small southern effect, though "the figure suggests that polarization among non-Southern legislators is the driving force."

[32] An analysis of both the polarization scores and the number of members from the North and South reveals that 63.9 percent of the House polarization comes from the South, even though the South only made up 33.3 percent of the House in the 108th Congress. The South is responsible for 47.4 percent of the Senate polarization, even though its members comprise only 26 percent of the Senate membership.

Panel A: The House of Representatives

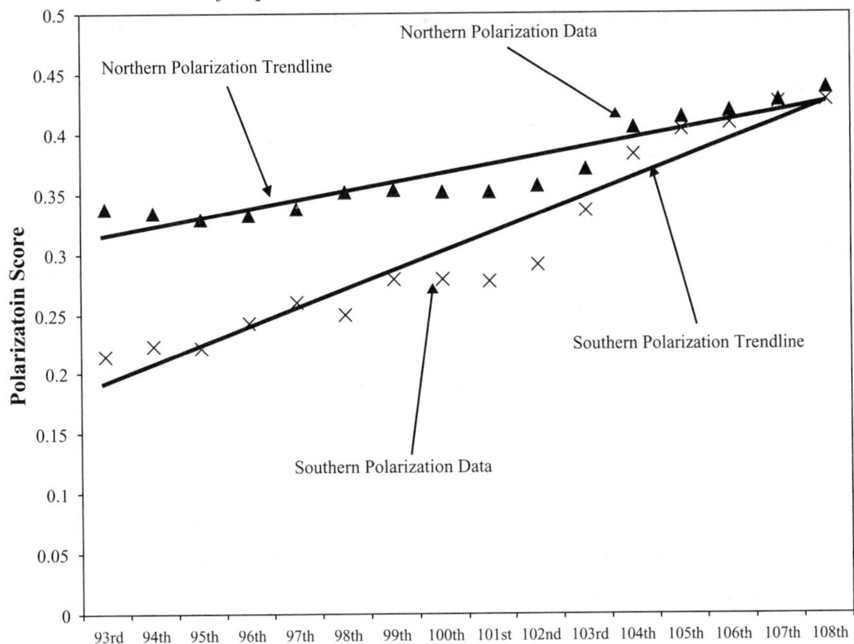

Panel B: The Senate

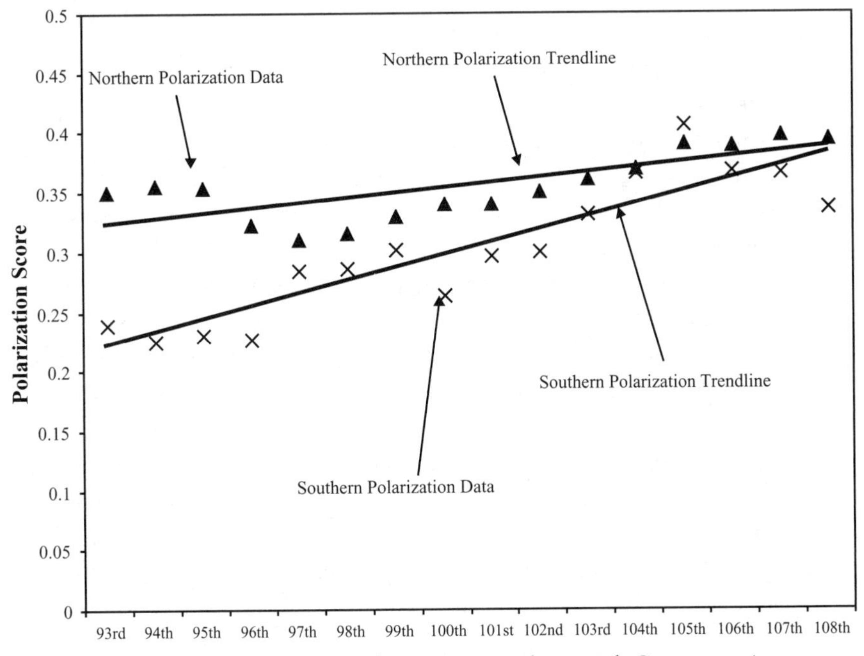

FIGURE 2.7. Polarization Scores by Region, 93rd to 108th Congresses (1973–2004).

turned McGee's position into a liability when he asked voters, "How efficient do you think the postal service is?" With that question as the cornerstone of his campaign, Wallop, a pro-environment, pro-choice Republican, defeated McGee. In his first congress, Wallop's DW-NOMINATE was 0.42, placing him in the middle third of all Republicans. As his career progressed, however, his very conservative military and foreign policy views prevailed, moving him to the extreme right wing of the Republican party. By the time he retired, Wallop's 0.78 DW-NOMINATE made him the second most conservative member of the Senate. Wallop's career adaptation score was the third largest in the Senate over the past 30 years. Members, upon being first elected to Congress, may have voted more moderately. Over the course of their careers, however, their records may have become more and more extreme. In explaining the timing of policy adoptions, Asher and Weisberg (1978, 393–4), Brady and Sinclair (1984), Burstein (1978, 1980), and Jones (1974) find small, but pervasive, member conversions.

Second, next door to Wyoming and two years after Wallop's retirement, in 1994, Helen Chenoweth, a Republican, challenged incumbent Larry LaRocco, a Democrat, for his western Idaho seat in the House. In two terms, LaRocco had built a fairly moderate voting record, scoring a −0.23 DW-NOMINATE in his second term (the House Democratic average was −0.34). In a highly contested Republican primary, Chenoweth, who demonstrated her conservative credentials by holding an endangered salmon bake fundraiser, came out on top. She went on to defeat LaRocco in the general election by painting him as a liberal lieutenant in Clinton's "War on the West." In her first Congress, Chenoweth, with a 0.76 score, was the fifth most conservative representative in the House. The difference between LaRocco and Chenoweth produced the fourth biggest change caused by the historic 1994 elections. Writing even before the Watergate Babies (1974 liberal Democrats), Newt's Lieutenants (1994 conservative Republicans), and the Bush Babies (2002 conservative Republicans), Burnham (1970), followed by a long list of others, attributes sudden swings in congressional policymaking to massive election turnover (see also Brady and Lynn 1973; Ginsberg 1973, 1976; and Brady 1978, 1991). Member replacement need not only happen in volatile elections. According to Clausen (1973) and Kingdon (1989), the changes brought about by member replacement can be more gradual. A slightly more conservative Republican may replace a more moderate Republican or a more reliable Democrat can replace a maverick Republican. In other words, not all replacements have happened as a result of wholesale electoral shifts such as those in 1974 or 1994.

Fundamentally, both member adaptations such as Wallop's and member replacements such as LaRocco-to-Chenoweth could have polarized the political parties in Congress. It is the numerous adaptations and replacements over the years that decimated the ideological middle in Congress. Individual member adaptations and replacements can occur at the same time in different legislative seats. Some members may be becoming more ideological at the same time as more extreme members replace more moderate members. Indeed, simultaneous member adaptation and member replacement are perhaps the most compelling and pervasive finding of those studying congress-to-congress changes (Asher and Weisberg 1978; Sinclair 1977, 1982; and Brady and Sinclair 1984). By comparing seat-by-seat changes congress-by-congress, Theriault (2005) finds that over the past 32 years, representative (*senator*) adaptation accounts for 35.2 (*38.0*) percent of the polarization in the House (*Senate*).[33] Any explanation, therefore, must take into account both the growing ideological voting of incumbents and the replacement of more moderate members by more ideological members.

VI. Conclusion

This chapter places the current polarization of political parties inside Congress into a broader context. Indeed, in the 108th Congress (2003–4), the House of Representatives was more polarized than it had been since the beginning of the twentieth century. The Senate reached its high water polarization mark in the 105th Congress (1997–8).

[33] Incidentally, these percentages are in the middle of the previous estimates. Fleisher and Bond (2003) find that the overwhelming majority – around 90 percent of the moderates in Congress – disappear as a consequence of replacement. Roberts and Smith (2003), on the other hand, maintain that member adaptation accounts for between 50 and 82 percent of the polarization of the parties during their respective polarizing phases (the 98th to 100th Congresses for Democrats and the 102nd to 104th Congresses for Republicans).

Nonetheless, for the past 32 years, the parties in both chambers have been becoming increasingly polarized.

Two additional findings from this chapter help describe the current era of party polarization. First, although the southern states have been leading the polarization trend, northern states have not been immune to it. Since 1973, more than one-third of the party polarization in the House and more than one-half in the Senate have taken place outside the South. Second, although the majority of the polarization has resulted from ideological members replacing more moderate members, congressional veterans have not been immune to the party polarization that surrounds them. Roughly one-third of the party polarization has come through the gradual adaptation of incumbents' migrating to their parties' ideological homes.

3

Explanations for Party Polarization

Political pundits and social scientists have offered various explanations for party polarization, including partisan redistricting (Carson et al. 2007 and Hirsch 2003, income inequality (McCarty, Poole, and Rosenthal 2006), constituency change (Oppenheimer 2005 and Stonecash, Brewer, and Mariani 2003), or institutional change (Lee forthcoming and Roberts and Smith 2003). These explanations have their roots in either members' constituencies or congressional institutions. Each of these studies presents evidence substantiating its argument. More often than not, however, the study does not rigorously test the alternative explanations. Taken as a group, these studies show that there are multiple causes of party polarization, but they typically fail on two other accounts. First, they do not present a comprehensive explanation for how these various causes relate to one another.[1] Second, they rarely provide an indication of *how* responsible each cause is *for* exacerbating the party divide. This chapter presents an integrated explanation that takes account of and builds off of the existing logic and evidence of these arguments and studies.

An explanation for party polarization, especially one that attempts to integrate the existing explanations, needs to be mindful of the lessons from the first two chapters. First, party polarization is not an artifact of any one voting score or ideology measure. Second, both the House

[1] See Sinclair (2006) and Mann and Ornstein (2006) for two recent books that examine the partisan divide more comprehensively.

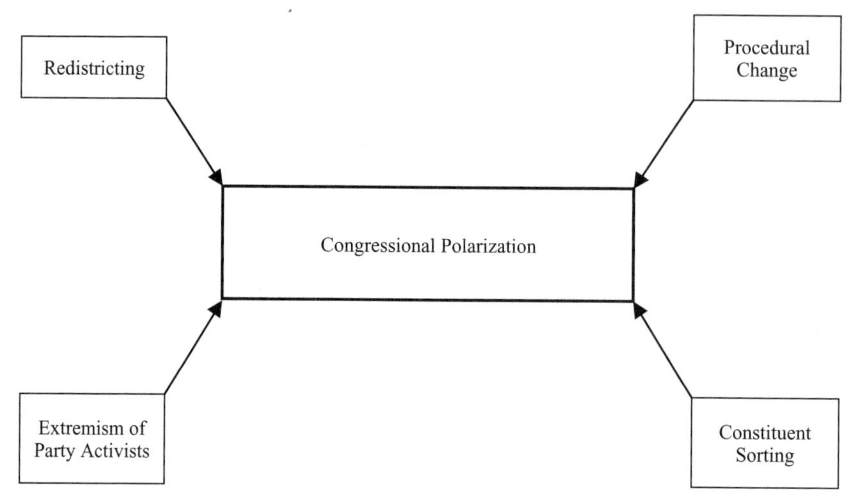

FIGURE 3.1. Current Understanding of Party Polarization in Congress.

and the Senate have polarized similarly over the same time period. Third, representatives and senators from both the South and the North have polarized, though the former has polarized slightly faster. Fourth, new members are more ideological than the members they replace, and existing members have also become more ideological over time, though the former is more responsible for polarizing the parties than the latter.

The various explanations for party polarization can be broken down into four broad categories: redistricting (chapter 4), geographic and political sorting of voters (chapter 5), party activist extremism (chapter 6), and institutional change (chapters 7 and 8). Much of the current literature reads as though these explanations are mutually exclusive and unrelated to one another (see figure 3.1). The integrated model uses these studies to develop a more complex understanding of the link among constituency change, institutional change, and party polarization.

If I were a chemist in a laboratory and I were trying to determine which of four elements caused a reaction, I would add one of the elements to a beaker and observe what happened. In three separate beakers, I would add the other elements and again observe what happened. The difference among the four would allow me to conclude with some degree of certainty which element caused the reaction. If they each caused some reaction, I could develop a test to measure the extent of the reaction and then offer relative assessments for each. Regrettably for my study, political scientists are not as lucky as chemists.

I do not dispute the extant claims made by the scholars studying party polarization in Congress. In their own way and to some extent, redistricting, the sorting of constituents, party activist extremism, and institutional change have each caused party polarization. This study integrates these explanations into one coherent argument and offers a relative assessment of the extent to which each contributes to the party polarization. No doubt, this integrated approach and relative assessment are not as neat and tidy as the chemists', but as political scientists, our data and our arrows of causation are subject to free will and human error. As such, I offer the integrated model to begin a much needed longer conversation about party polarization. Before integrating the explanations into one argument, I offer a recapitulation of each of the existing arguments and some of the evidence that has been used to substantiate each as a cause of party polarization. The conclusion of this chapter offers some important caveats to both the development and the subsequent testing of these explanations.

I. The Redistricting Explanation

By the end of 2001, everyone knew that the fix was in. Incumbents in the House of Representatives would sail to reelection, leaving only trampled democracy, bitter feelings, and Soviet-style elections in their wake. Thanks to redistricting, so the argument went, most incumbents would face minor or no opposition not only in 2002, but in every election through the next census in 2010. These drastic claims were made in respected news sources by political observers known for their modest assessments of political situations and conditions (Rothenberg 2002, Broder 2001, and Giroux 2001). Within a year, their predictions came true, as voters in 2002 returned 98 percent of the incumbents to their House seats. In 2004, only three members from outside Texas, which underwent redistricting in 2003, went down to defeat.

Those engaged in the craft of redistricting were being blamed not only for the demise of democracy in House elections, but also for the rampant partisanship and polarization that has subsequently spoiled

Congress. According to these arguments, the safe seats that were created through redistricting sent, for the most part, very conservative or very liberal members to Congress. "The ideological divisions in Congress," according to Bill Bishop, a reporter for the *Austin American-Statesman*, "are certainly a result of state legislators' ability and willingness to draw districts that overwhelmingly favor one party." He continues, "There is a cycle of intemperance. Homogenous communities gerrymandered into homogenous districts produce more extreme and uncompromising representatives."[2] Even former Senator Sam Nunn (2005), a cautious and respected former legislator, was outraged: "Both political parties have engaged in basically rigging congressional districts to the point where they are absolutely safe districts for one party or the other and I think that's detrimental to the kind of dialogue we need for bipartisanship."

Although little systematic evidence connected redistricting to polarization, the logic and the timing of the argument were too compelling to deny. Norman Ornstein wrote, "Congressional redistricting... has eliminated most competitive seats and thus removed most centrists and moderates from both parties."[3] An editorial in the *Omaha World Herald* noted, "Against this backdrop, statisticians provide an added wrinkle. Their studies indicate that the level of ideological polarization in Congress has intensified significantly over the past two decades. One reason: heightened attention to redistricting by the political parties in state legislatures, so that most U.S. House members tend to fall in one of two categories: hard-shell conservative Republicans or diehard liberal Democrats."[4] Perhaps Hirsch (2003, 215) offers the most damning criticism: "But today, a handful of congressional and state-legislative leaders pursuing a narrow partisan and ideological agenda are threatening to transform what should be our most democratic institution into something sclerotic and skewed." According to the argument, it is the polarization created by redistricting that has increased the acrimony in the House (Rothenberg 2001), perverted

[2] Bill Bishop, "A Steady Slide Toward a More Partisan Union," *Austin American-Statesman*, May 30, 2004, pp. A1, A8.

[3] Norman Ornstein, October 28, 2004, "A Divisive Election Will Only Worsen Existing Partisan Rifts," *Roll Call*, p. 7.

[4] "Divided, Not United Political Estrangement in Washington is Bad for the Country," *Omaha World Herald*, February 17, 2003, p. 6b.

the legislative process (Ornstein 2002), and led to political stalemate (Zone 2002).

To guarantee fair elections, which legitimize congressional policy making, a bevy of solutions have been offered to end incumbent-protection redistricting schemes. Congressman Earl Blumenauer (D-OR) thinks that a "popular movement" throughout America is needed to take redistricting away from the politicians.[5] Lisa Handley, a redistricting expert, advocates the British system where "civil servants redraw the lines to reflect population changes, and they do not take into account where incumbents live or which party will benefit."[6] Columnist George Will prefers the Iowa system, where redistricting decisions are left to a nonpartisan panel.[7] Several others prefer court-mandated solutions. Thomas Mann and Norman Ornstein look to the Supreme Court,[8] whereas a *Washington Post* editorial encourages action in state courts.[9] Governor Arnold Schwarzenegger wants retired judges to draw the lines with the expressed purpose of making elections competitive. Columnist William Raspberry offers perhaps the most unique solution: a return to a solution Illinois invoked more than 100 years ago to slow the rampant polarization following Reconstruction: the creation of three-member "super districts," which would eliminate the winner-take-all feature of our current single-member districts.[10]

In the face of such an assault, I sidestep these advocates' primary argument in order to evaluate their secondary argument. This study does not attempt to address the extent to which redistricting has led to an increased incumbency advantage, though reform advocates would be wise to remember the thorough debunking of that argument from the 1970s (Fiorina 1977, Ferejohn 1977; see also Abramowitz, Alexander, and Gunning 2006). A prima facie problem with the redistricting

[5] Quoted in Norman Ornstein, "High Court Should Halt Obsession with Redistricting," *Roll Call*, May 14, 2003, p. 6.

[6] Quoted in Fred Hiatt, "Time to Draw the Line," *The Washington Post*, May 3, 2004, p. A21.

[7] Quoted from the November 17, 2002, broadcast of "This Week with George Stephanopoulos."

[8] "Rescuing U.S. Democracy," *The Washington Post*, December 15, 2003, p. A30.

[9] Lyle Denniston, "US Courts to Hear Redistricting Cases Redrawing Maps for Partisan Gain Faces Challenge," *The Boston Globe*, December 9, 2003, p. A2.

[10] William Raspberry, "Do Cartographers Divine Electoral Results?" *The Houston Chronicle*, May 24, 2004, p. 18A.

explanation for party polarization is that it cannot explain the growing divide between the parties in the Senate. Most of the advocates for the redistricting explanation do not discuss the Senate or even realize that the Senate has polarized almost as much as the House. In fact, Keith Poole is so exasperated by the outlandish claims of this argument's proponents that at a recent political science meeting he carped: "It is not redistricting, it is not redistricting, it is not redistricting!" In a more formal venue, he and his coauthors argue, "It is not obvious that [redistricting controversies] are much more than a symptom of our political maladies rather than their cause" (McCarty, Poole, and Rosenthal 2006, 42).

II. The Geographic and Political Sorting of Constituents

As with the redistricting argument, this argument places the cause of party polarization in the members' constituencies. Instead of blaming those tasked with redrawing congressional districts, the proponents of the political segregation argument suggest that the parties have polarized through countless political reclassifications within and migrations of individuals between a multitude of communities throughout the United States. Voters in the United States have been sorted in two ways. First, at a political level, liberals increasingly vote for Democratic candidates and conservatives increasingly vote for Republican candidates (Fiorina 2006). Although this sorting has been driven mostly by the transformation of conservative southern Democrats into conservative southern Republicans, the same reclassifications have been going on throughout the rest of the country. The strong correlation between ideology and partisan identification as manifest in the mass electorate likely has its roots in either emboldened national party organizations or more party-disciplined elected officials. Whatever the cause, voters, districts, and even states split their votes less frequently between one party for one office and the opposite party for a different office than they once did.

Second, at a residential level, individual voters have sorted themselves into more politically homogeneous neighborhoods, communities, counties, congressional districts, and states. Pop culture suggests that Democrats choose to live near their local Starbucks for a convenient cup of joe and Republicans move to be closer to their favorite mega-church for a regular drink from the cup of salvation. Scholars have found that individuals increasingly select neighborhoods based on government services, income levels, and racial demographics, which are all highly correlated with political voting patterns (Oppenheimer 2005 and Gimpel and Schuknect 2004). Whether through the nascent political institutions of coffee houses and mega-churches or the more traditional explanations for migration patterns, Americans increasingly live in ideologically homogeneous areas quite independent of the manipulation of congressional district boundaries.

Although the degree to which Americans are divided into red and blue states is rigorously debated (see, for example, Fiorina 2006; DiMaggio, Evans, and Bryson 1996; and McCarty, Poole, and Rosenthal 2006), few question that Americans have politically sorted themselves ideologically (Abramowitz and Saunders 1998) and jurisdictionally (Brewer, Mariani, and Stonecash 2002; and Stonecash, Brewer, and Mariani 2003; Gimpel and Shucknecht 2003; and Oppenheimer 2005). As both sorting trends occurred within an ever more mobile American populace, voters are increasingly surrounded by people who share their educational level, income level, ethnicity, and race (Gimpel and Shucknecht 2003). As the constituents are geographically sorted, the members from their respective political parties are increasingly representing different constituencies with different underlying demographics. Democrats are increasingly representing constituents who are poorer and more ethnically diverse than Republicans (Stonecash, Brewer, and Mariani 2003). Unsurprisingly, these more polarized constituents elect more ideological members of Congress. Bryan Jones, in a *Seattle Times* story, nicely summarizes this argument: "Lawmakers elected from solidly safe districts have less incentive to compromise... Homogeneous districts add to the polarization of the political parties."[11]

Bishop (2004) presents perhaps the best visual of the political segregation argument by comparing presidential votes by county in two close presidential elections 28 years apart. In Jimmy Carter's defeat of Gerald Ford in the 1976 presidential race, only 26.8 percent of the voters lived in counties where one of the candidates beat the other by

[11] Quoted in David Postman, "Why So Many Races Lack One Thing: Competition," *The Seattle Times*, October 13, 2002, p. A1.

more than 20 percentage points. In the 2004 presidential race, that number jumped to 48.3 percent. Unlike congressional district lines, county lines, of course, are not subject to decennial (or more frequent!) changes.

The sorting argument overcomes the biggest criticism of the redistricting argument by plausibly explaining Senate polarization. So long as states have gone through the same sorting dynamics as counties, senators will be representing increasingly politically homogeneous states just as representatives are representing increasingly political homogeneous congressional districts. Whereas congressional district lines change, county and state lines, for all intents and purposes, are constant.

III. Extremism of Party Activists

Like redistricting and constituent sorting, the third cause, the extremism of party activists, also has its roots in the members' constituencies. If neighborhoods are becoming more homogeneous and district lines are increasingly being manipulated to deliver House seats to a particular party, members will increasingly face a more competitive primary and a less competitive general election. As the most important voter shifts from the median voter in the general election to the median voter in the primary, members become increasingly concerned with satisfying a more ideologically extreme constituent. As the threat of a serious primary opponent increases, so the argument goes, members cast increasingly ideological votes.

The validity of this argument depends critically on one trend and is exacerbated by a second. First, voters must be increasingly sorted into more homogenous constituencies through either redistricting or migration. Put simply, at least one of the first two causes of party polarization must be true in order for the extremism of party activists to be true. Second, if the primary electorate is becoming increasingly ideological, members will be forced to compete over an increasingly ideological median voter. The bigger these trends are, the more likely the extremism of party activists is contributing to the polarization of the political parties.

Much of the evidence for the first of these trends was explained and cited in the last two sections. Whether by redistricting or sorting, members' constituencies are increasingly becoming politically homogeneous. Sufficient evidence also exists for the second trend. Although it is hard to gauge the ideological predispositions of primary voters, we know the ideologies of two different definitions of "party activists" have become more extreme: respondents to the American National Elections Study who participate in at least three political activities (Fiorina 2006 and Layman and Carsey 2002) and delegates who attend the National Party Conventions (Herrera and Shafer 2004).

IV. The Institutional Explanation

In 1885, future president Woodrow Wilson (1956, 69), in an earlier career as a professor of politics and history, famously remarked, "Congress in session is Congress on public exhibition, whilst Congress in its committee-rooms is Congress at work." And so it was for at least the next 80 years. Shepsle (1989) characterizes the "Textbook Congress," which he claims reigned from World War II until at least the mid-1960s, as containing strong committee chairs, loosely organized political parties, and strong House norms and Senate folkways.

As the Textbook Congress evolved, the power that was at one time consolidated in the hands of strong committee chairs was divided and passed to at least three different groups of legislators (Sinclair 2000). First, with the Subcommittee Bill of Rights in 1974, subcommittee chairs were granted control over their legislative agenda and their committee staffs. Second, party members began giving their leaders more power in exchange for assuming more responsibility for their parties' fortunes in both the legislative and electoral arenas. Third, individual lawmakers began violating the norms of specialization and committee deference by offering amendments to committee bills on the floors and viewing more skeptically the decisions reached by the committees.

The transformation away from the Textbook Congress did not happen all at one time, nor did it happen all because of one factor. Some of the more important factors include: the congressional elections of 1958, 1964, 1974, 1980, 1992, and 1994, which brought scores of new members to Congress who came with their own ideas of how the system should work (Shepsle 1989 and Sinclair 2006); the diversification of members' constituencies as mandated by the 1960s' Supreme Court opinions requiring population-equal districts, which were exacerbated by politically charged redistricting plans (Shepsle 1989); the transformation of member offices into self-contained enterprises, which made the members independent from one another and their parties (Cain, Ferejohn, and Fiorina 1987, Shepsle 1989, and Smith 1989); reforms such as the Legislative Reorganization Act of 1946, the introduction of electronic voting in the House with the Legislative Reorganization Act of 1970, the Subcommittee Bill of Rights in 1974, and the Republican Caucus Rule changes in 1995, which had the overall effect of weakening committees (Shepsle 1989, Smith 1989, Aldrich 1995, and Evans and Oleszek 1997); explicit changes in the lawmaking process such as the Budget and Impoundment Control Act of 1974 and Reagan's overhaul of the budget-making process, which, for the first time since the spendthrift 1960s, forced members of Congress to make tough budgetary decisions (Sinclair 2000); the breakdown in personal relationships not only across members but also across parties, which coarsened the politics and hardened the lawmaking process (Sinclair 2000); and demands from the outside such as an increase in the complexity of issues needing to be addressed and the growth of organized interests, which forced changes and innovation (Smith 1989).

As committees lost power, the dichotomy established by Wilson between Congress on public exhibition and Congress at work became confounded. With sunshine laws in committee hearings, television cameras on the floors of both chambers, and a new breed of media-savvy members, Congress on public exhibition became Congress at work. Smith (1989, 1) claims, "The House and Senate floors were transformed into far more important arenas of substantive policymaking." He documents an increase in floor amending activity in both the House and Senate, an increase in the use of restrictive rules in the House, and an increase in the complexity of unanimous consent agreements in the Senate. Smith (1989, 234) argues that these changes "shift[ed] decisionmaking processes away from the traditional centralized-decentralized continuum and toward a more collegial, floor-oriented process." As electoral factors altered the relationship between members and their institution and as media pressure intensified the spotlight on Congress, floor procedures changed.

The transformation of legislative activity from the closed doors of committee hearing rooms to the House and Senate floor exacerbated the inefficiencies within the lawmaking process. As both chambers spent increasingly more time debating and voting on the increasing number of amendments, the streamlined legislative process on the floor was unraveling. As Schickler (2001) and Binder (1997) show through a careful read of the history and analysis of available systematic evidence, majority party members gave their leadership more power in structuring floor alternatives in an attempt to rein in members' amending activities.

The majority party leadership uses two different, though related, strategies to control the floor. First, the majority party leadership is responsible for scheduling legislation for the floor. Increasingly, they follow two commandments: (1) "Thou shalt not aid bills that will split thy party" and (2) "Thou shalt aid bills that most in party like" (Cox and McCubbins 2005, 24). As evidence of their complete control of the agenda since at least the 93rd Congress (1973–4), a majority of the majority party has never lost more than three final passage votes in any given Congress. In contrast, a majority of minority party members has lost as many as sixty-three times in one congress (Cox and McCubbins 2005, 92–3). As Cox and McCubbins (2005) show, the more control majority parties assert on the agenda, the more the legislative process exacerbates party polarization.

Second, when bills make it to the floor, they are increasingly given special rules, which significantly reduce the minority party's legislative opportunities to change the bill. In addition to granting more closed and modified rules, the Rules Committee began designing increasingly complex rules, such as queen-of-the-hill rules, self-executing rules, multiple-step rules, and anticipatory rules. The proportion of bills debated under restrictive rules has significantly increased over time. In the late 1970s, as few as 15 percent of the bills debated on the floor of the House had a restrictive rule. By the time Democrats lost control of the House, 70 percent of the bills had restrictive rules. Although Republicans followed through on their promise to open the floor up for more debates on amendments when they captured the House in 1994, by the 108th Congress (2003–4), the percentage of restrictive rules surpassed the Democrat's high water mark (Davidson, Oleszek, and Lee 2008, 252). These modifications in the rules process have made majority party control on the House floor easier. As individual members exercise less discretion on the floor, members face fewer opportunities to cast moderating roll call votes, which results in party polarization.

Not only have the agenda-setting and rule-making powers been accelerated by party polarization in Congress, but changes in the manner of debate in the House have also polarized the parties. Roberts and Smith (2003) show that when the House instituted electronic voting on the floor, the number of party votes – where a majority of one party votes against the majority from the other party – increased. This increase is especially marked during the periods of rapid polarization within the parties, which, according to them, is in the 1980s for the Democrats and in the late 1990s and early 2000s for the Republicans.

Although some of the changes in the legislative process are exclusive to the House (restrictive rules and electronic voting), other changes apply equally to the Senate (agenda setting, though to a lesser extent). Two additional changes to the lawmaking process are unique to the Senate. Holds and filibusters have become increasingly frequent actions on the Senate floor (Binder and Smith 1997, 10). Perhaps even more important than the use of filibusters is the threat of using a filibuster. Although the secrecy surrounding holds makes it difficult to quantify their growth, most political observers notice a sharp increase in their use (Binder 2004). Rather than advantaging party leaders, these trends advantage individual senators. Nonetheless, they have a tendency to exacerbate partisan warfare.

The increasing use of holds, filibusters, and the threats of using them has made the legislative process on the floor of the Senate more difficult. As a result, senators have come to expect their party leaders to develop floor procedures that ensure that important legislative business gets accomplished. More often than not, the leaders of both the majority and minority party have used complicated unanimous consent agreements to facilitate Senate passage. These more complex agreements necessarily have restricted senators' individual floor prerogatives in the interest of moving legislation through the Senate.

V. An Integrated Argument of Party Polarization

The primary problem with the extant studies of these explanations is that the scholars do not, for the most part, rigorously test any explanation other than the one they proffer. At the end of the day, we have sufficient evidence that each causes party polarization, but we do not know the relative importance of each, nor do we know how they affect one another. Science, in both chemistry and politics, is advanced when knowledge is accumulated and a more complete and accurate picture of a beaker's reaction or the real world is offered. Although individual findings are important steps along the way, an integrated understanding of a complex phenomenon necessarily brings the picture of that phenomenon into clearer focus.

The first step in an integrated argument for party polarization in Congress is the exogenous changes in members' constituencies. Either through the purposive act of redistricting or through political sorting and geographic-based political segregation, members' constituencies are more polarized. The effect of their increasing polarization is explored in chapter 4 (redistricting), chapter 5 (political segregation), and chapter 6 (extremism of party activists). Members' more ideologically polarized constituents have both a direct and an indirect effect on party polarization in both the House and the Senate. Directly, the first step is taken by the voters when they elect more polarized candidates to the House and Senate.

Legislators inside the U.S. Capitol take the second step. Even if not all moderate districts have vanished, the more polarized members coming from more partisan districts pursue more polarized politics by voting for more polarized party leaders who implement a more polarized legislative agenda and more polarizing legislative procedures. The effect of these institutional changes is explored in chapters 7 and 8.

These two steps are not taken in isolation from one another; rather, the first step provides the impetus for members to take the second step. The necessity of this first step has led social scientists and political observers to focus their attention on it almost to the exclusion of the second step. As the analysis in this book shows, the first step alone cannot account for the overwhelming majority of the party polarization that has occurred in the U.S. Congress. Nonetheless, without attention to the first step, no rationale exists for members to take the second step.

It is only when members, who come from increasingly polarized constituencies, meet in Washington, D.C., and elect leaders who implement their party rules that the current extent of party polarization comes into focus. The interaction of more polarized members within the legislative process is critical to comprehensively understand the divide between the parties on Capitol Hill. The effect of this interaction is explored in chapter 8.

In total, the exogenous change in members' constituencies should be weaker in the Senate because state legislators cannot redraw state

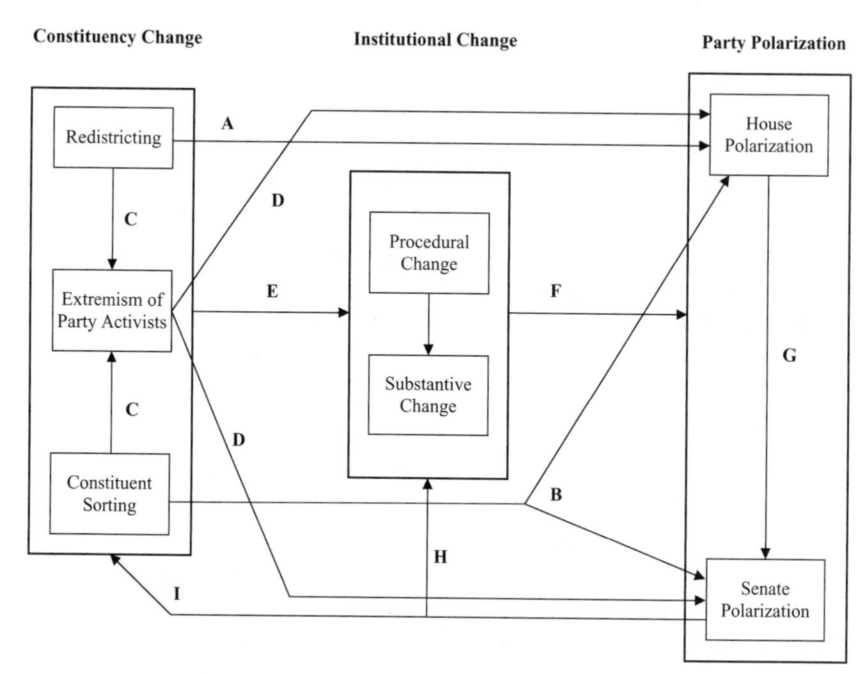

FIGURE 3.2. An Integrated Explanation for Party Polarization in Congress.

lines to serve political ends as they can representatives' district lines, and party leaders have less ability to dictate Senate legislative action. Nonetheless, polarization in the House has spilled over into the Senate. Chapter 9 explicitly examines how House polarization has affected (or infected) the Senate. In contrast to the disparate impression left by the disjointed political science literature and political pundits' editorials in figure 3.1, figure 3.2 depicts the integrated model to explain the 32-year rise of party polarization in the Congress.

VI. Adding Complexity to the Integrated Explanation

To buy my argument with the same amount of certainty with which the chemist's audience buys her argument, you have to believe that: (a) the arrows from the exogenous and endogenous factors nicely flow from one concept to another, and (b) party polarization in no way caused the redistricting revolution, migration patterns, the political sorting of voters, the extremism of party activists, or the institutional changes in

Congress. Proving either, let alone both, assumptions is an impossible task. Electoral rules, institutional rules, members, parties, and the people all interact and react in ways that make the arrows connecting these concepts and political actors difficult to trace and pin down.

Only a naïve understanding of the interaction of the various actors in the political arena would accept that the members' constituencies take the first step prior to the members taking the second step or that each of the arrows only goes in the direction shown in figure 3.2. Instead of being understood as two distinct steps in which the first is completed before the second is attempted, the relationship among constituency change, institutional change, and party polarization is more accurately understood as a vicious cycle. When the members' constituencies get a bit more polarized, the legislative process gets a bit more dominated by the majority party, which exacerbates party polarization. This exacerbated party polarization, in turn, drives the constituencies to become more sorted, which results in more divisive roll-call voting in Congress.

The vicious-cycle nature of the buildup to the current polarization between Democrats and Republicans in Congress implies that the arrows cannot nicely flow only from one actor to another. Just as every change in the vicious cycle affects the actions that come after it, so it is affected by all the changes that preceded it. Such an argument readily admits to constituency and institutional change, causing party polarization, but that party polarization, in turn, causes constituency and institutional change. Arrows H and I account for these additional complexities to the integrated explanation depicted in figure 3.2.

Constituency change is presented before institutional change because this flow makes more sense to me than the reverse order given that members are notoriously risk averse (Jacobson 1987). If their relationship with their constituents has not changed, why would risk-averse members embark on a series of changes that end in partisan warfare? Nonetheless, the integrated explanation does not require that you accept this flow.[12] It only requires that you believe that both

[12] Incidentally, a nice sub-literature is developing in the party polarization literature on what came first. See Hetherington (2001) and Jacobson (2000) for arguments about the chicken and the egg. At the end of the day, I am only concerned that there is a chicken that can lay an egg – the integrated explanation, to continue with the animal analogies, does not have a dog in that fight.

constituency change and institutional change cause party polarization. The value added by this study to our understanding of Congress is in recognition that both cause polarization and in parsing out the relative contributions of each to the current polarization between the Democrats and Republicans in Congress.

VII. A Conclusion of Caveats

A chemist would show you how the addition of each element to a beaker would cause a reaction or not. The relative arrows could be appropriately evaluated, and a complex assessment could be reached. In political science, it is not that easy. Nonetheless, in the succeeding six chapters, I proffer tests that help parse out and evaluate these connected and interconnected concepts. The results from no individual test are likely to compel you to buy any one arrow over another. Only through a whole battery of tests can the evidence for or against the integrated model be appraised and the individual explanations assessed. It is to these tests that I now turn.

PART II

CONSTITUENCY CHANGE

Part II of this book examines the connection between the increasing partisanship of members' constituencies and the growing divide between the parties on Capitol Hill (arrows A, B, C, and D of figure 3.2). Redistricting, ideological sorting, and geographic sorting provided the initial jolt and the extremism of party activists provide the sustaining power that directly – and then indirectly, through the legislative process – polarized the political parties in Congress.

Figure P.1 shows the conceptual difference among the districting-based explanations for party polarization. Consider a state with twelve residents and four congressional districts. In the initial district lines, the state has two districts with one Republican and two Democrats (Districts 2 and 4) and two districts with two Republicans and one Democrat (Districts 1 and 3). In each of these four districts, a moderate member is likely to be elected. In panel A, the state goes through redistricting after a census. The state legislators decide to protect their incumbents by getting rid of partisan dissent in each of the districts, such that all four districts now contain partisan homogeneity. By the end of the decade, we would not be surprised to see two conservative Republicans replace the two moderate Republicans and two liberal Democrats replace the two moderate Democrats. In each of these districts, the incumbent is vulnerable only in a primary.

In panel B, the initial set-up is similar, though two of the Democrats are now classified as being conservative Democrats and two of the Republicans are classified as liberal Republicans. We would expect the

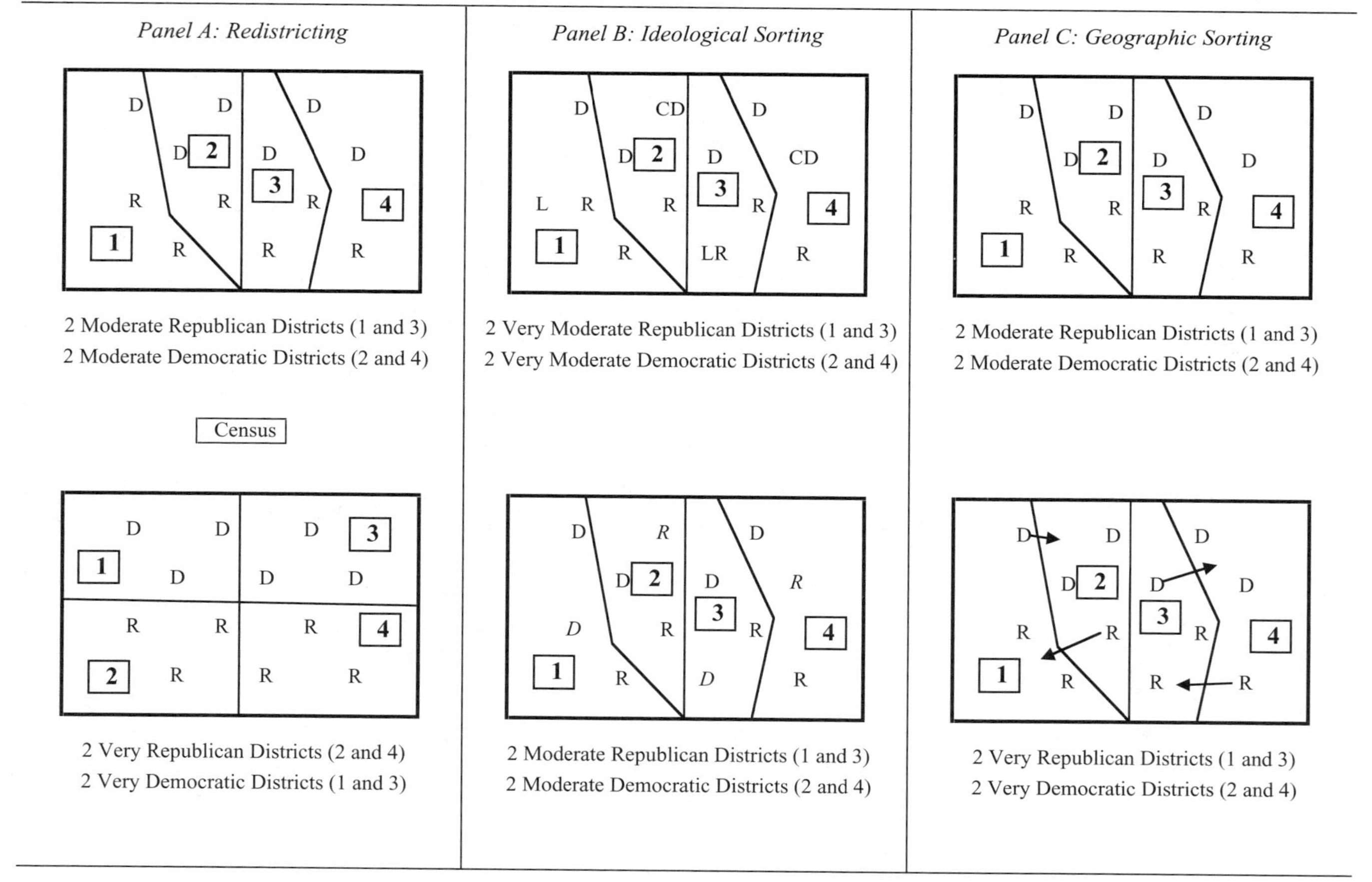

FIGURE P.1. Districting-based Explanations for Party Polarization.

members to be even more moderate because the slightest ideological bent could rattle these cross-pressured voters to vote against their party in favor of their ideology. By the end of the decade, suppose that the two conservative Democrats decide to switch parties and join their fellow conservatives in the Republican party and vice versa for the liberal Republicans. Again, by the end of the decade, after the voters have ideologically sorted, the districts are likely to elect more polarizing members, though in this particular case the legislators go from being very moderate to being slightly less moderate.

In panel C, the initial set-up is exactly the same as it was in panel A. This time, however, the state decides to keep the same lines after the census. Now suppose, by the end of the decade, the odd voter out in each district decides to move into a district with her like-minded partisans. If all four districts lose their opposition voter and gain a fellow partisan, we would expect all four districts to end up with more ideologically extreme members.

The end result in all three panels is similar: a more polarized constituency in which serious competition is most likely to happen in the primary. If any of the constituency trends are happening, the party activists become more powerful because their voices are amplified in party primaries. The effect of the activists' extremism, in turn, will be greater as the district becomes more politically homogeneous. The increasingly polarized districts caused by redistricting and constituent sorting – both ideological and geographic – directly polarized roll call voting above and beyond the kinds of issues and the types of votes that members faced on their chambers' floors.

Chapter 4 focuses on redistricting (arrow A from figure 3.2); chapter 5 analyzes ideological and geographic sorting (arrow B); and chapter 6 investigates the extremism of party activists (arrows C and D). Constituency change also can indirectly affect polarization by changing the kinds of issues and types of votes that members face. Part III explores the impact of constituency change on the changes in the institutions and procedures within Congress.

4

Redistricting

Georgia gained one seat in the 1990 round of reapportionment. In creating the new district and altering the old districts to achieve population-equal congressional districts, the Democratic state legislature and Democratic governor pursued multiple objectives: protect the Democratic incumbents in the House, maximize the number of Democratic districts, to divide up the constituency of its lone Republican congressman (Newt Gingrich), and gain the Department of Justice's assent as mandated by the preclearance provision in the Voting Rights Act of 1965. Although the state legislature passed and the governor signed various plans, the Department of Justice, under a directive from President George H.W. Bush, rejected them because they failed to maximize minority representation. Eventually the state legislature relented and created a third black district in the Atlanta suburbs.

The "bleaching" of the districts surrounding the black majority districts and a Republican wave in the wake of Clinton's first two years in the White House radically changed the state's congressional delegation. In the 102nd Congress, the last one using the 1980 district lines, Georgia voters sent one liberal African American Democrat, six moderate Democrats, two conservative Democrats, and one even more conservative Republican to the House. In the 107th Congress, the last election using the 1990 census data, Georgia sent two liberal African American Democrats, one moderate African American Democrat, and eight more or less conservative white Republicans to Congress (see panel

A of figure 4.1). The Democratic legislature and governor's best-laid plans went seriously awry. The delegation, in addition to being much more conservative in the 107th Congress (Georgia's DW-NOMINATE average went from −0.036 in the 1980s to 0.189 in the 1990s), was much more ideologically dispersed, going from a polarization score of 20 percent in the 102nd Congress to 51 percent in the 107th Congress.

Another state whose congressional delegation became more conservative and more ideologically polarized over the same time period was Oklahoma. In going from a delegation of four Democrats and two Republicans in the 102nd Congress to one Democrat and five Republicans in the 107th Congress, Oklahoma's polarization score went from 25 percent to 44 percent (see panel B of figure 4.1). Although its polarization did not increase as much as Georgia's, Oklahoma could have been another case in which the redrawing of lines in the early 1990s drastically affected its House delegation. Such a conclusion, however, contradicts the description that Oklahoma's congressional redistricting "was not a point of controversy" (*Congressional Districts in the 1990s* 1993, 605). In fact, but for a few line changes to accommodate the shifting population within Oklahoma, the congressional district lines in 2000 were the same as the lines that produced Oklahoma's 102nd Congress delegation.

This pair of vignettes suggests that the make-up of a state's congressional delegation can change drastically as a consequence of congressional redistricting, but that drastic redistricting is not necessarily required. Another pair of vignettes might have shown that drastic line drawing as well as minimal line drawing led to very little change in the ideological composition or polarization of a state's congressional delegation. In short, redistricting may be a factor – but it is not the only factor – that can explain party polarization in Congress.

A broader historical perspective on the redistricting and polarization stories, which is rarely offered in journalistic accounts of current congressional district reconfigurations, strengthens the link between the two. It was not until the mid-1960s, when the Supreme Court mandated regular line drawings to produce population-equal districts, that the incumbency advantage and party polarization began to grow. This redistricting revolution has been blamed for the demise of competition in congressional elections (Tufte 1973). Given the confounded relationship among districts, members, competitive elections, and ideology,

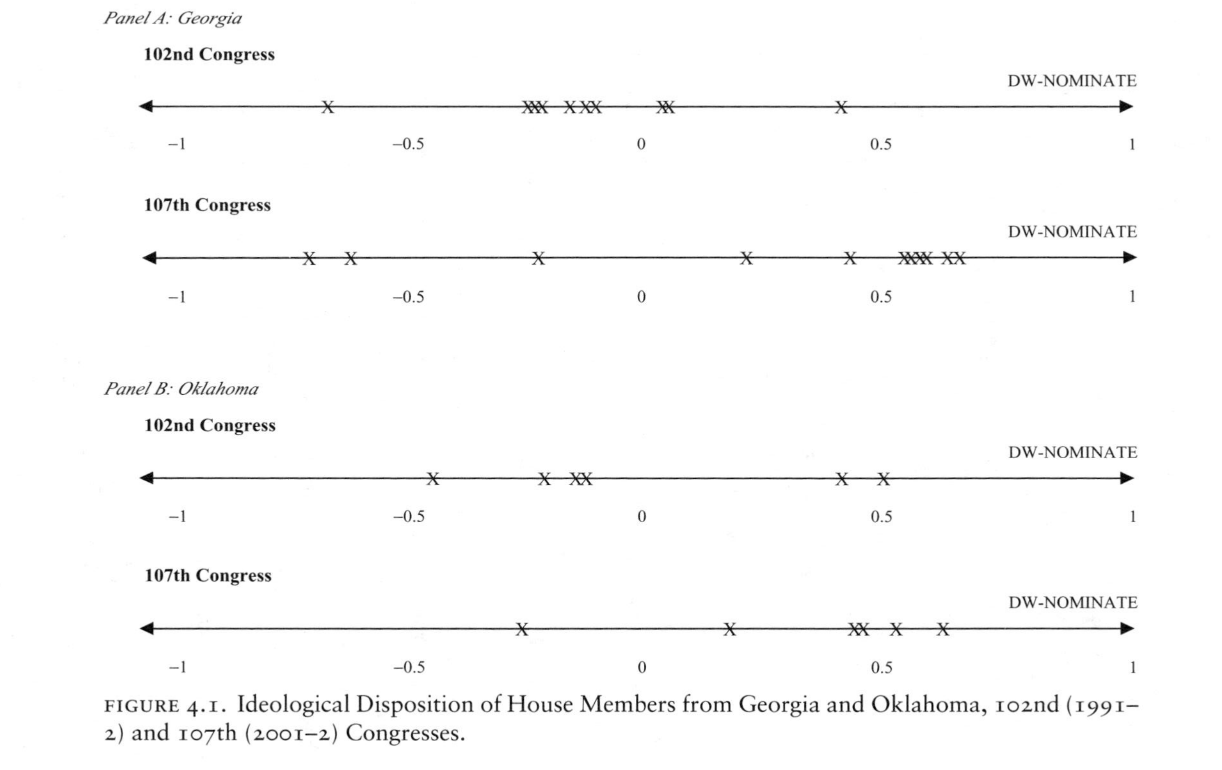

FIGURE 4.1. Ideological Disposition of House Members from Georgia and Oklahoma, 102nd (1991–2) and 107th (2001–2) Congresses.

it is at least curious that the rise of the incumbency advantage and party polarization both have their roots in an era when the Supreme Court was mandating the massive changes in members' constituencies brought on by redistricting throughout the states. Although a number of scholars have debunked the connection between redistricting and the incumbency advantage (Ferejohn 1977, Cox and Katz 2002, and Abramowitz, Alexander, and Gunning 2006), a new generation of political pundits and scholars suggests that the new highly charged partisan redistricting of the 1990s and 2000s has more dramatic implications than the more benign redistricting of the 1960s and 1970s. With modern computer technology, line drawers have more computational power than ever to analyze census data and election results to control the partisan make-up of congressional districts and, consequently, the partisan make-up of their states' congressional delegations. Political observers point to these practices as causes of polarization: "Redistricting has produced far fewer competitive congressional districts, a fact that has lead (sic) to greater polarization in the conduct of the House."[1] In this current era of redistricting, it has become a popular refrain that legislators are no longer chosen by their constituents, but rather that the constituents are chosen by the legislators.

This chapter explores the degree to which redistricting explains the party polarization in the U.S. Congress. The first section analyzes the ideological disposition of the new districts created and the old districts destroyed by decennial line drawings. The second section explores the consequence of redistricting by examining the aggregation of the same presidential votes under both the old congressional lines and the new congressional lines. The third section inspects more closely the actual redistricting schemes that states have utilized during different redistricting cycles. The fourth section assesses the effect of redistricting by analyzing how House polarization changes in relation to Senate polarization. Finally, the fifth section summarizes the overall analysis, suggesting that redistricting has indeed caused party polarization in the House of Representatives over the past 30 years, but probably not as much as the redistricting explanation advocates would have us believe.

[1] Dan Balz, "Partisan Polarization Intensified in 2004 Elections," *The Washington Post*, March 29, 2005, p. A4.

I. The Ideology of New and Obliterated Districts

Carson et al. (2007) argue that the new districts created during redistricting elect more ideological members of Congress than the preexisting districts. To test this relationship, they link congressional districts over time from the 1960s to the 2000s. If one district has at least 50 percent of its constituents from an antecedent district, the two districts are "linked." If a district does not have at least 50 percent of its constituents from an antecedent district, they call it a "new" district. They find that members from these new districts have more polarized roll call voting records than members from linked districts. In the 1992 round of redistricting, for example, they find that the sixty-three members from new districts were almost 25 percent more ideological than the members who were elected in old districts.[2]

I devise an alternative method for classifying districts that is based on the states that gain or lose House seats during reapportionment. I maintain that Carson et al.'s (2007) logic of comparing new and linked districts presents an incomplete picture. For every new district that is created, an old district is destroyed in a state that lost congressional representation in reapportionment. Sometimes the addition or subtraction of districts results in massively redrawn lines. Other times, the overall effect is muted when those charged with redistricting add the new district in the region of the state that experienced the most growth or delete a district in the region that saw the biggest decline, causing relatively minor reverberations throughout the rest of the state. Although McCarty, Poole, and Rosenthal (2006) find that the redistricting explanation is overblown, they do recognize that the effect of reapportionment is the "principal way" in which districting-based explanations cause polarization. They maintain that, though this effect is real, it is rather small in magnitude.

To determine the "new" and "obliterated" districts, instead of examining the constituents, I look to the incumbents' behavior. As the percentage of incumbents running for reelection rises, the task of deciding which of the districts is new and which obliterated becomes easier.

[2] Carson, Crespin, Finocchiaro, and Rohde (2007) graciously gave their data to me. The forty-one Democrats (*21 Republicans*) who were elected from new districts had an average PR score of −0.442 (*0.432*); the 217 Democrats (*156 Republicans*) elected from old districts had an average PR score of −0.330 (*0.392*).

Consider first states that gain seats. The "new" district in a state that gained representation in the House is the district without an incumbent running in it.[3] When vacancies lead to multiple open seat races in a particular state, I revert to Carson et al.'s (2007) "linked" districts to determine which one is "new." All the districts that are not new in a given redistricting cycle are classified as "continuing districts," which are parallel to Carson et al.'s (2007) "linked" districts.

Consider Nevada before and after the 2000 census. In the 1990s, Nevada had two districts. The first district, containing 231 square miles, was centered in Las Vegas and included Henderson. The second district, which was 474 times larger than the first district, encompassed the rest of the state. After the 2000 reapportionment, Nevada gained a third district. To account for the population explosion in the greater Las Vegas area, the first district shrank by more than 20 percent to 177 square miles. The second district also lost some of its area, though a much smaller percentage (less than 4 percent). The new third district took Henderson from the old first district and Overton and Bunkerville from the old second district. At the end of the day, Shelley Berkley, the representative from the old first district, decided to run in the new first district, and Jim Gibbons, the representative from the old second district, decided to run in the new second district. So, through a process of elimination, the "new" district was the third district. Nevada's first and second districts were classified as "continuing districts."

Again, by looking at the behavior of incumbents and going through a process of elimination, the "obliterated" districts are also revealed. The "obliterated" district is the one whose representative was not elected to a subsequent term in the House. Consider Oklahoma during the same redistricting cycle as the Nevada example. In 2000, the Oklahoma congressional delegation was devastated to learn that it would lose one of its six congressional districts. Of the six members in the 107th Congress, four successfully ran for reelection; two opted for retirement. J.C. Watts represented the southwest corner of the state. His district remained largely intact and the candidate he endorsed, Tom Cole, won the general election. Wes Watkins, a Democrat turned Republican, who had long represented district 3, the "little Dixie"

[3] The descriptions of the new and old districts in the respective editions of the *Almanac of American Politics* and *Politics in America* helped classify the districts into the proper categories.

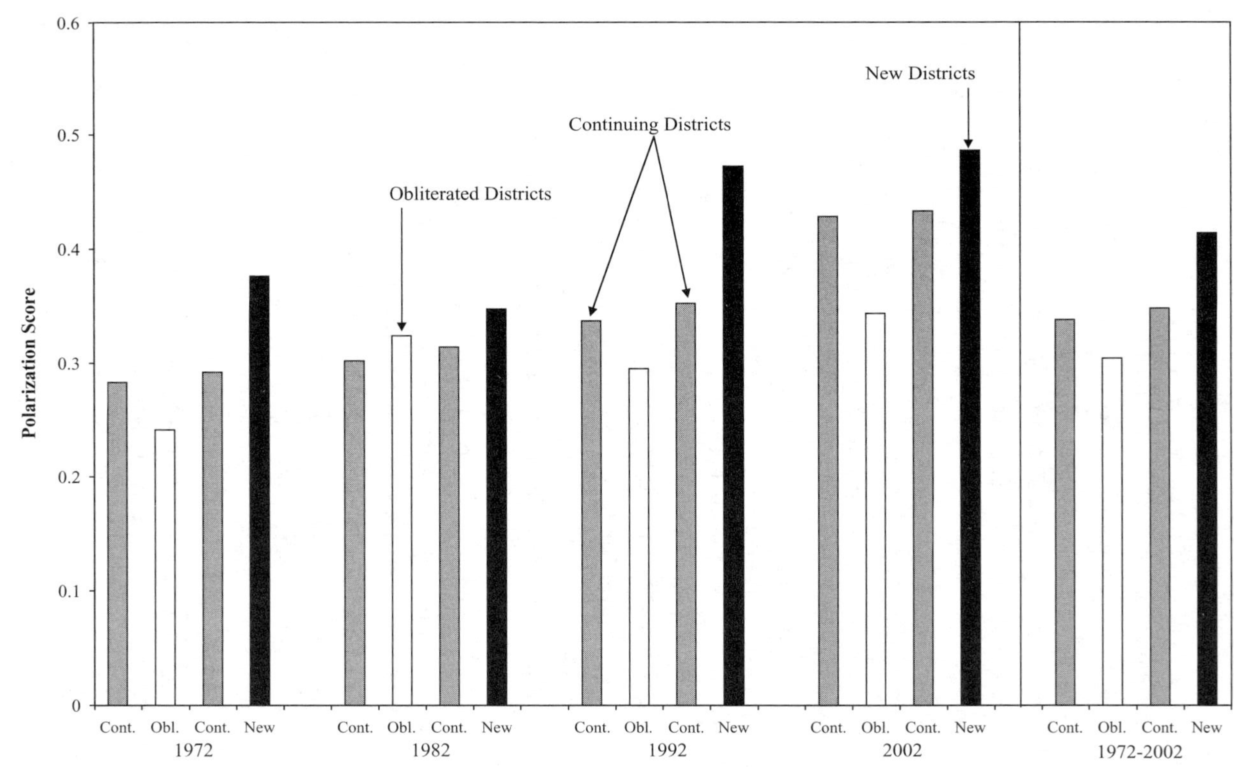

FIGURE 4.2. Polarization Score for Members from Continuing, Obliterated, and New Districts, 1972, 1982, 1992, and 2002.

portion of Oklahoma in the southeast corner of the state, also retired. His old district 3 was split into the four surrounding districts (three of which returned incumbents to Congress; the fourth elected Cole). Although both Watts and Watkins retired, only Watkins's district was considered to be "obliterated." Watts's old district, as well as the other four districts whose members continued serving into the 108th Congress, are classified as "continuing," even though all of their borders and several of the their numbers changed (for example, Frank Lucas, who represented the panhandle and western Oklahoma, represented nearly the exact same area even though his district number changed from 6 to 3).

Jon Porter, the representative from Nevada's third district, and the other 11 representatives from "new" districts in 2002 had a polarization score of 0.44, which was roughly 25 percent higher than the scores of members elected from the other 424 districts. Not only were the 12 members elected from new districts more ideological than the members elected from continuing districts, but so, too, were members elected from new districts in 1972, 1982, and 1992 (black bars in figure 4.2). In fact, over the four elections, the members from new districts were, on average, 16.2 percent more polarized than those members from continuing districts ($p = 0.02$). These results nicely mirror the results found by Carson et al. (2007). The difference between the representatives from new and continuing districts does not significantly decrease over the course of the decade; rather, by the end of the decade, these new districts were electing members who were 20 percent more polarized than the representatives in continuing districts.

Not only were the 63 members elected from new districts more ideological than the members elected from continuing districts, but also members who were redistricted out of the House, like Oklahoma's Wes Watkins, were less ideological (the white bars in figure 4.2) than the members from the continuing districts. Although the difference between continuing and obliterated districts is not as stark as the difference between continuing and new districts, obliterated districts are, on average, 6.2 percent less polarized than continuing districts ($p = 0.41$).[4] The percentage difference between new and obliterated

[4] Again, Carson, Crespin, Finocchiaro, and Rohde's (2007) categorization substantiates this finding. In the 2000 round of redistricting, they found that twenty-seven districts

districts is greatest in the 1990s' redistricting and is least in the 1980s' redistricting.

Across all four redistricting periods, the continuing districts elected representatives that were 3.2 percent more polarized than the continuing districts' representatives in the previous congress. In contrast, the new districts created in states that gained congressional representation were 27.5 percent more polarized than the obliterated districts in states that lost congressional representation. As such, the redistricting destroyed and created districts that were 24.3 percentage points more polarized than the continuing districts.

In a polarizing period, the DW-NOMINATE scores for veteran legislators may be a bit attenuated because they are anchored by the legislators' service in a less polarized chamber. As such, the more apt comparison to these obliterated and new districts is continuing districts that have, respectively, retiring and newly elected members. The 279 newly elected members from continuing districts were 17.9 percent more polarized than retiring members from continuing districts, which is 9.6 percentage points less than the polarization created by reapportionment changes. The ideological changes brought about by the new members in old districts explain almost the entire 3.2 percent gap in continuing districts. The fraction of the gap that remains is a consequence of member adaptation (Theriault 2006).

II. A Direct Test of Redistricting's Effect on Polarization

Perhaps the best test for the redistricting explanation of congressional party polarization would directly compare the aggregation of the exact same votes within the old and new district lines (see also Abramowitz, Alexander, and Gunning 2006). This comparison directly shows how redistricting affects the grouping of the votes within congressional districts. The 1980 presidential election results between Carter and Reagan were initially reported by the districts created after the 1970s census. After the 1980 round of redistricting, the exact same 1980

were obliterated. On average, the members that represented them had a polarization score of 0.34. The polarization score of the members whose districts continued to exist was 0.43. These numbers are statistically significantly different from one another at the 0.0091 level.

presidential voters were reported by the newly created districts.[5] The parallel data are also available for the 1988 election between Dukakis and Bush and the 2000 election between Gore and Bush. Both sets of lines aggregate the exact same votes. I analyze these "crossover elections" because they show the pure effect of the changes in the lines.[6]

The results from a direct comparison of the presidential vote totals under the old and new congressional district lines cast doubt on the redistricting explanation (see panel A of figure 4.3). Although the standard deviation slightly increased for the new districts in the 1990s' redistricting, the standard deviation of the Republican Presidential Vote (RPV) is *lower* in the new district lines for both the 1980s' and 2000s' rounds of redistricting. These results indicate that the new district lines in the 1980s and 2000s, when aggregating old presidential votes, yielded less polarized congressional districts. In the 1990s, redistricting slightly increased the polarization; however, the magnitude of this polarization is smaller than the decreased polarization brought about by redistricting in the 1980s and 2000s.

Not only is there little difference in the standard deviations of the RPV, but also there is little difference in overall strength of partisanship in the districts. For example, the presidential candidate – Bush or Gore – who secured the most votes in a district in the 2000 election using the 1990s' districts received 61.30 percent of the two-party vote (see panel B of figure 4.3). In the new lines adopted for the 2000s, the proportion jumped 0.04 percent all the way to 61.34 percent. The change is similarly small in the 1980s and 1990s rounds of redistricting. Advocates of the redistricting explanation would be hard-pressed to claim that the 0.11 percent change in the 1980s redistricting, the 0.63 change in the 1990s redistricting, and the 0.04 change in the 2000s redistricting were sufficient to cause the parties to polarize so drastically over the past 30 years.

These summary measures may be too blunt an instrument to detect the subtle changes brought about by redistricting. Although the

[5] The 1984 edition of *Politics in America* reports how the new districts would have voted in the 1980 presidential election.

[6] The 1994 edition of *The Almanac of American Politics* reports how the new districts would have voted in the 1988 presidential election. Gary Jacobson selflessly provided the breakdown of the 2000 presidential vote based on congressional district lines in 2002.

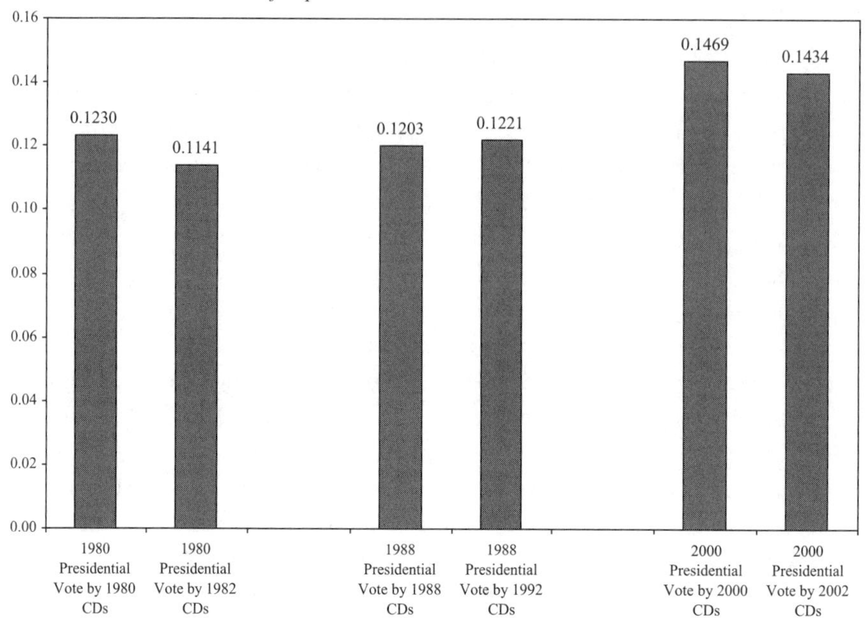

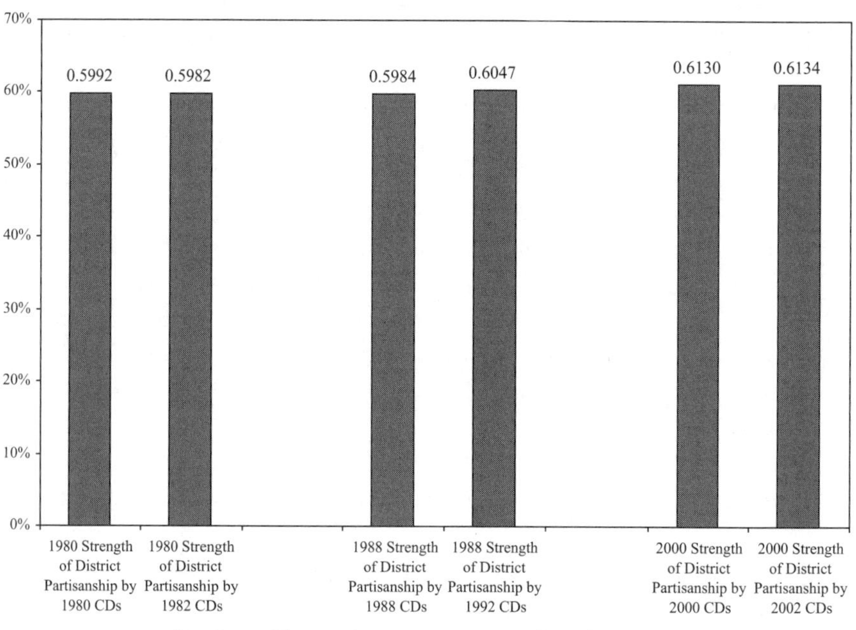

FIGURE 4.3. Partisan Change in Districts Brought About by Redistricting, 1980s, 1990s, and 2000s.

standard deviation and percentages did not change much, a more fine-tuned classification of safe districts reveals a definite redistricting effect. Figure 4.4 shows the percentage of safe districts (black and gray), where one presidential candidate did 5 percent better, or very safe districts (black), where one candidate did 10 percent better than they did nationwide in cross-over elections. Presumably, safe and very safe districts elect more ideological members of Congress. According to the 1980 presidential vote, either Reagan or Carter did 10 percent better than their nationwide average in 31 percent of the districts according to the 1970 districts lines and did 5 percent better than their nationwide average in 62 percent of the districts. The parallel numbers using the same individual votes aggregated by the 1980s lines are 31 percent and 63 percent. The 1990s and 2000s rounds of redistricting had a slightly larger effect, especially on the very safe districts, where one presidential candidate did more than 10 percent better than he did nationwide. The very safe districts usually came about as a result of creating majority-minority districts.

As an aside, the largest trend in figure 4.4 is not the differences created by redistricting; rather, it is the increasing trend of safe districts within the same district lines. Although the effect of redistricting appears to be minor, the trend toward safer districts is quite dramatic (see also Stonecash, Brewer, and Mariani 2003). For example, between the 1988 and 2000 elections, 6 percent more districts became very safe, and 7 percent more districts became safe even though the exact same 1990s redistricting plans were in use. As such, an analysis of redistricting may not be picking up the true effect of district-based explanations for party polarization. The following chapter presents more evidence along these lines.

III. Redistricting Category Analysis

Based on the new census numbers, the House of Representatives is reapportioned every 10 years. Following a series of Supreme Court opinions from the 1960s, states must use the new census data to create population-equal districts, even if their overall number of seats remained the same. States whose population only affords them one representative in the House have the easiest task because the state

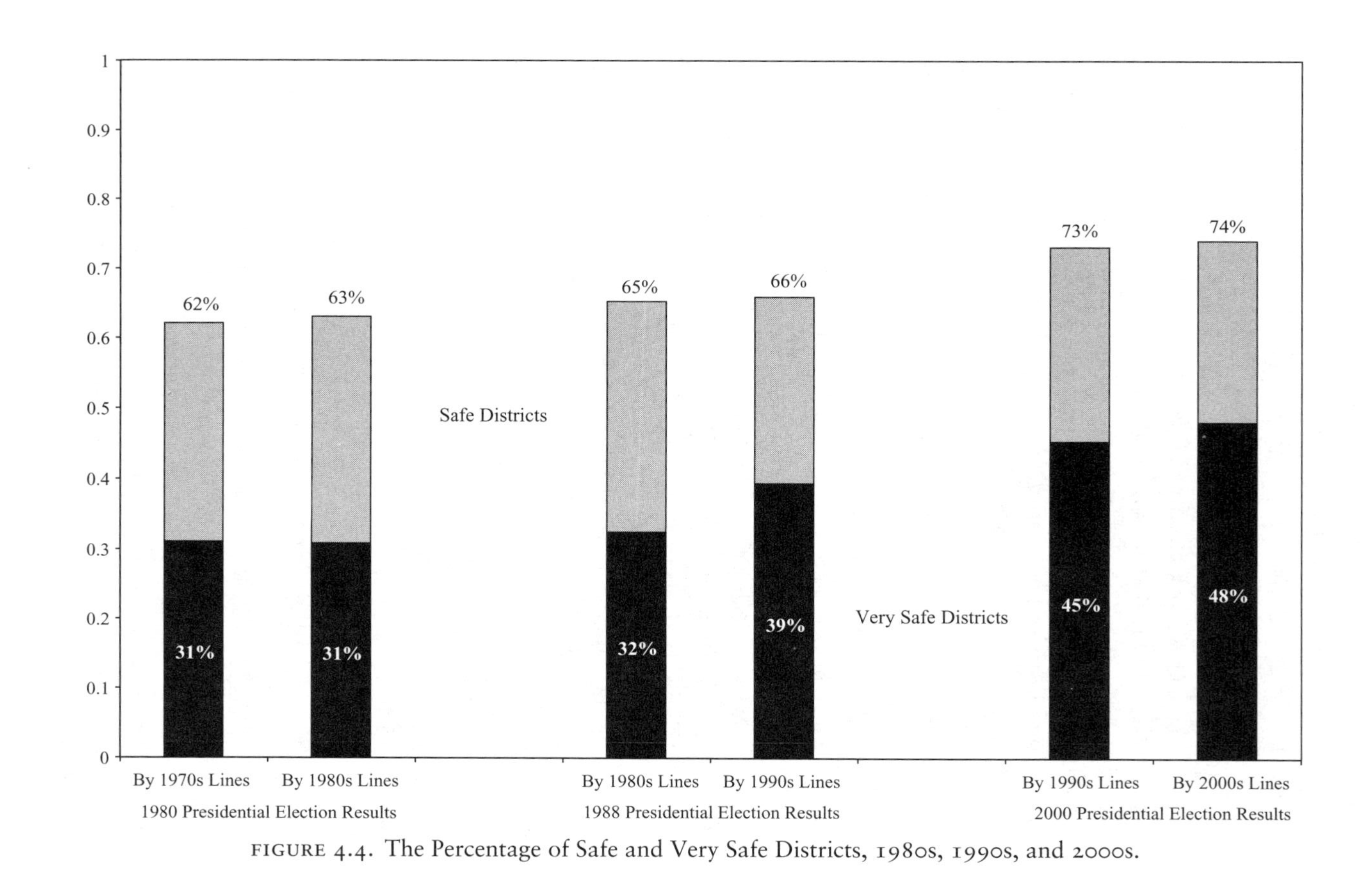

FIGURE 4.4. The Percentage of Safe and Very Safe Districts, 1980s, 1990s, and 2000s.

boundary is their district line (such is the case with Alaska, Delaware, Montana, North Dakota, South Dakota, Vermont, and Wyoming in 2002). Other states make only minor adjustments to their existing lines to equalize population. For example, Rhode Island, with two representatives, has had the same basic lines since 1842, except for a 20-year period in the early twentieth century when it was granted a third representative.

On the other hand, other states, prompted by shifting populations, changing political fortunes, or varying numbers in their congressional delegation, undergo wholesale line redrawing. A typical example of a state in this category is California, which has seen its delegation increase from 38 members in the 1960s to 43 members in the 1970s to 45 members in the 1980s to 52 members in the 1990s and, finally, to 53 members in the 2000s. Although its population growth and shifting demographics have forced line changes, California's legislators notoriously used more than shifting populations to draw the new district lines. Several of these plans have become legendary in the gerrymandering Hall of Fame. First, the infamous Burton lines, adopted after the 1980 reapportionment, transformed a 22–21 margin for Democrats in the 97th Congress (1981–2) to a 28–17 margin in the following congress, even though the Republican areas grew faster than the Democratic areas (*Congressional Districts in the 1980s* 1983, 29). Second, the incumbency protection plan that followed the 2000 reapportionment divided the state delegation into 20 safe Republican seats and 33 safe Democratic seats. In fact, every district under the new lines would have given Gore either less than 46 percent or more than 54 percent of the two-party vote in 2000, whereas 11 districts under the 1990s' lines fell in the 46 to 54 percent range (Jacobson 2004, figure 10–1).

Characterizing redistricting plans can yield important evidence in evaluating the extent to which redistricting has caused party polarization in Congress. I use the journalistic accounts of the new districting plans provided by the *National Journal* and *Congressional Quarterly* to categorize each state's new districting plan. If a state either did not change its district lines or adjusted them only to account for population shifts without changing the partisan complexion of any district, I coded the state as experiencing "minor redistricting changes." If a state changed the partisan make-up of any of its districts, I coded the state as experiencing "major redistricting changes."

If redistricting is the cause of party polarization, it must be that the states with radically redrawn lines have led the political parties to their ideological poles. Quite simply, district lines cannot be responsible for more polarized members if the same district lines at one point elected moderate members. I should note that not all states that radically redraw their lines do so with the intent of creating more partisan districts. For example, in 2002, Iowa approved completely new lines with the intent of creating more competitive elections as mandated by state law. The new lines prompted two of Iowa's five members to move so that they could run in more comfortable districts. Only Congressman Steve King, who ran in the only district that remained largely intact, surpassed 60 percent of the two-party vote in the 2002 congressional elections. I maintain that Iowa's 2001 incumbency-damaging scheme occurs much less frequently than California's explicitly political redistricting schemes.

I use two sets of data to test for differences in the redistricting categories. First, I examine how the new district lines affected the aggregation of presidential voters in crossover elections (Reagan versus Carter in 1980, Bush versus Dukakis in 1988, and Bush versus Gore in 2000). In this analysis, I examine the two-party percentage of the presidential candidate receiving the most votes in the particular district. Second, I test the redistricting's effect on members' polarization scores. To dampen the effect of either any one particular legislator or any one set of congressional election results, I average the members' polarization scores from a particular district across an entire decade to arrive at a 10-year average polarization score for each district. If redistricting has caused the parties to polarize, states with major redistricting changes should have a bigger difference between the old and new lines than states with minor redistricting changes.

Table 4.1 shows the results for these two separate analyses over the past three redistricting cycles. In the 1980s, the 355 districts in states that experienced major line changes did not yield more partisan districts, as measured by the 1980 presidential votes, than the 80 districts in states with minor line changes. In contrast, the representatives from the substantially redrawn states polarized almost three times as much as the representatives from states that underwent minor line

TABLE 4.1. *Redistricting's Effect on Polarization, 1980s, 1990s, and 2000s*

	Number of Districts	Districts' Winning Presidential Vote by Crossover Election[a]				Decennial Member Polarization Score[b]			
		Before	After	Difference	P > |t|	Before	After	Difference	P > |t|
1980s Redistricting									
Minor Changes	80	0.577	0.576	−0.001	0.981	0.238	0.252	0.014	0.258
Major Changes	355	0.604	0.603	−0.001	0.839	0.304	0.342	0.038	0.000
Difference			0.000			0.024			
1990s Redistricting									
Minor Changes	95	0.582	0.580	−0.002	0.864	0.314	0.394	0.080	0.000
Major Changes	340	0.602	0.611	0.009	0.165	0.329	0.402	0.073	0.000
Difference			0.011			−0.007			
2000s Redistricting									
Minor Changes	80	0.592	0.591	−0.001	0.912	0.382	0.399	0.017	0.352
Major Changes	355	0.618	0.618	0.000	0.921	0.405	0.441	0.036	0.000
Difference			0.001			0.019			
Total Redistricting Effect									
Minor Changes	255	0.584	0.582	−0.001	0.864	0.311	0.351	0.040	0.000
Major Changes	1050	0.608	0.611	0.003	0.494	0.346	0.395	0.049	0.000
Difference			0.004			0.009			

[a] Changeover elections are those presidential elections in which voting data exist by congressional district for both the old and the new districts. The data exist for the presidential vote aggregated by both the 1970s' and the 1980s' congressional districts for the 1980 election; by both the 1980s' and 1990s' election for the 1988 election, and by both the 1990s' and 2000s' districts for the 2000 election. The numbers in these columns are the averages of the winning candidate's two-party vote in the congressional districts.

[b] The Decennial Member Polarization Score is the DW-NOMINATE for Republicans and negative one times the PR score for Democrats. These columns average the polarization score for the members who served in the five congresses within each district. For the 2000s' decade, the statistic is based only on the 108th Congress (2003–4).

redrawing. In the 1990s, the states that underwent major changes polarized more according to the crossover elections and less according to members' polarization scores than states with minor changes. In the 2000s, the redrawing of the district lines had no effect whatsoever on the aggregation of votes in the 2000 presidential election, though the states that underwent major redistricting polarized more than twice as much as the states experiencing minor redistricting. In total, the table presents some evidence for the redistricting explanation. Though the data vary from cycle to cycle, when the results are aggregated across all three redistricting cycles, the districts that underwent major redistricting changes cast more partisan presidential votes and elected more polarized members than districts experiencing only minor redistricting changes.

In addition to being classified by the amount of redistricting, the 2000 redistricting plans can be characterized along two other dimensions. First, I compare the extent of polarization within states that did not redistrict (the seven listed earlier) and states where redistricting was primarily delegated to a nonpartisan or bipartisan commission (Arizona, Connecticut, Hawaii, Idaho, Indiana, Iowa, New Jersey, and Washington) with states that conventionally redistricted (the rest). No difference existed within the categories in the crossover election analysis. Contrary to expectations, states that used commissions had members that polarized almost 50 percent more than members from states that did not use commissions (see panel A of table 4.2).

Second, I compare states that adopted redistricting plans that were described by the *National Journal* or *Congressional Quarterly* as "incumbent protection plans" (California, Illinois, Louisiana, Missouri, New Jersey, North Carolina, Texas, Virginia, West Virginia, and Wisconsin) with states that did not attempt explicitly to advantage incumbents with new district lines (see panel B of table 4.2). The line drawing in these incumbent-friendly states yielded a 0.6 percent advantage for the winning presidential candidate in comparison to states without incumbency protection plans. Additionally, the incumbency-friendly districts yielded members who polarized one-third more than members from states that did not pass incumbent-friendly plans. Although the commission analysis yielded counterintuitive results, the results from the incumbency protection plans analysis yielded the results most consistent with the redistricting analysis.

TABLE 4.2. *The Effect of Commission Plans and Incumbency Protection Plans on Party Polarization, 2000s*

	Number of Districts	Districts' Winning Presidential Vote[a]				Decennial Member Polarization Score[b]			
		2000	2002	Difference	P > |t|	1990s	2000s	Difference	P > |t|
Panel A: The Effect of Commissions									
No Redistricting	7	0.630	0.630	0.000	0.996	0.378	0.364	−0.014	0.791
Commisssion	53	0.595	0.594	−0.001	0.953	0.391	0.445	0.054	0.044
Subtotal	60	0.599	0.598	**−0.001**	0.956	0.390	0.435	**0.045**	0.066
Regular Redistricting	387	0.615	0.616	**0.001**	0.936	0.402	0.433	**0.031**	0.001
Difference			**0.002**			**−0.014**			
Panel B: The Effect of Incumbency Protection Plans									
No Redistricting	7	0.630	0.630	0.000	0.996	0.378	0.364	−0.014	0.791
Non-Incumbency Protecting Redistricting	262	0.609	0.607	−0.002	0.807	0.396	0.427	0.031	0.010
Subtotal	269	0.610	0.608	**−0.002**	0.809	0.396	0.425	**0.029**	0.007
Incumbency Protecting Redistricting Plans	166	0.618	0.622	**0.004**	0.693	0.408	0.447	**0.039**	0.008
Difference			**0.006**			**0.010**			

[a] Average of the presidential candidate who received the most votes in each congressional district in the 2000 election based on the 1990s' district lines and the 2000s' district lines.

[b] The Decennial Member Polarization Score is the DW-NOMINATE for Republicans and −1 times the PR score for Democrats. These columns average the polarization score for the members who serve in the five congresses within each decade. For the 2000s' decade, the statistic is based only on the 108th Congress (2003–4).

IV. A Multivariate Assessment of Redistricting

The Senate polarization scores can be used to provide a clean test for determining whether redistricting is a cause of House party polarization. The political factors influencing member voting in the House presumably have a similar effect upon senators. These factors include the legislative agenda, world crises that might have arisen, and the political environment. One factor, redistricting, necessarily only will have an impact in the House. Redistricting, if it is a cause of House party polarization, should have an effect above and beyond the correlation between the House and Senate party polarization scores.

The dependent variable in this analysis is the House polarization score by congress. Column A of panel A in table 4.3 shows the bivariate relationship between the House and Senate polarization scores. Not surprisingly, the relationship is quite strong, leaving very little unexplained variance for all of the other independent variables, let alone redistricting. This analysis employs two different measures for redistricting. First, redistricting takes on a value of "1" when the House goes through reapportionment and redistricting. Second, the new district variable, adopted from Carson et al. (2007, table 1), is the number of new districts created each Congress. Because of the political nature and timing of redistricting, parties are frequently too rushed to take complete advantage of new district lines. Frequently, the full impact of redistricting is only fully realized in the second election after redistricting. As such, both operationalizations of redistricting contain a 50 percent lag, so that the second congress after reapportionment and redistricting is coded as "0.5," and the new district variable is the sum of the new districts created this congress plus one-half the new districts created in the previous congress. The results for these two operationalizations are reported in columns B and C, respectively. Although both coefficients are correctly signed, neither comes close to achieving statistical significance. In predicting House polarization, the consequences of redistricting and the creation of new districts appear to have little effect.

Given the strong relationship between party polarization in the two chambers, any variable would have difficulty achieving statistical significance. Additionally, the development of DW-NOMINATE scores makes it extra difficult for redistricting to have a statistically significant

TABLE 4.3. *Redistricting's Effect on Party Polarization in the U.S. House, 93rd to 108th Congress (1973–2004)*

	(A)	(B)	(C)
Panel A: Dependent Variable is the House Polarization Score:			
Senate Polarization	1.327**	1.327**	1.318**
	(0.08)	(0.08)	(0.08)
Redistricting Indicator		0.009	0.00004
		(0.01)	(0.000)
Number of New Districts			0.058
			(0.04)
Constant	−0.092**	−0.097**	−0.092**
	(0.03)	(0.03)	(0.03)
N	16	16	16
R^2	0.953	0.953	0.953
Panel B: Dependent Variable is the House Replacement Score:			
Senate Replacement	0.203	0.154	0.139
	(0.20)	(0.20)	(0.19)
Redistricting Indicator		0.680	0.025
		(0.53)	(0.01)
Number of New Districts			0.025*
			(0.01)
Constant	0.517*	0.304	0.165
	(0.24)	(0.29)	(0.28)
N	16	16	16
R^2	0.067	0.170	0.289

*Statistically significant at 0.10; **statistically significant at 0.05.

affect upon House party polarization. Because DW-NOMINATE scores force members to adapt linearly over time, the scores for a particular congress are affected by the scores of the surrounding congresses. Consider the consequences that new district lines would have on both a veteran and freshman member. If the veteran voted in line with the new district, her DW-NOMINATE would be anchored by her previous voting record, forcing her to have what would appear as only a tiny or moderate change on her score.[7] As such, the scores for veterans will be attenuated. Now suppose that a new member is elected from the district. If he votes exactly as the old member had voted, he

[7] Poole and Rosenthal (1997, 74) assure that higher polynomial specifications had little effect on the generation of these scores.

would end up with a different DW-NOMINATE, because, as a consequence of serving in his first congress, which is more polarized, his score would not be anchored by his service in more moderate congresses. As such, the DW-NOMINATE scores for new members should be more sensitive to redistricting's effect than the scores for returning members.

To isolate more cleanly the influence of redistricting, in panel B of table 4.3, I conduct a parallel analysis to panel A using the House replacement polarization score as the dependent variable in place of the overall House polarization score and the Senate replacement polarization score in place of the overall polarization score as an independent variable.[8] As column A shows, the relationship between the replacement polarization scores in the two chambers is not nearly as strong as the overall polarization score. The results in column B show that although the redistricting indicator variable does a better job of predicting House replacement polarization than House polarization scores, it still does not achieve statistical significance. Column C shows that the new district variable also more accurately predicts the House replacement polarization score. Its statistical significance level breaks the 0.10 barrier, but not the more conventional 95 percent confidence level. Substantively, the new district variable at its maximum value (in 1992) has three times the effect of Senate replacement polarization on House replacement polarization.

V. Conclusion

Four tests from this chapter provide some evidence that redistricting has caused the parties in the House to polarize. Statistically significant findings show that new districts are more polarized than old districts (figure 4.2), new congressional lines yield more polarized voting patterns than old congressional lines (figure 4.4 and table 4.1), states that purposefully partisan redistrict yield more polarized districts and representatives than states that do not (table 4.2), and congresses with newly redistricted members in the House polarize above and beyond the Senate (table 4.3). Although these findings, especially when they are aggregated, certainly suggest that redistricting should be included

[8] See Theriault (2006) for the values of these scores.

in a list of causes of party polarization, they do not, either individually or aggregately, give an assessment of the degree to which polarization is caused by redistricting. The analysis in this conclusion suggests that redistricting causes between 10 and 20 percent of the party polarization that has occurred in the House of Representatives over the past 32 years.

Members elected from the 64 new districts over the past four redistricting periods were 27.5 percent more ideological than the 64 representatives from districts obliterated in redistricting. In contrast, the 1676 districts that continued to exist were 3.2 percent more polarized than the continuing districts of the previous congress. In comparing the polarization within the district categories, redistricting, as made manifest in obliterated and new districts, has caused 24.2 percent of the polarization in the U.S. House of Representatives since 1973. Taking into consideration the retiring and new members in the continuing districts does not change this estimate because the larger polarization among the former category of members would significantly reduce the average polarization in the continuing districts of the members who did not retire and were not new.

Although the standard deviation and strength of partisanship indicate that redistricting causes very little aggregate change, the percentage of districts that are classified as "safe" and "very safe" exhibit bigger changes. Over the past three redistricting cycles, the percentage of safe districts has increased 1.3 percent as a consequence of redistricting and 6.9 percent as a consequence of political change over the course of the decade. More dramatically, the percentage of very safe districts has increased 8.7 percent as a result of redistricting and 9.3 percent as a result of political change over the course of the decade. Redistricting, then, has led to 16 percent and 48 percent of the total change in the percentage of safe and very safe districts, respectively, though this test does not assess the ideological extremity of the members elected from these districts.

In the past three redistricting periods, 85 districts, on average, were in states that underwent minor changes, which accounts for slightly less than 20 percent of all districts. These districts sent representatives to Congress who were, on average, 4.0 percent more polarized than the districts' previous representatives. The more than 80 percent of the districts that were in states that underwent major redistricting changes, in contrast, sent representatives who were 4.9 percent more polarized than the districts' previous representatives. Taking into consideration the difference in polarization between districts from states with major changes and districts in states without major changes and the frequency of each kind of district, redistricting has caused about 15 percent of the polarization between the parties in the U.S. House of Representatives.[9]

The multivariate tests are largely inconclusive. A forced conclusion from them is that they point to some, but not an overwhelming amount of, evidence for the redistricting explanation. Although the redistricting indicator variable does not achieve statistical significance, it is always in the correct direction. The number of new districts achieves a low standard of statistical significance only in the replacement equation.

Given that the four tests employ different data and different statistical methodologies, it is somewhat surprising that they yield similar results. Concluding from any one of the tests that redistricting *causes* a particular percentage of party polarization is hasty. Nevertheless, the accumulation of tests point to significant evidence suggesting that redistricting accounts for between 10 and 20 percent of party polarization in the U.S. House.

[9] The 16 percent figure comes from simple arithmetic (data from table 4.1). Over the past three redistricting periods, 255 districts underwent minor (or no) changes. These districts became 4 percent more polarized. One thousand and fifty districts underwent major changes and elected members who were 4.9 percent more polarized. Multiplying the frequencies by the polarizations reveals that the total change was 6165, of which only 945 can be accountable to redistricting (the 0.9 percent difference multiplied by the 1050 districts). Dividing 945 by 6165 reveals the 15 percent reported in the text.

5

The Political and Geographic Sorting of Constituents

Michigan's Livingston County is strategically situated. It is less than an hour's drive from both the state capitol in Lansing and the auto manufacturing international headquarters in Detroit. Even as *the* industry in Michigan has shed high-paying low-skilled jobs, Livingston County's population has experienced growth almost unrivaled in the state, increasing more than 166 percent over the past 30 years. In contrast, Wayne County, where much of Detroit is located, has lost almost 23 percent of its population over the same time period.

Livingston and Wayne are not only experiencing divergent population changes, but also as the residents politically sort themselves, move in, and leave the area, the demographics of these counties have similarly diverged. Wayne was 27.7 percent African American in the 1970s. In the 2000 census, that percentage increased almost 15 percentage points to 42.2 percent. Although the median household income in Wayne County has tripled over the 30 years, its residents went from earning about 1 percent more than Michigan's median to earning nearly 9 percent less. Although Livingston's black population has not changed much (in the 2000 census, it was still less than one-half of 1 percent), the residents' increase in earnings has nearly doubled those in Wayne. Whereas Livingston's median household earned almost 9 percent more than Michigan's median in 1970, it now earns more than 50 percent more than the state's median.

The coupled population and demographic transformation of these counties has had a significant influence on their residents' voting habits.

In the Nixon versus McGovern presidential election in 1972, Wayne gave the Democrat a surplus of 79,036 votes, which more than made up for the 9,222 Republican surplus in Livingston County. While the Democratic percentage in Wayne was 11.5 percent greater for McGovern than his percent statewide, Livingston was 11.5 percent more Republican than the state. As Wayne has become more Democratic, Livingston has become more Republican. In the Bush versus Kerry presidential election in 2004, Wayne gave the latter 342,297 more votes than the former. Livingston, on the other hand, gave the former 24,869 more votes than the latter. Wayne was 18.1 percent more Democratic than the state, and Livingston was 15.2 percent less Democratic than the state.

The counties' demographic and voting divergence is replicated in the congressional districts that include these counties. In the 93rd Congress, Livingston was one of four counties in the Sixth Congressional District, which was 5 percent African American and had a median income 15 percent above the national average. In the 108th Congress, Livingston was one of four counties in the Eighth Congressional District, which was still 5 percent African American and had a median income 26 percent above the national average. Although six congressional districts reached into Wayne County in the 93rd Congress, the heart of the county (and Detroit) was in the First Congressional District. It was 30 percent white and had an income 4 percent above the national average. In the 108th Congress, only four congressional districts reached into Wayne County. The successor of the old First Congressional District was the Fourteenth Congressional District, which was again 30 percent white. Thirty years later, however, the district's income was 18 percent below the national average. The income divergence was replicated in the districts' political voting records. In the 2004 election, Bush won 54 percent of the vote in the Eighth Congressional District and only 17 percent in the Fourteenth Congressional District.

The counties' representation in Congress has also changed – at least nominally. In the 93rd Congress, Livingston was represented by Congressman Charles Chamberlain, "an often voluble Republican" with a DW-NOMINATE score of 0.29 (Barone, Ujifusa, and Matthews 1972, 373). Thirty-two years later, Representative Mike Rogers represented Livingston County, which is where his home is located. Rogers, a "compassionate conservative," had a DW-NOMINATE score of 0.42 in the 108th Congress (Barone and Cohen 2005, 875).

Whereas the representative from Livingston in the 108th Congress was 16 years younger than his counterpart in the 93rd Congress, Wayne's representative in 2003 was 32 years older than his earlier counterpart. The firebrand liberal from Wayne called for Nixon's impeachment in May 1972, a month before the Watergate break-in, for his conduct in the war against the Viet Cong. Thirty-one years later, the firebrand liberal from Wayne called for Bush's impeachment for mishandling the war in Iraq. The firebrand, of course, is the same John Conyers, who was the second longest serving representative in the 108th Congress (eclipsed only by his fellow Wayne County resident, John Dingell). His DW-NOMINATE score has held steady around −0.8 over the course of his career. The six members who represented at least a part of Wayne County in the 93rd Congress had an average polarization score of 44.7 percent. In the 108th Congress, that percentage, calculated on only the four members who represented Wayne, increased to 51.8.

Bill Bishop's (2004) analysis shows that Livingston and Wayne are not unique, though perhaps a bit more exaggerated than the typical county. He finds that the percentage of people living in counties that cast lopsided ballots aggregately in presidential elections, which he defined as giving either candidate more than 60 percent of its votes, increased from 26.8 percent in 1976 to 48.3 percent in 2004. This phenomenon of polarization across fixed boundaries is not only happening at the county level. The percentage of voters in states won by a presidential candidate with equally lopsided presidential votes increased even more dramatically. In 1976, only six states, with 4.7 percent of the U.S. electorate, cast 60 percent or more of the two-party vote for either Jimmy Carter or Gerald Ford. In 2004, 19.5 percent of the electorate lived in one of the 17 states where either John Kerry or George Bush won with more than 60 percent of the two-party vote.

These county-level and state-level analyses show that perhaps the underlying logic of the redistricting explanation is correct, but that its advocates take the argument one step too far. Perhaps House districts, like counties and states, have become more politically segregated, which exacerbates the polarization within them. Perhaps, consistent with the redistricting argument, more conservative districts are electing more conservative members and more liberal districts are electing more liberal members. But, perhaps, the effect of redistricting is exaggerated because it ignores the transformation that occurred in states like Oklahoma in the 1980s and 1990s, where more homogeneous districts have elected more polarizing members even though the district lines had changed only marginally. Perhaps all geographic jurisdictions, independent of having moving boundaries (congressional districts) or not (states and counties), have become more politically homogeneous over the past 32 years.

The demographic and political changes in Livingston and Wayne counties are an example of only one out of the two "sortings" that are analyzed in this chapter. "Sorting" at two different levels helps explain the homogenization of political jurisdictions quite independently of the malleability of their boundaries. First, as exemplified by Livingston and Wayne counties, scholars who have been studying demographic trends at a neighborhood level find that, although perhaps not explicitly, more and more individuals are moving closer to their ideological soul mates (Bishop 2004, Oppenheimer 2005, and Giroux 2005). Although property taxes, daily commutes, and the quality of public schools are dictating these decisions, these factors are not unrelated to politics. This geographic sorting has been coupled with and exacerbated by an ideological sorting of voters into more coherent political parties. As conservative voters increasingly identify with the Republican party, not only does the Republican party attempt to maintain the conservatives' newfound loyalties with conservative proposals, but the Democratic party adopts more liberal policies because it no longer needs to worry about keeping the conservatives in the fold.

This chapter analyzes the extent to which the voters' sorting has polarized the U.S. Congress. I test the argument in three steps, which comprise the first three sections of the chapter. The first section examines the link between ideological predisposition and partisan identification. The second section tests if jurisdictions have become more demographically or politically homogeneous. Additionally, it shows the extent of the political sorting into ideologically pure parties and the ramifications that has on congressional elections. If voters are not segregating themselves into like-minded districts and states, then the argument, at its face, could be rejected. The third section tests whether more consistent and segregated constituencies elect more ideologically charged members. The fourth section offers a comprehensive assessment of the degree to which political segregation, in combination with redistricting, has caused party polarization in Congress. In total, geographic and partisan sorting have a real effect on polarizing Congress, accounting for between 15 and 30 percent of the divergence between the parties in both the House and the Senate.

I. Ideological Sorting of Voters

Political scientists have been finding fewer and fewer voters who claim to be either liberal Republicans or conservative Democrats (Hetherington 2001, Galston and Kamarck 2005, and Abramowitz, Alexander, and Gunning 2006). As the parties at the national level have separated, the American public has increasingly sacrificed its prior party labels on the altar of ideological consistency. Even those scholars who question the electorate's polarization recognize that the voters have ideologically sorted themselves (Fiorina 2006).

In 1972 – the year of McGovern's candidacy – about 25 percent of Democratic party identifiers also classified themselves as conservatives. By the 2004 election, that number was cut nearly in half. During that same time period, liberals went from comprising 36 percent of the Democratic party to 51 percent. Liberals in the Republican party went from nearly 13 percent in 1972 to under 6 percent in 2004 (see figure 5.1 for the composition of the parties by ideological placement). Conservatives, on the other hand, who were slightly more than half of the Republican party in 1972, now comprise nearly 70 percent of the party.

The greater consistency in partisan and ideological alignment transcends into greater voting consistency. Liberals voted for the Democratic candidate in congressional elections 86 percent of the time in 2004 (up from 75 percent in 1972) and John Kerry received a whopping 90 percent of their vote in the 2004 presidential election (up from McGovern's 69 percent in 1972). Likewise for conservatives and the Republican party. Congressional candidates received 79 percent of the conservative vote in 2004 and George Bush got a whopping 88 percent of their vote in the 2004 presidential election.

Panel A: The Democrats

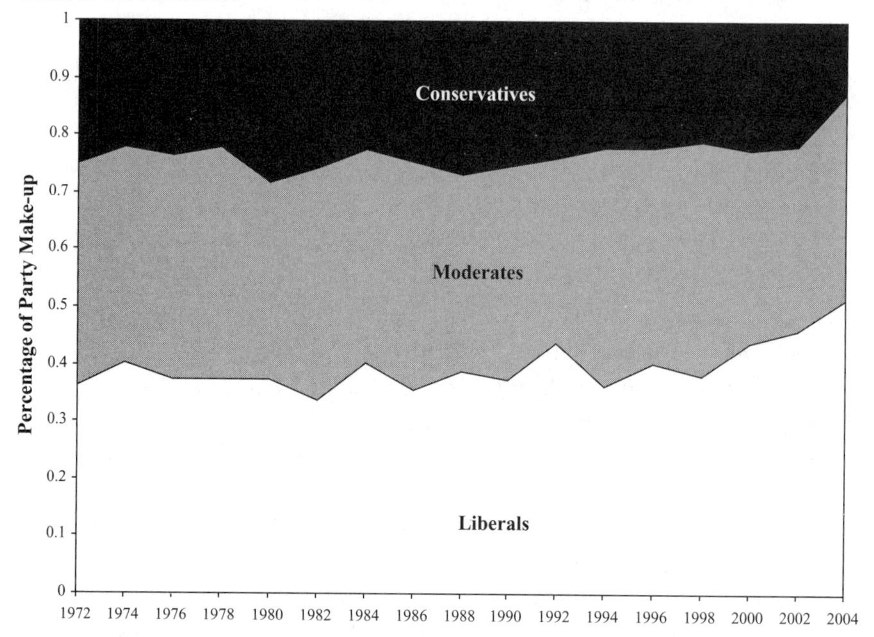

Panel B: The Republicans

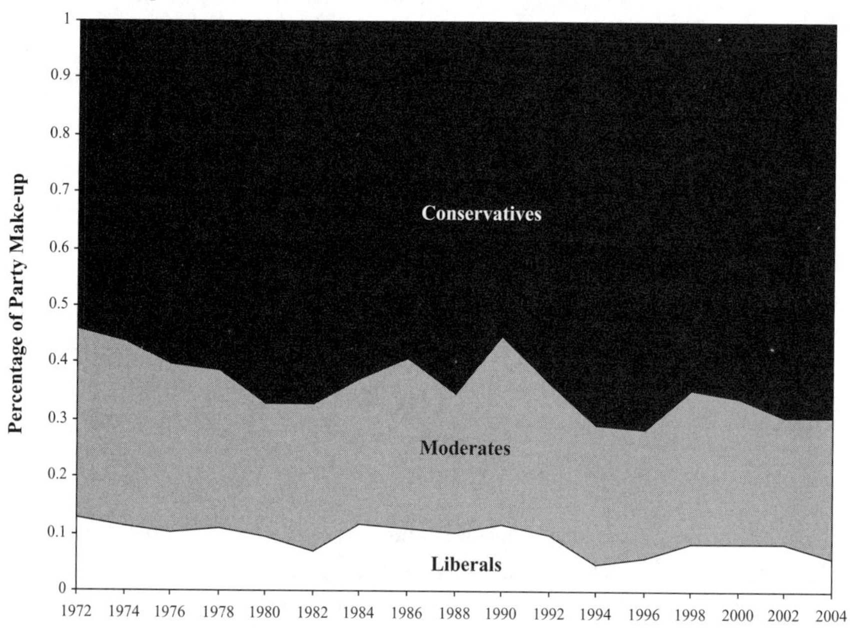

FIGURE 5.1. Ideological Make-up of Self-Identified Partisan Voters, 1972–2004.

II. Sorting into Homogeneous Jurisdictions

Ideological sorting is both more prevalent in the literature and more understood among the American public. Geographic sorting is more complicated and less examined. I evaluate the political segregation argument with two tests. First, I evaluate whether members' constituencies have been demographically diverging. Second, I examine the partisan results of elections in congressional districts and states over time. In short, the disparity in both demographics and political outcomes has grown considerably between Democrats and Republicans in both representatives' districts and senators' states.

Demographic Polarization in Members' Constituencies

The introduction of this chapter shows that, for whatever reason, the residents in southeast Michigan are increasingly residing in neighborhoods where the residents look alike and earn similar salaries. That trend is not only apparent in Livingston and Wayne counties, but also in congressional districts and states throughout the United States. The standard deviation of non-white residents within congressional districts increased almost 17 percent from the 1970s' districts to the 2000s' districts (see panel A of figure 5.2). The spread of income increased even more. The standard deviation of median income increased more than 50 percent, even after controlling for inflation (the spread for nominal median income increased more than five fold). These results are consistent with McCarty, Poole, and Rosenthal's (2006) much more rigorous analysis on the income disparity between districts represented by Republicans and districts represented by Democrats.

The divergence of demographics across states, like the congressional districts, has increased (see panel B of figure 5.2). The standard deviation of the percentage of non-white residents in the states has increased almost 18 percent since the 1980s (for whatever reason, the non-white spread in the 1970s was just a bit smaller than it was in the 2000s). While the spread of nominal median income across states has increased almost four fold, the real income spread has only increased 19 percent since the 1970s.[1]

[1] Giroux (2005) shows how the districts represented by the two parties vary even in the percentages of the district that are urban, suburban, exurban, and rural.

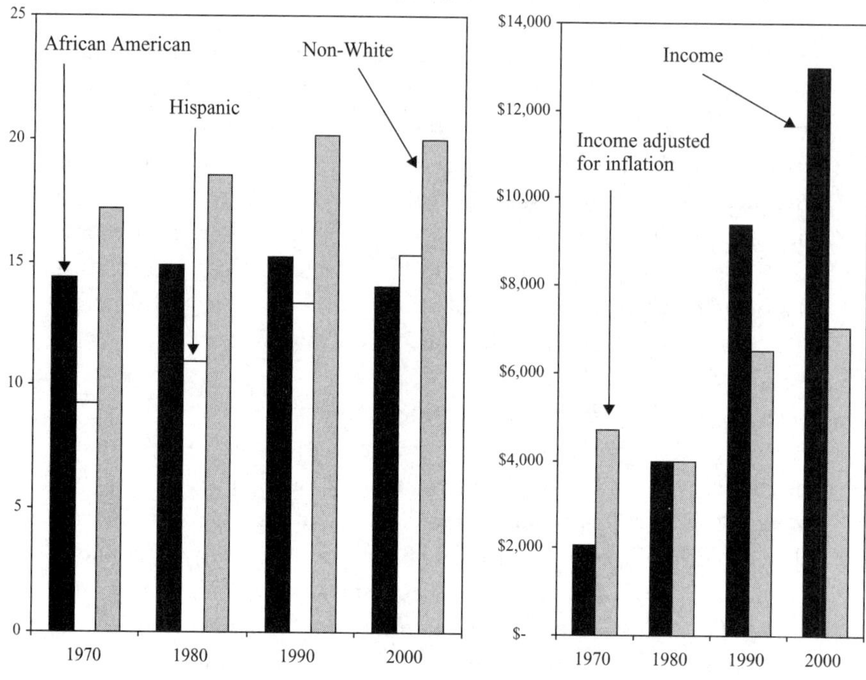

Panel B: The Standard Deviation across States

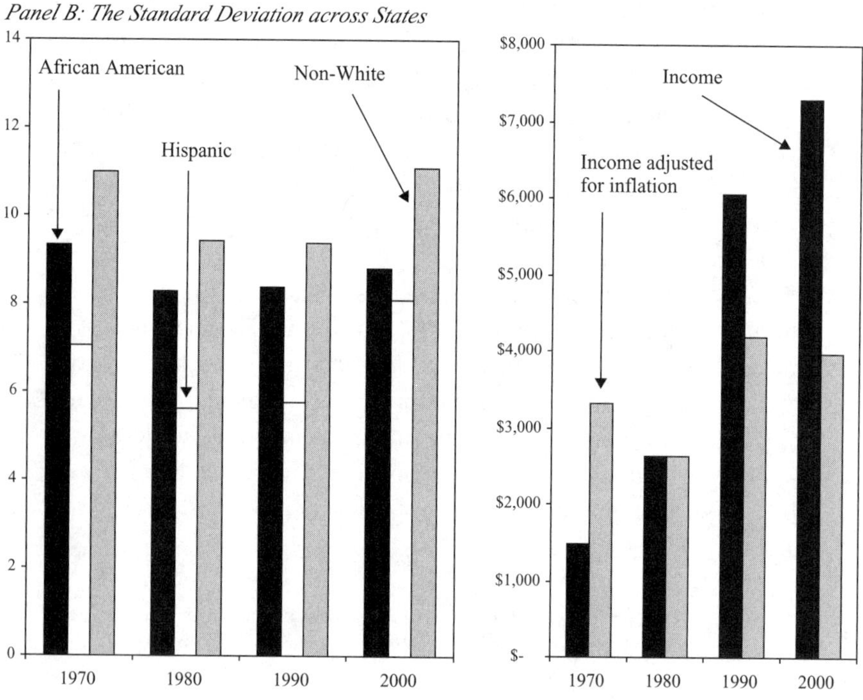

FIGURE 5.2. The Spread of Race and Income, 1970s, 1980s, 1990s, and 2000s.

Partisan Outcomes by Congressional District and State

Political scientists typically use a congressional district's presidential vote as a proxy for its partisanship (Ansolabehere, Snyder, and Stewart 2001; Bond, Campbell, and Cottrill 2001; Hirsch 2003). Although most of the analysis has been restricted to congressional districts, the same rationale exists for using a state's presidential vote as a proxy for its partisanship. Throughout this book, I use the two-party vote that the Republican presidential candidate received (henceforth, RPV for Republican Presidential Vote) within congressional districts and states as a proxy for the constituents' partisanship. The standard deviation of the RPV measures the heterogeneity of the presidential election results throughout all congressional districts and states. For example, if every state and congressional district gave George W. Bush 51 percent of its two-party vote, the standard deviation of the districts and states would be zero. The more imbalanced the results across the districts and states, the greater the standard deviation.

The standard deviations of the RPV from 1972 to 2004 for both congressional districts (denoted by circles) and states (denoted by asterisks) have noticeably increased (see figure 5.3). The line running through both series is the time trend, and it is nearly parallel in the two. Even though both trends are relatively flat until the 1992 election, the standard deviations increase 0.004 and 0.002 per election for districts and states, respectively. The results, especially from the past four elections, show that some districts and states are casting a higher percentage of their votes for the Republican candidate, while other districts and states are casting a lower percentage for the Republican. Since the Bush-Clinton contest in 1992, the standard deviation of RPV has increased 17.3 percent among districts and 20.1 percent among states. A time trend (not depicted) indicates that over the past four elections, both standard deviations have increased almost 0.01 per election.

The bigger standard deviations for the demographic variables and presidential voting for counties and states do not, alone, imply that districts and states are becoming more internally homogeneous. They only show that the differences among districts and states are growing. As districts and states become more demographically and politically distinct, they become more likely to be aligned with one of the political parties.

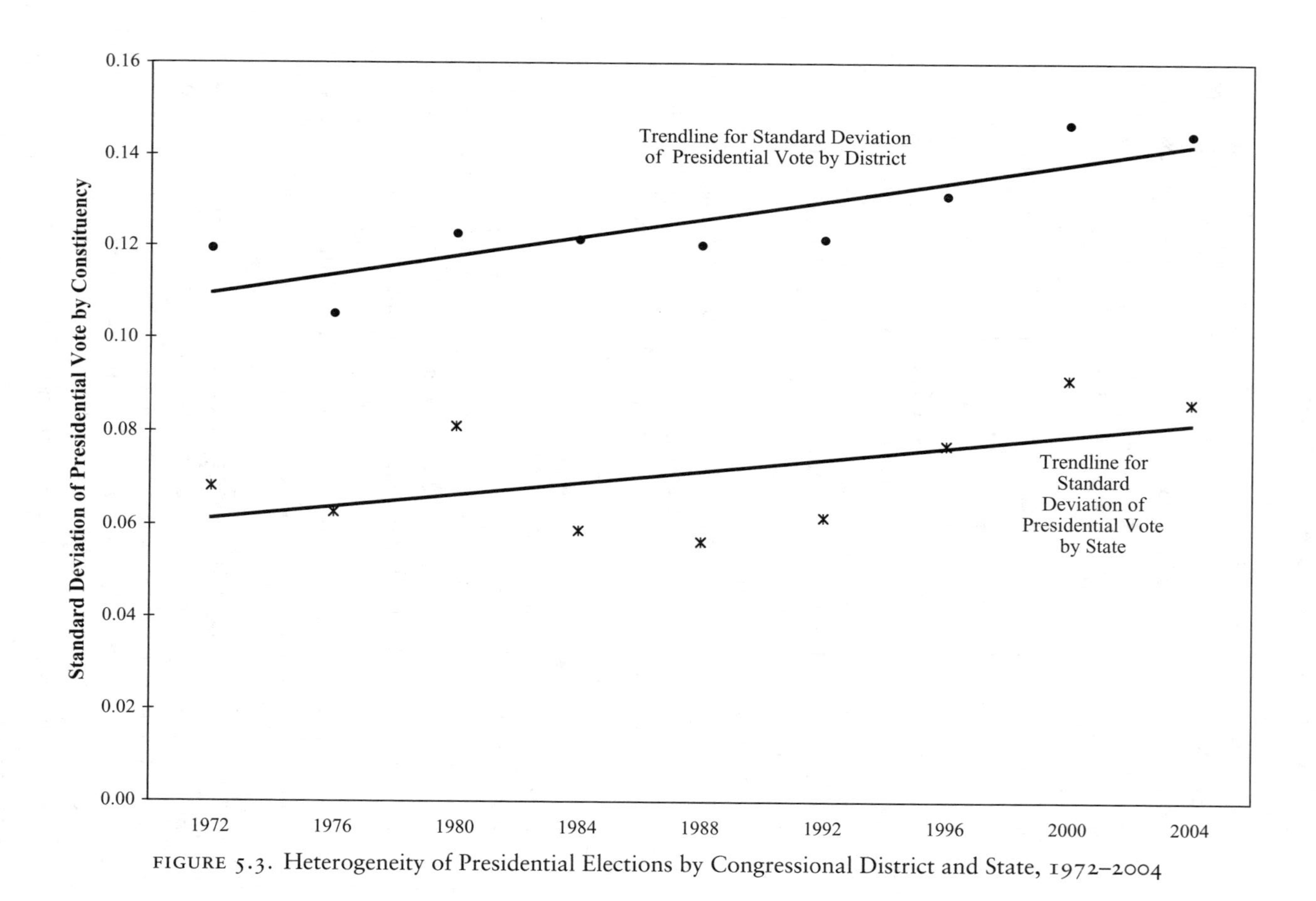

FIGURE 5.3. Heterogeneity of Presidential Elections by Congressional District and State, 1972–2004

The Partisanship of Members' Constituencies

The results reported in this chapter up until this point concerned only demographic divergence and the spread of partisan ballots in presidential contests. To test whether these changes have filtered down to congressional representation, I examine the underlying partisanship of the constituencies – as measured by presidential voting – represented by Democrats and Republicans in Congress. To take account of landslide presidential elections, I compute the constituencies' Republican Presidential Vote Advantage (RPVA), which compares the Republican presidential vote in a particular constituency to the Republican nationwide average. The "corrected" Republican percentage subtracts the Republican presidential candidate's margin from each of the congressional districts' results. For example, Nixon beat McGovern in 1972 by 24 points nationwide. To compute the partisanship of Arizona's Third District in 1972, the 24 points are subtracted from the 58–42 Nixon victory, revealing an 8 percentage point anti-Republican district, reflecting that Nixon did 8 percentage points worse in this western Arizona district than he did nationwide.

As constituencies have become more ideologically homogeneous, they are also casting increasingly consistent ballots between presidential and congressional elections. In the 93rd Congress (1973–4), Republicans in the House represented districts that gave Nixon, on average, 5.4 percent more of the two-party vote than he received nationwide. Democrats, on the other hand, represented districts where Nixon did 4.2 percent worse than he did nationwide. This 9.6 disparity arising from the 1972 election more than doubled, to 20.5 percent, after the 2004 elections. Panel A of figure 5.4 shows the development of these numbers over time.

The disparity in the Senate increased even more (see panel B). In the 93rd Congress, Republicans came from states where the RPVA was 1.4 percent. Democrats came from states with a −1.0 RPVA percent. This 2.4 percentage point disparity more than tripled, to 8.1 percent, in the 2004 elections. Put simply, the constituencies of the party caucuses on Capitol Hill were more than twice as partisan in the early 2000s as they were even 30 years before.

Consistency across Races in the Same Election

If the partisanship of residents is becoming more consequential, it should increasingly be more determinative for different races during

Panel A: The House of Representatives

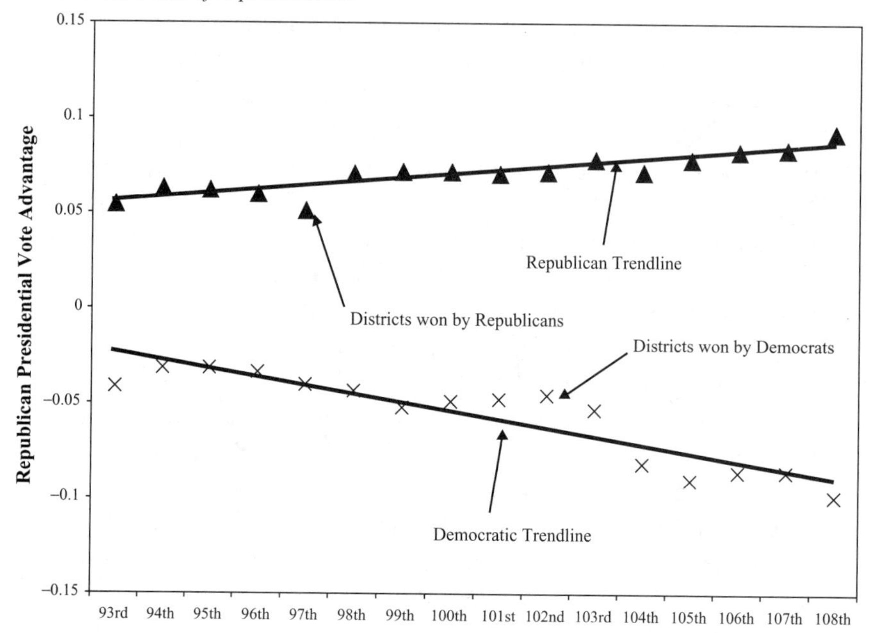

Panel B: The Senate

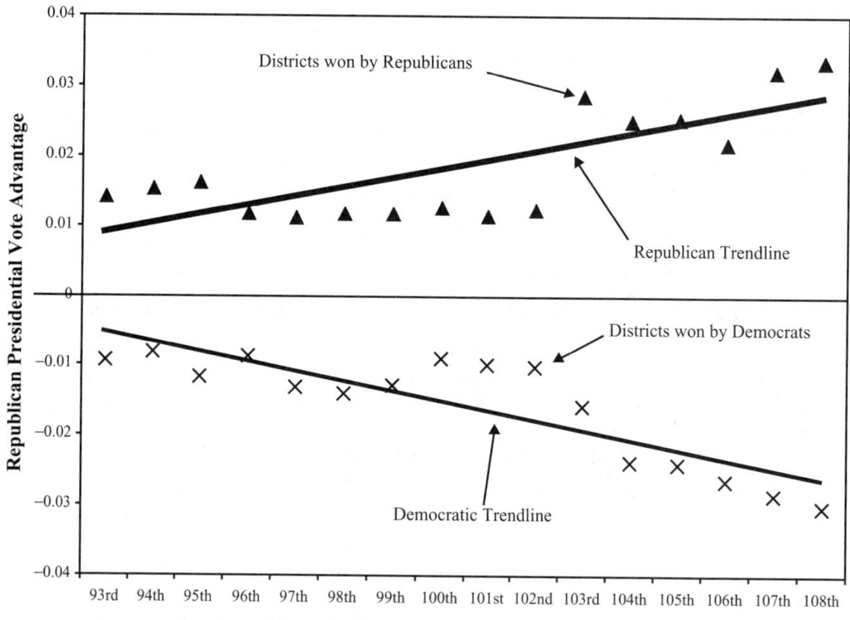

FIGURE 5.4. Partisanship of the Parties' Constituencies, 93rd to 108th Congresses.

the same election. Over the past three decades, so the argument goes, districts have become so dominated by constituents from one party or the other that few districts remain where voters "split" their partisan results between the presidential and congressional races. The light gray bars in panel A of figure 5.5 show the decrease in the number of districts that vote for candidates of one party for the U.S. House and candidates of the other party for president. Fewer than one in seven districts split their presidential and congressional results in 2004, reflecting a steady decline from a high of nearly 45 percent of all districts in 1972 and 1984.

The problem with the split district analysis is that as the presidential race becomes more one-sided, the number of split districts necessarily increases if the winning presidential candidate does not have long coattails. For example, the reason that the number of split districts was highest in 1972 and 1984 is because Republican presidential candidates Richard Nixon and Ronald Reagan were coasting to huge victories at the same time as Democrats were racking up huge margins in the House. The only way for such divergent election outcomes to co-exist is if many districts voted for Nixon and Reagan at the same time that they sent Democratic candidates to the House. When the presidential election is more competitive, as it was in 1976 and 1980, we see that the number of split districts is significantly lower.

I take account of these landslide elections in two different ways. First, I again use the Republican Presidential Vote Advantage in a particular constituency. The percentage of split districts based on the RPVA is represented as black bars in figure 5.4. The second alteration of the split districts data creates a higher standard for the definition of a split district. In both the light gray and black bars, if a Democratic candidate for president gets 50.1 percent of the vote – either in raw (light gray) or corrected (black) percentages – and the Republican congressional candidate gets 50.1 percent of the vote, the district is classified as "split" even though the vote margins may have differed by as few as a hundred votes. The higher standard forces both congressional candidates and corrected presidential candidates to get more than 55 percent of the vote before determining whether the district truly split its results. The percentages of the split districts that pass the higher standard are depicted as dark gray bars in figure 5.3. The impression from the light gray bars suggests that the number of split districts has decreased

Panel A: Split Results between House and Presidential Candidates

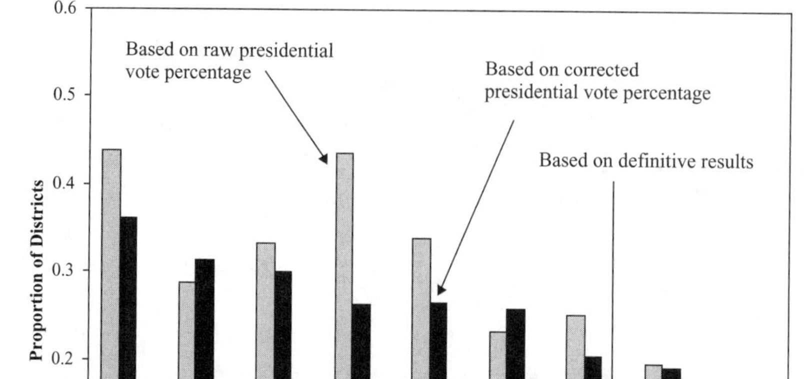

Panel B: Split Results between Senate and Presidential Candidates

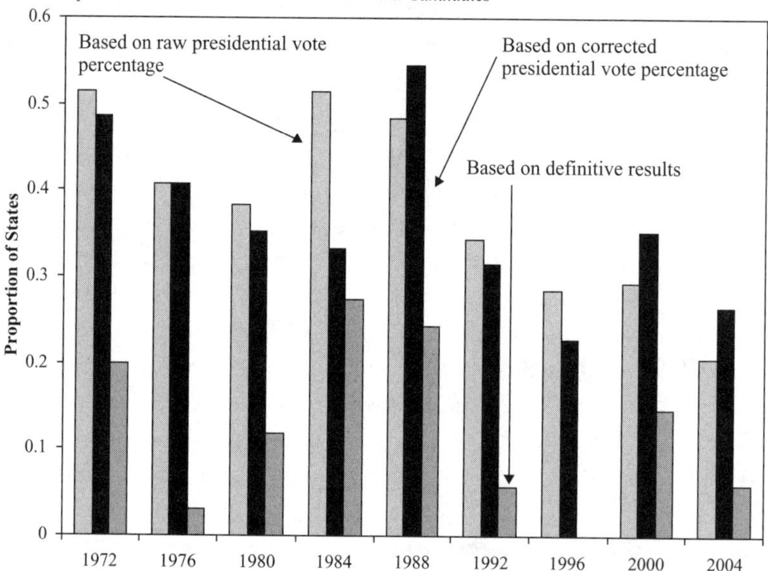

FIGURE 5.5. "Corrected" Percentages of Districts and States Splitting Results between Congressional and Presidential Candidates, 1972–2004.

by more than two-thirds from 1984 to 2004. The corrected and higher standard also shows a marked decline – 49 and 50 percent, respectively – though not nearly to the same extent as the raw split district results.

Panel B of figure 5.5 shows the percentage of states splitting their election results between presidential and senate candidates. It tells a similar story to the House split districts analysis. Up through the 1988 election, it was as common for states to split their results as it was for them to vote for candidates of the same party. Since then, however, the percentage has seriously declined to a low of 21 percent in the 2004 election.

Consistency Across Elections

If partisanship is becoming more politically consequential, it should be becoming not only more determinative for different races during the same election, but also should yield more consistent results across elections. For example, a state or a district that previously gave the Republican presidential candidate 52 percent of its vote and has more recently been giving him 58 percent of the vote should be returning Republican congressional candidates more reliably to the House and Senate.

Panel A of figure 5.6 depicts the Republican, Democratic, and mixed senate delegations for the states from the 93rd to the 108th Congresses (1973–2004). The overwhelming trend in the figure, especially since the 96th Congress (1979–80), is the reduction in the percentage of states that have sent a mixed delegation to the Senate. From then until the 108th Congress (2003–4), the number of states sending mixed delegations has decreased almost 50 percent, from twenty-seven states to fourteen.

Because each House district only ever sends one member at a time to Congress, the House's data in panel B of figure 5.6 is not an exact parallel to the Senate's panel A. Panel B shows the number of congressional districts per decade that sent all Republicans, all Democrats, or a mix of Democrats and Republicans to the House. In the 1970s, 154 districts sent at least one Democrat and one Republican to the House. In the 1980s, that number fell to sixty-eight before increasing to 117 for the 1990s. The turbulent 1994 elections understate the voting consistency of House districts in the 1990s, as forty-two of the 117

Panel A: States' Senate Delegations, 93rd to 108th Congresses (1973-2004)

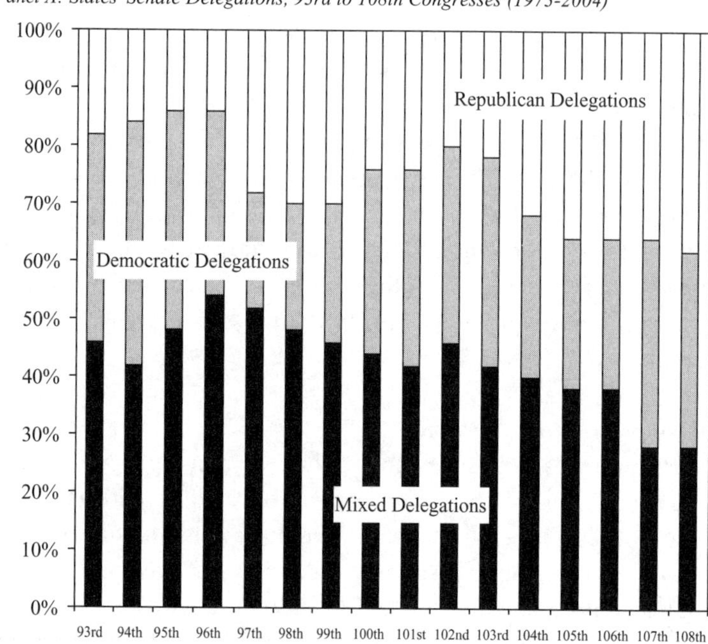

Panel B: House District Election Outcomes across Decades, 1970s, 1980s, 1990s

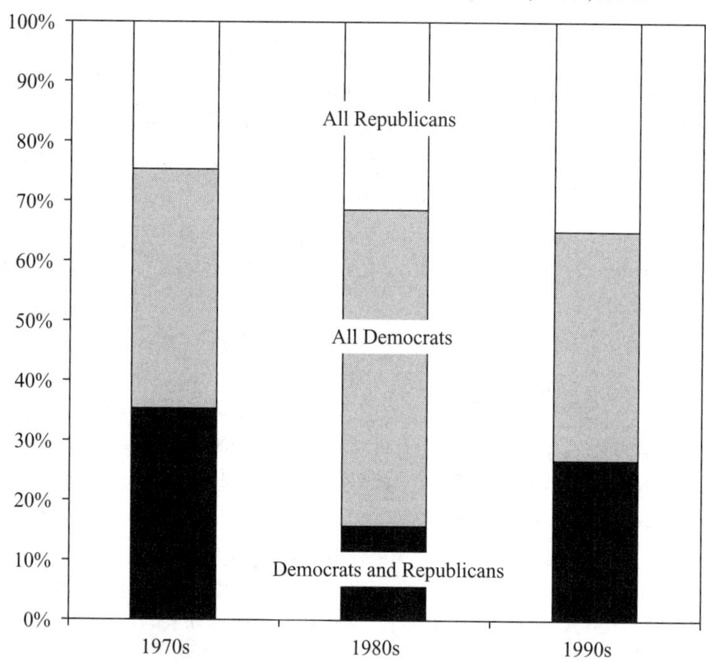

FIGURE 5.6. Consistency across Elections in Congress.

districts that sent at least one member from both parties to the House in the 1990s voted for the same party in the 1994, 1996, 1998, and 2000 congressional elections.

Figures 5.4 through 5.6 show that as political jurisdictions have become more partisan, they have increasingly elected the same party for different races during the same election. Additionally, they aggregately show that states and districts are casting increasingly partisan ballots not only within elections but also across elections. When these results are combined with figure 5.1 showing the growing consistency between voters' ideology and political party, only the first step in the sorting argument is verified. The changes in the constituencies can only have a consequence on the Congress if they are reflected in the constituencies' representatives.

III. The Ideology of Members from Strong and Weak States

Ample evidence exists for sorting's first step: increasingly, voters who are more consistent in their ideology and partisanship and who live in more varied districts and states are casting increasingly partisan ballots within and across election cycles. This section analyzes the second step, which requires that these increasingly partisan constituencies elect increasingly ideological members. To evaluate this step, I divide members into two groups based on their constituencies' RPVA. Republican members that represent constituencies that gave Republican presidential candidates more than 5 percentage points more than the candidates' national average are classified as coming from "strong" districts or states. Members representing constituencies that gave the Republican presidential candidates less than 5 percentage points above their national average are classified as coming from "weak" districts or states; likewise for Democrats.

Ted Kennedy is the prototype of a senator in the first category. His Democratic partisan identification matches the partisan preferences of his state, Massachusetts. Kent Conrad of North Dakota represents the classic weak state. Although a Democrat, his state regularly votes for Republican presidential candidates. Even though Conrad's lowest victory margin since his first reelection in 1992 was 16 percentage points, the highest percentage that a Democratic presidential candidate has gotten since then was Clinton's 40 percent in 1996. A division based on the constituencies' partisanship permits a distinction between the polarization brought about by the homogenization of members' constituencies and the polarization brought about by members' polarization scores controlling for their constituencies.

Two trends become apparent in this categorization. Consider, first, the number of members and senators coming from safe and weak constituencies. By the 99th Congress (1985–6), the number of members coming from safe districts exceeded the number of members coming from weak districts (see panel A of figure 5.7). By the 108th Congress, almost twice as many members came from safe districts. In the Senate (panel B), the lion's share of the senators serving in the 1970s and 1980s came from weak partisan states. Over time, the disparity between categories shrinks such that, by the 108th Congress, almost as many senators come from safe states as weak states.

The next step requires that the members from these safer constituencies vote more ideologically than the members from weak constituencies. Consistent with the hypothesis, representatives (likewise, *senators*) in the safest districts (*states*) went from a 0.36 (*0.36*) polarization score in the 93rd Congress to 0.48 (*0.44*) in the 108th Congress.[2] But, somewhat unexpectedly, the members from the weakest districts also became more polarized over time (see figure 5.8). Representatives (*senators*) in the weakest districts increased from 0.24 (*0.27*) to 0.33 (*0.33*).

IV. Conclusion

The evidence in this chapter suggests that both steps of the political segregation argument are valid: as the voters have become ideologically sorted and as the constituencies of members have become more demographically, economically, and politically divergent, these constituencies have elected more ideologically charged members. What the evidence does not show is the magnitude that these effects have on the overall party polarization. Regrettably, the trends of political

[2] These polarization scores are computed using DW-NOMINATE scores. First, Democrats' scores are multiplied by −1, so that they are on the same scale as Republican members. Second, all the scores within the categories are averaged to arrive at the reported polarization score.

Panel A: The House of Representatives

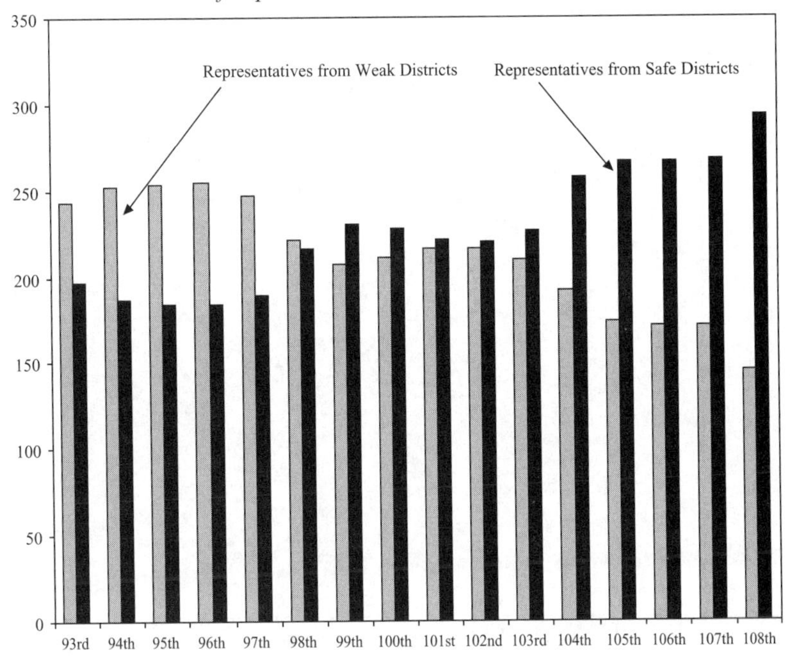

Panel B: The Senate

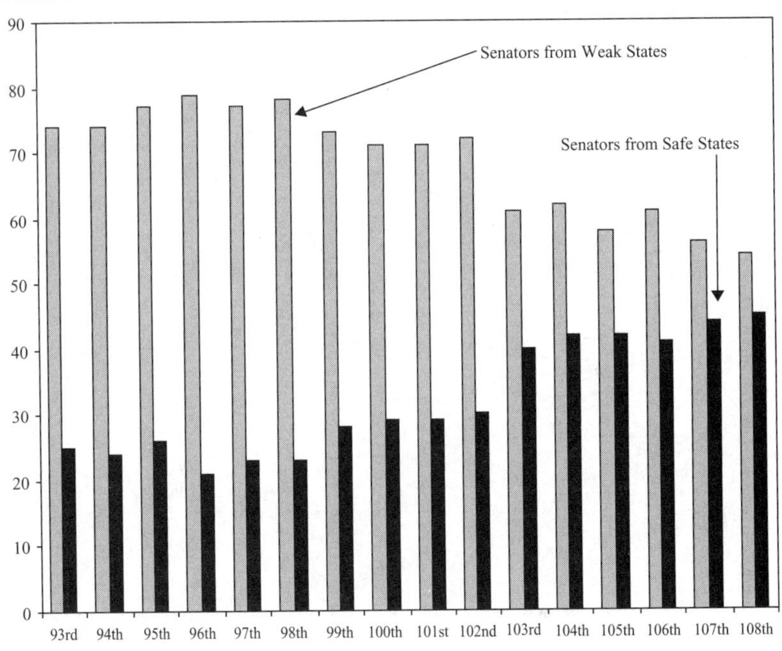

FIGURE 5.7. Members' Electoral Safety, 93rd to 108th Congresses (1973–2004).

Panel A: The House of Representatives

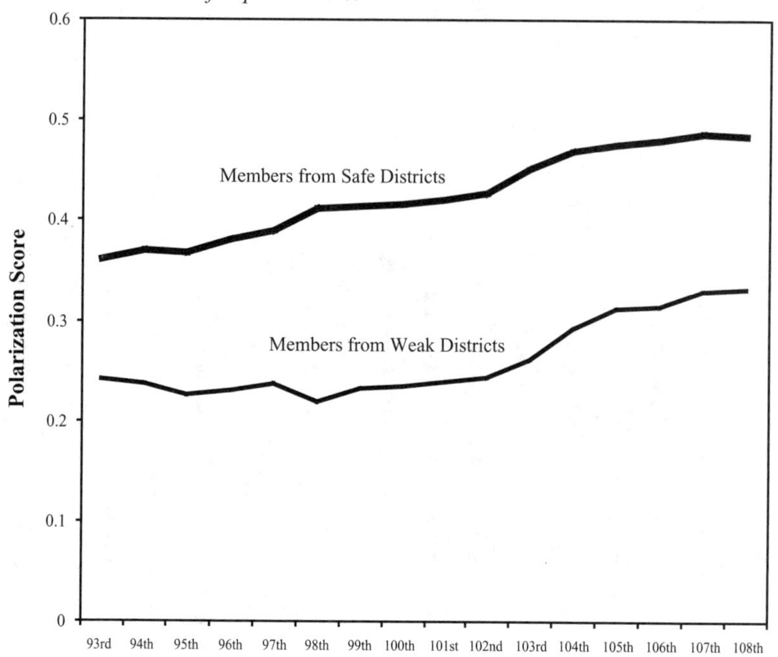

Panel B: The Senate

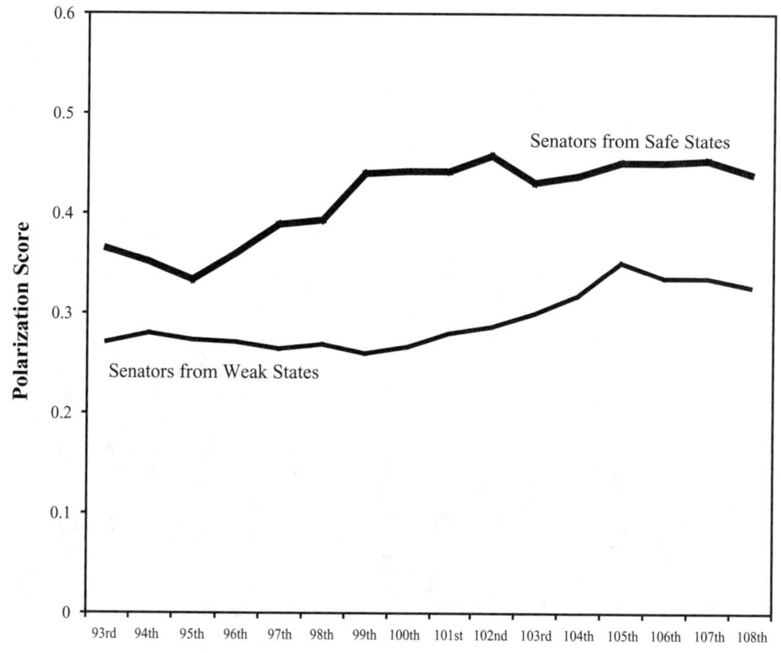

FIGURE 5.8. Members' Polarization Score by Electoral Safety, 93rd to 108th Congresses.

and geographic sorting cannot be analyzed independent of redistricting changes. As such, this conclusion evaluates the entirety of increasingly partisan constituencies on party polarization inside Congress.

Before presenting the actual data from the 93rd to the 108th Congresses, let me present a more simple hypothetical Senate to drive the logic of this analysis. Suppose this Senate has five members in two congresses. In the first congress, suppose that the three senators from weak states have polarization scores of 0.2 and suppose that the two senators from safe states have polarization scores of 0.3. In Congress A, the polarization score would be 0.24. If constituents sort themselves or are sorted such that one of the weak states becomes a safe state and the respective polarization scores remain the same, the polarization of the senate would increase to 0.26 because Congress B would have two weak state senators with polarization scores of 0.2 and three safe state senators with 0.3 polarization scores. The constituencies of the senators would be responsible for the entire increase in the Senate's polarization.

Now, suppose that, in addition to one seat shifting from a weak state to a safe state, all the senators become a bit more polarized, such that the three senators from the safe states have polarization scores of 0.35 and the two weak state senators have 0.25 polarization scores. In Congress B, the Senate's polarization score would be 0.31, which is an increase of 0.07 from Congress A. The shift of one member from weak to safe caused 0.02 of that increase and the remaining 0.05 of the increase came about because all of the senators, even those with the exact same constituencies, became more polarized. In going from Congress A to Congress B, we could say that 29 percent (0.02/0.07) of the polarization was a consequence of constituency change (moving the one senator from a weak state to a safe state), whereas the remaining 71 percent (0.05/0.07) came about as a consequence of changes above and beyond constituency change (polarizing all senators, regardless of weak or safe state designation, 0.05).

The comprehensive analysis extends this logic to the chambers comprising 535 members over 16 congresses. To show the magnitude of the increasingly partisan constituencies on party polarization, I conduct a counterfactual analysis, first holding the average ideology scores across time constant and varying the frequency of the members within the safe and weak categories and then holding the frequencies across time constant while varying the average ideology scores within categories.

This counterfactual combines the trends from figures 5.7 and 5.8 to ascertain the effect that more partisan constituencies have on party polarization independent of the increased polarization of all members without regard for their constituency. As represented by the gray shaded area (see figure 5.9), if the number of representatives within the two categories did not change, the House would have been only 3.9 percent more polarized in the 108th Congress (2003–4) than it was in the 93rd Congress (1973–4). By each category becoming more ideological (the black shaded area), the polarization of the House grew by 11.1 percent. When these changes are summed over all the 93rd-108th Congresses, the growing ideological separation between the parties controlling for the more partisan constituencies has caused 70.4 percent of the House polarization over the last 32 years. Only 29.6 percent of the House polarization was caused by the increase in partisanship of the representatives' constituencies.

The parallel analysis for the Senate is even more one-sided than the House. If the ideology did not change within the individual categories, and only the number of senators from strong and moderate states changed, the Senate in the 108th Congress would have been only 1.4 percent more polarized (the gray shaded area of panel B). If the number of senators within categories did not change, and only the ideology within categories changed, the Senate in the 108th Congress would have been 7.4 percent more polarized (the black shaded area). These figures suggest that 14.8 percent of the polarization in the Senate is caused by the states' growing partisanship. Senators' increased ideological voting above and beyond the growing ideological polarization of their constituencies brought about the remaining 85.2 percent of the polarization. These assessments suggest that the increased partisan constituencies have a definite impact on congressional polarization, though, again, probably a smaller influence than this theory's proponents suggest.

From the previous chapter, we know that redistricting has caused between 10 and 20 percent of House polarization. If we know that the total effect of the increasing partisanship of members' constituencies has caused at most 30 percent, we know that redistricting changes and the political and migratory sorting of constituents have caused about half of that polarization. Because the Senate does not undergo redistricting, its analysis more crisply reveals the amount of polarization

Panel A: The House of Representatives

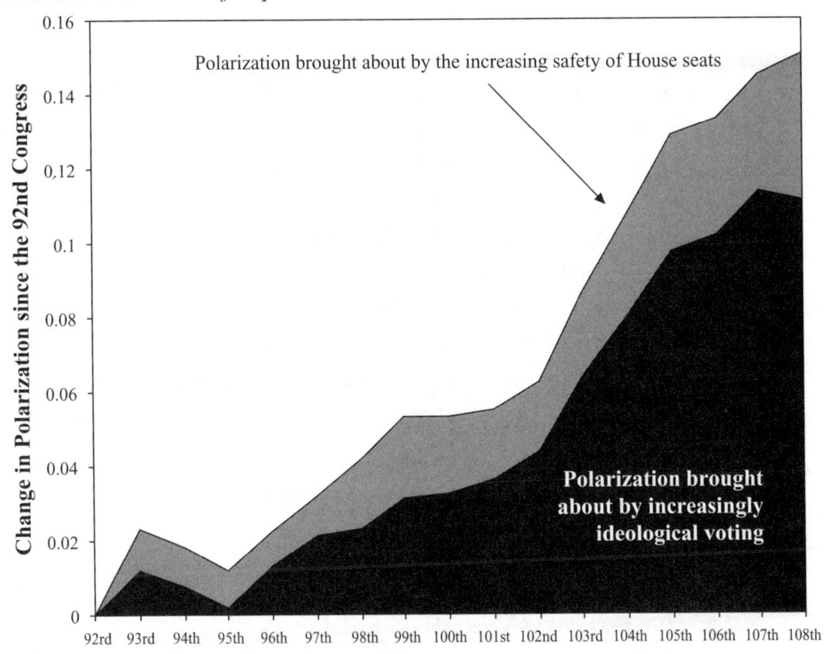

Panel B: The Senate

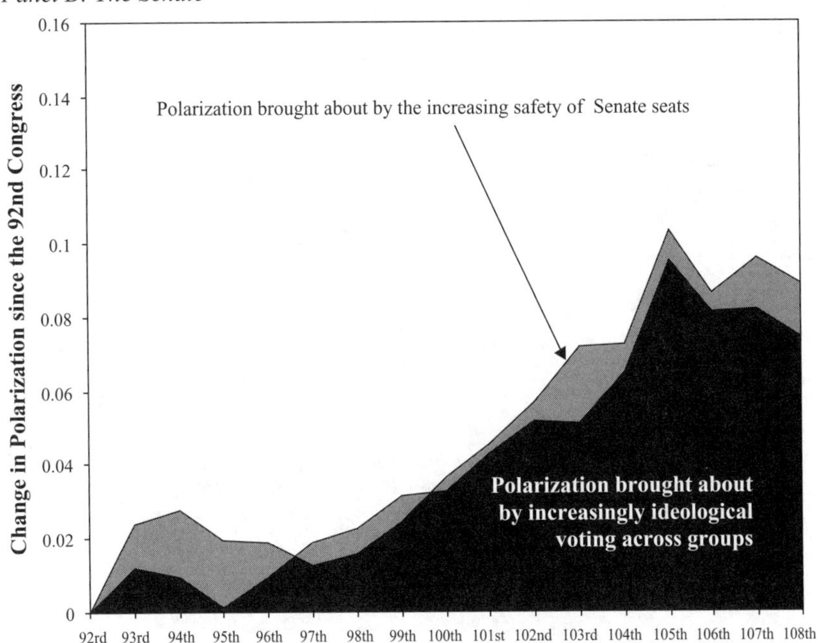

FIGURE 5.9. Polarization Brought about by the Underlying Dynamics of Political Segregation, 93rd to 108th Congresses.

brought about by political segregation. The increased polarization of states has caused around 15 percent of Senate polarization.

This analysis shows concretely the first problem with social scientists and political observers who ignore the interaction of changes in members' constituencies with the legislative process. More than two-thirds of the House polarization and 85 percent of the Senate polarization must be explained by something other than the growing partisanship of the members' constituencies. The lion's share of polarization in both chambers is brought about by the growing ideological voting of members above and beyond their constituencies' growing partisanship.

6

Extremism of Party Activists

In the 104th Congress (1995–6), the Oregon delegation was, perhaps, the most powerful state delegation in the Senate. Senator Mark Hatfield, who was first elected in 1966, chaired the Appropriations Committee. His colleague, Senator Bob Packwood, who entered the Senate two years after Hatfield, chaired the Finance Committee. Although Oregon had voted for Democratic presidential candidates in every election between 1988 and 2004, Democrats could not defeat these long-serving moderate Republicans, though both senators faced increasingly spirited contests.

Although their presentations of self were very different, Hatfield and Packwood walked a very similar electoral strategy. They frequently had to defeat more conservative Republicans in their party primaries and then appeal to enough moderates in Portland so that the Democratic candidates could not use a huge Portland surplus to override the Republican majority throughout the rural parts of the state. Through their moderate ideologies (Hatfield's DW-NOMINATE score was −0.02 and Packwood's was 0.03) and the powers of incumbency, they both survived. In the 104th Congress, however, both long-serving senators saw the proverbial handwriting on the wall.

Packwood's years of womanizing and ethical transgressions caught up with him in 1995, when he resigned rather than face certain expulsion.[1] Hatfield, on the other hand, found his brand of moderate

[1] See Duncan and Lawrence (1997, 1193).

politics built on a long-standing opposition to military intervention increasingly difficult to practice in a Republican party dominated by Newt Gingrich and his conservative foot soldiers. During the 1995 debate on the Balanced Budget Amendment, Hatfield offered his resignation to Senate Majority Leader Bob Dole so that his vote against it would not cause the defeat of the proposed constitutional amendment. Even though Dole refused his resignation, an insurgent group of conservative senators, several of whom were first elected in 1994, called for the Republican party leadership to strip him of his chairmanship, a move that was not quickly thrown aside. In the end, he kept his chairmanship, but few doubt that the controversy affected his decision to retire at the conclusion of the 104th Congress.

With two open seats in a state that had not had an open Senate seat since the 1960s, activists in both parties were poised to force the Oregon senate delegation into the era of polarization. In the special election, Ron Wyden, "an-out-of-touch liberal" with 16 years of experience in the House, won the Democratic primary, and Gordon Smith, who had most recently served as the president of the state senate and was criticized for being "a pawn of the rabidly anti-choice and anti-gay Oregon Citizens Alliance," won the Republican nomination. Wyden defeated Smith by fewer than 19,000 votes in the first all-mail election for a U.S. Senate seat (more than 1.1 million ballots were cast). In his first full congress in the Senate, Wyden had a −0.41 DW-NOMINATE score.

Though he had suffered a stinging defeat, Smith, after some equivocation, ran for Hatfield's open seat, which he won by more than 50,000 votes. His DW-NOMINATE score in his first congress was 0.21. The move from Packwood to Wyden and Hatfield to Smith explains why Oregon ranked near the top of senate delegations experiencing the greatest amount of polarization (as reported in table 2.3), even though, by most accounts, Oregon's new senators continue in the bipartisan tradition of their predecessors.

These transitions underline the importance of party activists in the filling of congressional seats. Although little systematic evidence has been offered, political scientists have speculated that part of the explanation of party polarization has its roots in primary elections, which are typically dominated by party activists (Fiorina 2006). In order to appeal to party activists and in order to keep them at bay in subsequent reelection efforts, congressional candidates can no longer be singularly focused on winning general elections. As a sign of the difficulty moderate candidates face, no Hatfield or Packwood protégés ran in either party's primary. Would-be moderate candidates knew that surviving a primary dominated by ideologues was next to impossible.

This chapter explores the influence that party activists have on members of Congress. The first section describes the ideological extremity of party activists. The second section compares the ideology of senators from states that elect senators of the same party to states that elect senators from different parties. The third section more directly explores the growing extremism of party activists and its effect on member ideology. I uncover several pieces of evidence showing that the extremism of party activists has directly affected the voting behavior of members of Congress. The results from the data analysis in this chapter suggest that the effect of party activists on party polarization in Congress is in the same ballpark as the effect of members' constituencies.

I. The Extremism of Convention Delegates

Going back to the days of Andrew Jackson and Martin Van Buren, the party activists were, first and foremost, professionals who sought victory at the polls. Issues and ideologies necessarily took a back seat to winning elections. Only through electoral success could the spoils of office be enjoyed. Beginning in the 1960s, however, political scientists noticed that these elites were increasingly "purists" or "amateurs" who were more concerned with advocating proper issue positions than they were with winning elections (Wilson 1962 and Wildavsky 1965). As this new breed of party activist replaced the party professionals, the Democratic and Republican elites became increasingly polarized.

Although the polarization among the "elites" is true across the board, political scientists analyze at least three different kinds of elites: those who hold elected office, those engaged in multiple political activities, and those attending their parties' national nominating conventions. All three types of elites are both more ideological than the mass electorate and more polarized than they used to be. Although this book is generally concerned with polarization among office holders, this chapter examines the effect of polarization of elites by examining the extent to which the growing ideological purity of the national parties' convention delegates has polarized the Congress.[2] Henceforth, the terms "elites," "activists," and "convention delegates" are used interchangeably.

At about the time that the purists were taking over the political parties, McCloskey, Hoffman, and O'Hara (1960) discovered that Democrats who attended their national party convention were more liberal than Democratic identifiers in the public and that Republican convention delegates were more conservative than Republican identifiers. Their findings, based on the convention delegates in the 1950s, have been confirmed by more than 50 years of data. Fiorina (2006, 17), who relies upon *New York Times* polls, shows how much more polarized convention delegates were than party identifiers on a whole host of issues. For example, whereas Democratic identifiers were only 13 percent more likely than Republican identifiers to want more government action to solve the nation's problems, Democratic delegates to the national convention were 72 percent more likely than Republican delegates.[3]

Not only were the convention delegates more ideological than other partisan identifiers, but also they were more ideological than they used to be. For example, 5 percent of 1980 convention delegates from both parties thought that abortion should never be permitted and 36 percent thought it should always be permitted. By 2000, the never category more than doubled, to 11 percent, and the always category rose 13 percentage points, to 49 percent.[4] The American electorate's view of abortion also polarized over the time period, but not nearly as much as the convention delegates' view.[5]

The convention delegates have not only polarized on abortion and other issues involved in the growing cultural divide between Democrats

[2] Polarization and ideological separation are, of course, two sides of the same coin. For elite polarization among those engaged in multiple political activities, the only category of elites not examined in this book, see Fiorina (2006, 67–70) and Layman and Carsey (2000).

[3] Fiorina analyzes data from the polls taken by the *New York Times* and CBS News. He finds similar gaps on a wide range of questions, including tax cuts, anti-terrorism laws, the United Nations, gay relationships, and "traditional" values.

[4] Data come from the 1972, 1980, 1984, 1988, 1992, and 2000 Convention Delegate Studies. Due to the imbalance between the number of Republican and Democratic responses in the Convention Delegate Studies, I weight each observation such that each party makes up exactly half the sample.

[5] According to the National Election Study (http://www.umich.edu/~nes/nesguide/gd-index.htm), approximately 1 percentage point more Americans thought that abortion should never be permitted and 4 percentage points more thought that abortion should always be permitted.

and Republicans, but also on other issues, which, theoretically, are not linked to the cultural divide. Layman, Carsey, and Horowitz (2006) develop separate composite measures for cultural, social, and racial issues. They find that the difference between parties' convention delegates has grown at least 25 percent between 1984 and 2000 on all three sets of issues.

Delegates to the respective party conventions have not only grown more polarized on individual issues and composite measures of their issues positions, but also in self-placing their ideology.[6] Figure 6.1 shows this growing divide and compares it to changes among the American public. It shows, first, that the convention delegates are more ideological than the American public and, second, that while both have become more polarized over time, convention delegates have polarized more. In 1972, 2 percent of Americans classified themselves as "extremely liberal" or "extremely conservative." In contrast, almost 4 percent of convention delegates placed themselves at the end points of the ideological continuum.[7] In 2000, the percentage of extreme ideologues in the public increased to 5 percent, whereas nearly 15 percent of convention delegates self-identified as "extreme."

The self-reported ideological placement of the convention delegates probably understates the change they have had on the political landscape. As the activists have become more extreme, they have become more willing to sacrifice electoral victory on the altar of position purity. As such, not only have their views become further away from the moderates who decide general elections, but also the campaigns they force on their candidates are exceedingly irrelevant at a minimum or, more likely, off-putting to moderate voters.

[6] Herrera (1992) finds a high degree of accuracy in the self-placement of ideology among convention delegates. He finds that around 90 percent of them who proffer a definition of "conservative" and "liberal" do so accurately.

[7] Only in the 1972 Convention Delegate Study did the responses for the ideological self-placement question differ. For that year only, the responses were: "radical," "very liberal," "somewhat liberal," "moderate," "somewhat conservative," "very conservative," and "reactionary." For all other years in the Convention Delegate Studies and the NES studies, the responses were: "extreme liberal," "liberal," "somewhat liberal," "moderate," "somewhat conservative," "conservative," and "extreme conservative." This labeling change in 1972 minimizes the gap between convention delegates and the American public and maximizes the growing polarization of the convention delegates, though when the 1972 data are deleted from the analysis, convention delegates still show a marked increase in "extreme" ideological placement over time.

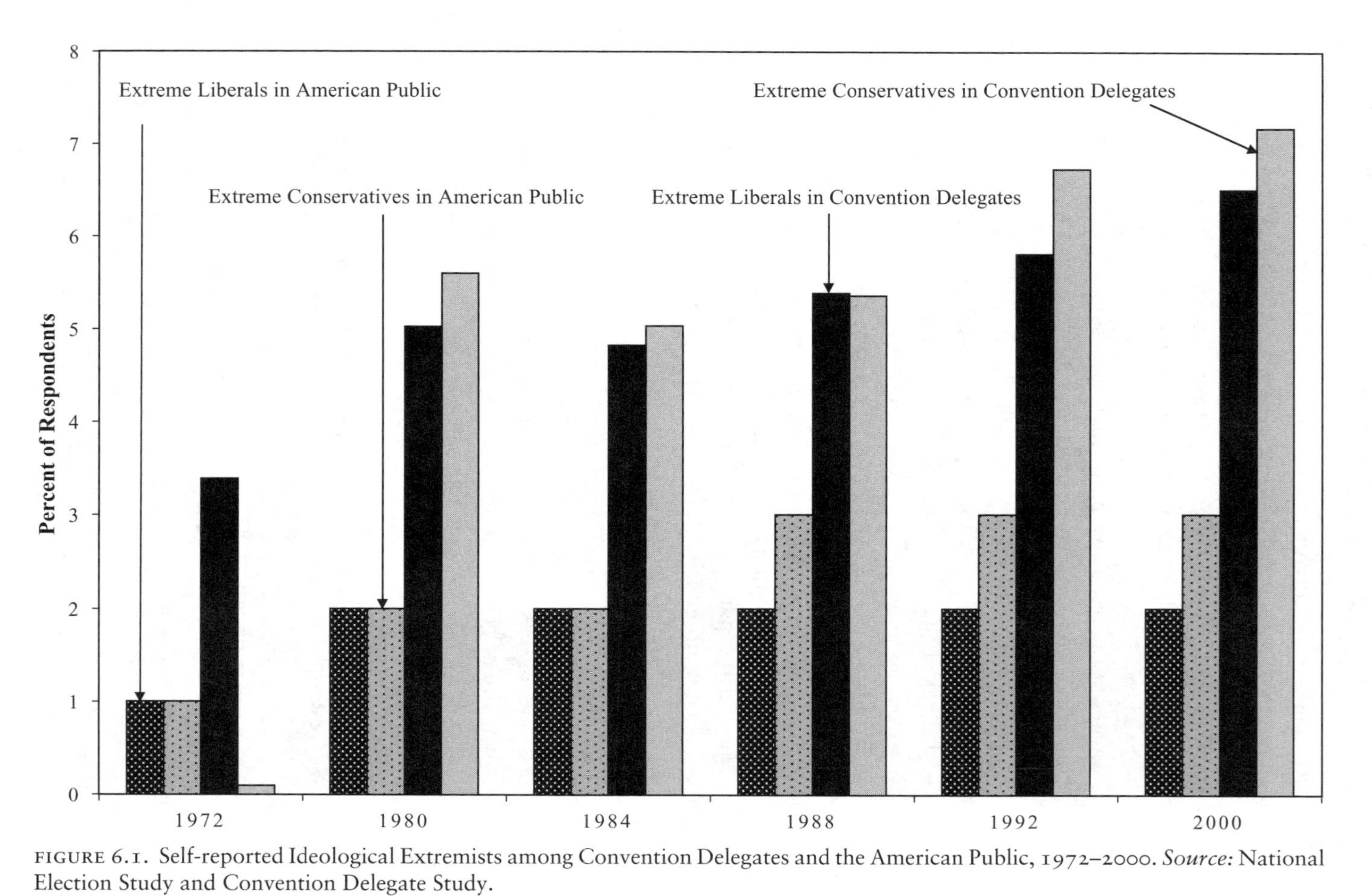

FIGURE 6.1. Self-reported Ideological Extremists among Convention Delegates and the American Public, 1972–2000. *Source:* National Election Study and Convention Delegate Study.

The small change in the American electorate, compared with the larger changes in convention delegates, nicely parallels the small changes in polarization brought about by redistricting and political migration described in chapters 4 and 5 and the larger changes in party polarization witnessed in chapter 2. This chapter shows that these parallel changes are probably more than coincidental.

II. The Impact of State Delegations on Senators' Ideologies

The previous section shows evidence that elites, as defined by convention delegates, have become more ideological over time. The previous chapter shows that constituencies at both the district and state levels have, at the same time, politically and geographically sorted themselves. The uniqueness of representation in the Senate establishes a natural experiment that can measure the impact that both of these changes have had on member polarization. The motivation for using state senate delegations to get at the distinction between the constituencies' partisanship and the pull of party extremists is presented in a vignette about two states: Kansas and New Mexico.

Kansas has only elected Republicans to the U.S. Senate in the post–World War II era. During that time, only one Democratic presidential candidate (Lyndon Johnson in 1964) received more votes than the Republican presidential candidate. Although Kansas was and remains a solidly Republican state, it has become even more Republican over the past 32 years (Frank 2004). In the 1970s, it was providing Republican presidential candidates with 5 percent more of the two-party vote than they were getting nationwide. In the 1990s, that Republican advantage nearly doubled to 9 percent.

During the same 32 years, the Kansas delegation to the Senate became much more conservative. The seats that had long been held by pragmatists Nancy Kassebaum (average DW-NOMINATE of 0.15) and Bob Dole (0.31) gave way to hardcore conservatives Pat Roberts (0.39) and Sam Brownback (0.47). The change in polarization brought about by these ideological transformations put Kansas in the top ten of the most polarized senate delegations (see table 2.3). What these changes in ideology do not reveal is the extent to which the senators were reacting to changes in the partisanship of the state versus changes in the ideological extremism of the Republican party activists.

In the 108th Congress, Roberts and Brownback may have been more conservative because the state was more conservative or because the Republican party activists in the state were more conservative.

New Mexico, unlike Kansas, has a tradition of electing a split delegation to the Senate. In the 93rd Congress, New Mexico sent Pete Domenici (a Republican with a 0.22 DW-NOMINATE score) and Joe Montoya (a Democrat with a −0.24 DW-NOMINATE score) to the Senate. In 1976, New Mexicans sent a unified Republican delegation when Jack Schmitt defeated Montoya by gathering 57 percent of the vote. Six years later, New Mexicans opted to return to a split delegation when they voted for Schmitt's opponent, Jeff Bingaman. In the 108th Congress, New Mexico continued to send a more conservative Republican, Domenici (0.29), and a more liberal Democrat, Bingaman (−0.32), to the Senate.

In the 1970s, Republican presidential candidates did less than one one-hundredth of a percentage point better in New Mexico than they did nationwide. By the 1990s, the Republicans fell back a bit – New Mexicans provided Democratic candidates with an advantage 2.4 percent greater than their nationwide average. While Bingaman might be more liberal than Montoya because of the slight Democratic slant in the state, the same explanation cannot possibly explain Domenici's more conservative voting record. New Mexico, in this sense, is like Oregon, where the slight tilt toward the Democratic presidential candidates cannot possibly explain why Smith is more conservative than Hatfield or Packwood.

The only constituency-based explanation for Smith's and Domenici's more conservative voting records in the 108th Congress is that they are trying to mollify Republican party activists in their state. So it is with any senator from a split delegation. As the Senate has become more polarized, senators from unified delegations may be responding to the general partisanship of the state or the ideological extremism of the activists in the state. Furthermore, the personal opinions of the senators may be becoming more ideological. But if these changes are brought about only by their constituencies, senators from split delegations must be responding to their party's activists. While pinning Smith's or Domenici's conservative voting habits to a particular cause is exceedingly difficult, as the trend broadens, the conclusions become more valid. See figure 6.2 as evidence of the growth in partisanship

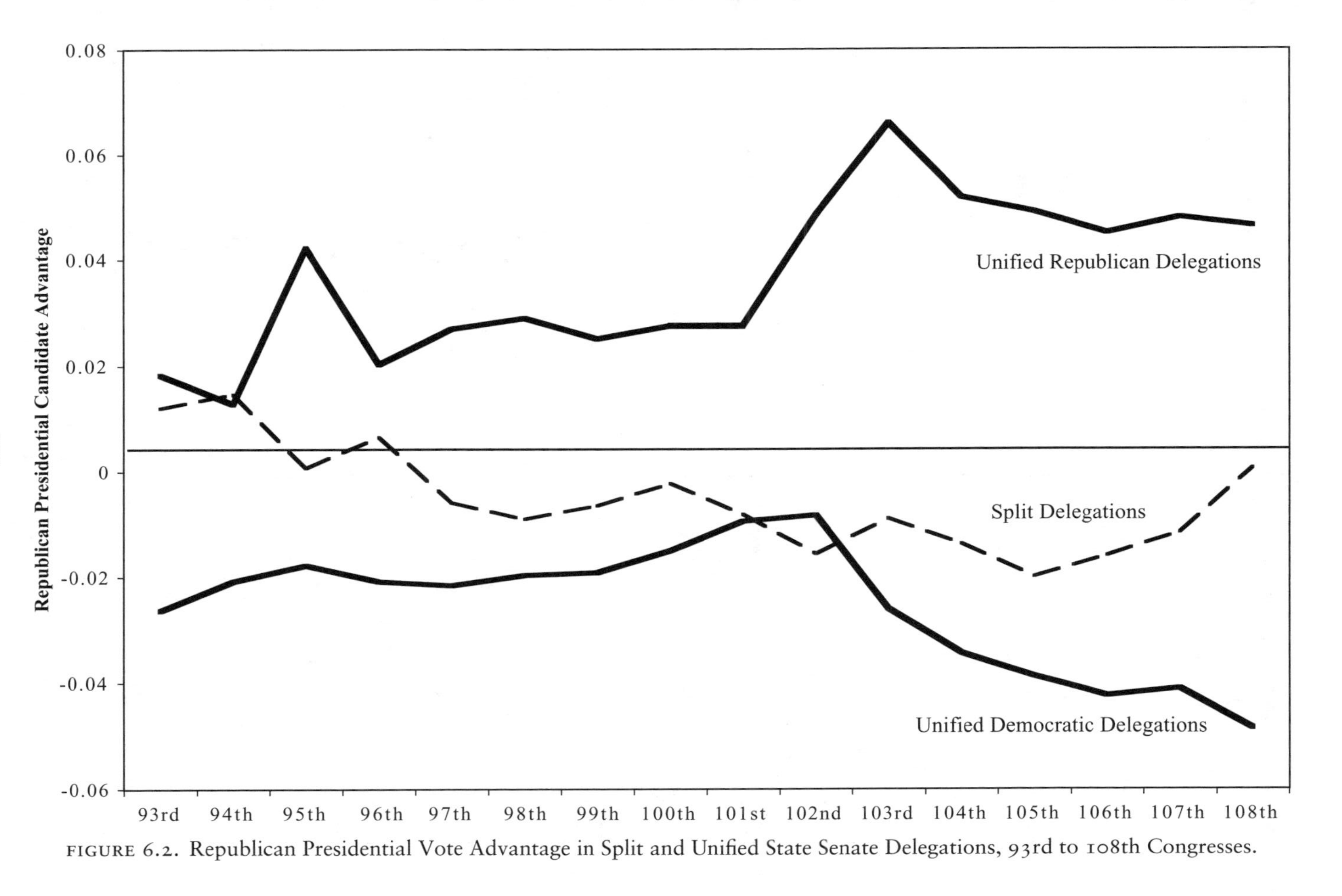

FIGURE 6.2. Republican Presidential Vote Advantage in Split and Unified State Senate Delegations, 93rd to 108th Congresses.

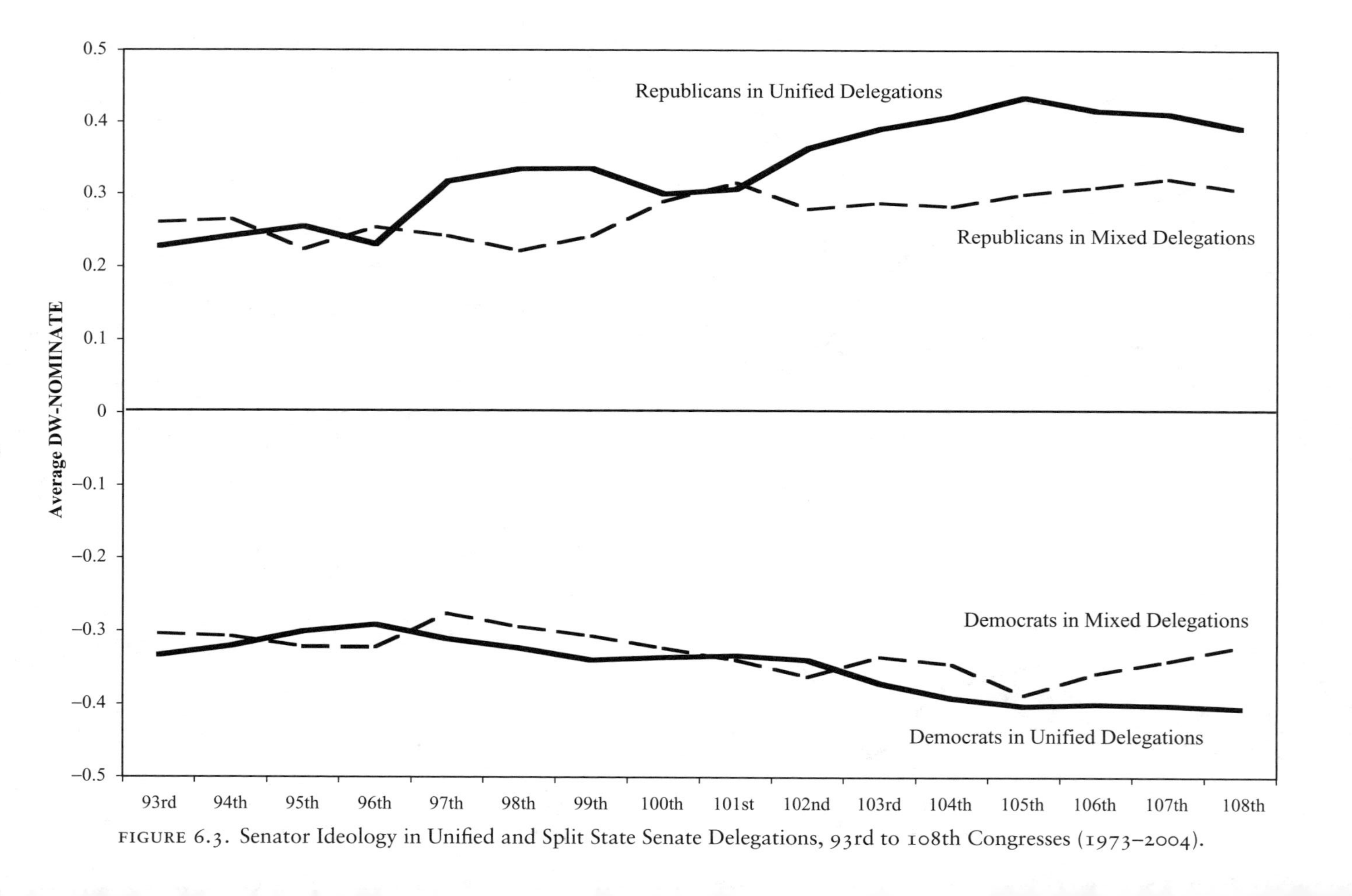

FIGURE 6.3. Senator Ideology in Unified and Split State Senate Delegations, 93rd to 108th Congresses (1973–2004).

of the Republican-unified and Democratic-unified state Senate delegations.

The Republican presidential vote advantage of states that sent a mixed-party delegation to the Senate has, unsurprisingly, danced around 0 since 1972. Over the same time period, the average lean of states that send unified delegations has more than doubled even as the number of states sending unified delegations has increased. Surprisingly, senators in the 1970s did not vote systematically any different whether or not their Senate counterpart was on the same side of the aisle (see figure 6.3). It was only in the 97th Congress (1981–2) that a divide in the voting between senators from these two delegations opened up. In the 108th Congress, Democrats from unified delegations were 0.08 (or 21 percent) more liberal than Democrats (like Bingaman and Wyden) from split delegations; Republicans (like Roberts and Brownback) from unified delegations were 0.09 (or 29 percent) more conservative than Republicans (like Smith and Domenici) from split delegations.

Between 1973 and 2004, Democrats from split delegations became 0.004 more liberal with each passing congress whereas Democrats from unified delegations became 0.007 more liberal. Republicans from split delegations became 0.005 more conservative in comparison to Republicans from unified delegations, who became 0.014 more conservative each congress. Over the 16 congresses, the number of senators from split delegations shrank from 49 to 26.

A back-of-the-envelope analysis suggests that the effect of extremism among party activists is responsible for about as much of the party polarization as the constituencies' overall partisanship.[8] This

[8] This assessment is based on the assumption that senators who experience both the extremism of party activists and the partisanship of their constituents (like Brownback and Roberts) are polarizing 0.0105 each congress, which averages the 0.007 for Democrats and 0.014 for Republicans; in comparison, senators who only experience the extremism of party activists (like Domenici and Bingaman) have polarized 0.0045. In the 108th Congress, there were three times as many senators from unified delegations as from split delegations. Taking into consideration both the frequency and the polarization of the senators for unified and split delegations reveals that the polarization caused by party activists equals the polarization brought about by polarizing constituencies. Senators from unified and split delegations have experienced a 0.0045 increase as a consequence of party activists. Senators from unified delegations have experienced another 0.006 polarization as a consequence of the growing partisanship of their general electorate. Given that unified delegations are three times as common

simple analysis makes two assumptions that may be hard to accept. First, it assumes that senators in unified delegations respond to party activists in the same way as senators in split delegations. Second, it assumes that senators in split delegations are not responding any differently than their 1970s counterparts to the overall partisanship of their constituents.

A More Sophisticated Analysis

Accepting the back-of-the-envelope analysis as true without further validation would be foolhardy. Although the following analysis is more sophisticated, the basic premise that split and unified delegations reveal the effect of party activist extremism and general constituency partisanship is unchanged. That assumption is unpacked in the next section.

The dependent variable in the more sophisticated analysis is the senators' DW-NOMINATE scores. The independent variable of interest is the Republican delegation variable, which takes on a value of "1" for senators from unified Republican state delegations, "0" for senators from mixed state delegations, and "−1" for senators from unified Democratic state delegations. This variable, as it did in the preceding analysis, assumes that the constituency-driven changes in senators' ideologies from states with mixed delegations are only responsive to the party activists, whereas senators from unified delegations are responsive to both party activists and the general electorate. To account for a possible change in relationship over the 32 years, the Republican delegation variable is interacted with time. The only control variable, in addition to time, is Republican party identification, where "1" is a Republican and "0" is a Democrat. It is also interacted with time to allow for a changing relationship over the 16 congresses comprising this data analysis.

The model performs well (see table 6.1). All of the principal component variables are statistically significant at the 90 percent level, and the overall R^2 is 0.75. Because of the time interactions, it is difficult to interpret the substantive meaning of the Republican delegation

as split delegations, the general electorate is responsible for 0.018 of the polarization. Multiplying the 0.0045 by three for the unified delegations and adding that to 0.0045 for the split delegations reveals that party activists are also responsible for 0.018 of the polarization.

TABLE 6.1. *The Effect of Mixed and Unified State Delegations on Senate Polarization, 93rd to 108th Congresses*

Time	−0.004*
	(0.002)
Republican Unified Delegation	0.003
	(0.003)
Republican	0.523***
	(0.03)
Time * Republican Unified Delegation	0.003
	(0.003)
Time * Republican	0.009**
	(0.003)
Republican * Republican Unified Delegation	0.004
	(0.04)
Time * Republican * Republican Unified Delegation	0.005
	(0.004)
Constant	−0.294***
	(0.02)
N	1619
Pseudo-R	0.745

Note: Dependent variable is the senators' DW-NOMINATE score.
*Statistically significant at 0.1; **statistically significant at 0.05; ***statistically significant at 0.001.

variable. To measure the impact of the senator's delegation, I generate predicted DW-NOMINATE scores for Republicans and Democrats, in mixed and unified delegations, in the 93rd through the 108th Congresses. For example, the DW-NOMINATE for a Republican senator from a split delegation increases from 0.23 in the 93rd Congress to 0.31 in the 108th Congress, an increase of 0.08. A Republican senator from a unified state delegation increases from 0.24 to 0.43 (an increase of 0.19). In other words, the DW-NOMINATE for a Republican senator from a unified state delegation increases 138 percent more than one from a mixed state. The parallel percentage for the Democrats is 67 percent.[9]

The congress-by-congress changes, when weighted by the frequency of senators falling into each of the categories, reveal the extent of

[9] The DW-NOMINATE for a Democratic senator from a split delegation went from −0.30 to −0.36 (a change of −0.06). A Democratic senator from a unified state went from a DW-NOMINATE score of −0.30 to −0.40 (a change of −0.10).

the polarization brought about by senators from unified and mixed delegations. Consistent with the earlier analysis, this analysis assumes that senators from unified states react to both party activist extremism and the growing partisanship of the general electorate, whereas senators from split states only react to the growing extremism of party activists. The polarization changes and frequencies within these categories reveal that 61 percent of the polarization in the Senate is a consequence of party activist extremism, and 39 percent is a consequence of the increasing partisanship of senators' general electorates.

III. The Impact of Party Activists' Extremism on Member Polarization

Although the results from the previous section seem plausible, they require the leap of faith that the bluntness of state Senate delegations can be used to tease out distinctions between the influence of a state's general partisanship and the influence of state party elites. This section presents analysis that matches data from the Convention Delegates Study with member voting scores to yield a more direct test of the relationship between party elite (as defined by convention delegates) and elected officials. This more refined analysis substantiates the general thrust of the findings from the previous section.

The Convention Delegates Study has been ongoing for six iterations. In 1972, 1980, 1984, 1988, 1992, and 2000, Warren Miller and Richard Herrera (as well as various colleagues throughout the years) have ascertained the opinions of the delegates to presidential nominating conventions (Miller and Jennings 1986, Herrera 1992, Herrera and Shafer 2003). In many respects, the questions in the Convention Delegates Study parallel the questions asked of respondents in the American National Election Studies. I use the opinions of the delegates to derive estimates for the ideological extremism of party activists in members' constituencies. To preserve the anonymity of the respondents, the studies do not report the delegates' states, instead coding the geographic variable into nine regions.[10]

[10] Richard Herrera graciously gave me the state codes for the 2000 study so that I could compare the state results with the region results. In none of the analysis that I did for 2000 did the results appreciably change between using the state codes and the regional codes. Although the state codes were more refined than the regional codes,

The analysis has two key independent variables: the ideology of the party activists and the partisanship of the general electorate. The Convention Delegates Studies asked many questions that could have served as the measure for the members' party activists, including questions about their strength of partisan feelings, their opinion on various public policy matters, their preferences for spending on a multitude of government programs, and their temperature on a feeling thermometer of the parties. I decided to use the answers on the self-placement of their ideology as the proxy for their ideological extremism. The overwhelming advantage of using ideological self-placement is that the question was asked in all iterations of the Convention Delegates Study.[11] Frequently, the self-reported ideology is fraught with mistakes and nonresponses. These problems are minimized because of the elite's sophistication. All of these measures are highly correlated, and the 2000 results change only marginally when any of the other possibilities replace ideological self-placement in the data analysis. If the extremism of party activists is driving party polarization, Republican members should be responsive to the Republican convention delegates; likewise for Democrats. As the activists become more extreme, so, too, should their elected officials. To see whether members are also responsive to the general partisanship of their constituency, I include the constituencies' Republican presidential vote advantage. I also control for the members' partisanship with a Republican indicator variable, which is coded "1" if the member is a Republican; "0" otherwise.

The dependent variable is the members' DW-NOMINATE score. Parallel analyses are performed on senators and representatives for the

frequently the state estimates were based on only a few respondents. The initial analysis and the follow-up diagnostics suggest that these two effects probably cancelled each other out. The regional codes include: New England (Connecticut, Maine, Massachusetts, New Hampshire, Rhode Island, and Vermont), Middle Atlantic (Delaware, New Jersey, New York, and Pennsylvania), East North Central (Illinois, Indiana, Michigan, Ohio, and Wisconsin), West North Central, (Iowa, Kansas, Minnesota, Missouri, Nebraska, North Dakota, and South Dakota), Deep South (Alabama, Arkansas, Florida, Georgia, Louisiana, Mississippi, North Carolina, South Carolina, Texas, and Virginia), Border States (Kentucky, Maryland, Oklahoma, Tennessee, and West Virginia), Mountain States (Arizona, Colorado, Idaho, Montana, Nevada, New Mexico, Utah, and Wyoming), Pacific States (California, Oregon, and Washington), and External States (Alaska and Hawaii). As a check on face validity, the most conservative region for both the Democrats and the Republicans is the Deep South and the most liberal region for both parties is New England.

[11] As verification that the regional score does not drive the results, the correlations among individual self-placement, the state average, and the regional average are all high.

members who serve in congresses immediately following a national convention in which the Convention Delegates Study was implemented.[12] To see whether the relationships between the substantive independent variables and the dependent variable have changed over time or are different between the parties, I include a time trend and a Republican indicator variable, which are fully interacted with the two key independent variables (and each other). Additionally, because an assumption of ordinary least squares regression is that the observations are independent from one another, I include member random effects specification to account for the panel nature of the data (i.e., different observation from the same member over time). With this correction, Senator Ted Kennedy's observation in the 93rd Congress is independent from his observation in the 97th as well as all the other congresses in which he served.

The models for both the House and the Senate perform well. In both models, the members' partisanship, their general constituencies' voting patterns, and their party activists' ideological self-placement are all key predictors of their DW-NOMINATE score (see table 6.2). Additionally, both models have overall R^2 values above 0.75. Because the interaction terms make it difficult to parse out the independent effects of the variables of interest, I present figure 6.4, which shows the substantive impact of the regression results for both the House (panel A) and the Senate (panel B).

The first bar in panel A in figure 6.4 shows the impact of changing an otherwise average Democratic House member into an average Republican.[13] The second and third bars show the impact of moving a Republican and Democratic representative, respectively, from a Democratic friendly district to a Republican friendly district.[14] For example, a typical Republican from a Democratic-leaning district (two

[12] These include the 93rd Congress (for 1972 convention), the 97th Congress (1980), the 99th Congress (1984), the 101st Congress (1988), the 103rd Congress (1992), and the 107th Congress (2000).

[13] In this analysis, "average" means a representative from a district that had a Republican presidential vote advantage of 0 and an ideology of its state party activists of 4.06 in the 101st Congress (1989–90).

[14] For this analysis, I calculate the impact of changing a member's districts from two standard deviations below the mean to two standard deviations above the mean. I separate the Democrats from the Republicans so that the standard deviation changes are reasonable within each party.

TABLE 6.2. *The Effect of Partisanship, Constituency, and Party Extremists on Members' DW-NOMINATE Scores*

	The House of Representatives	The Senate
Time	0.022***	0.021*
	(0.01)	(0.01)
Republican Presidential Vote Advantage	0.611***	0.146
	(0.05)	(0.19)
Republican	1.020***	0.948***
	(0.06)	(0.11)
Party Extremist Ideology	0.165***	0.115***
	(0.01)	(0.02)
Time * Republican Presidential Vote	−0.014***	0.019
Advantage	(0.004)	(0.02)
Time * Republican	−0.046***	−0.035*
	(0.01)	(0.02)
Time * Party Extremist Ideology	−0.009***	−0.008**
	(0.002)	(0.003)
Republican * Republican Presidential Vote	−0.051	0.841**
Advantage	(0.11)	(0.28)
Republican * Party Extremist Ideology	−0.164***	−0.116***
	(0.02)	(0.03)
Time * Republican * Republican	−0.007	−0.058**
Presidential Vote Advantage	(0.01)	(0.02)
Time * Republican * Party Extremist	0.015***	0.011**
Ideology	(0.002)	(0.004)
Constant	−0.737***	−0.659***
	(0.04)	(0.07)
N	2630	605
R^2 Within	0.063	0.095
R^2 Between	0.845	0.777
R^2 Overall	0.847	0.779

Note: Dependent variable is the members' DW-NOMINATE score. Models include member random effects to account for the dependence of observations from the same members. *Statistically significant at 0.05; **statistically significant at 0.01; ***statistically significant at 0.001.

standard deviations below the average for Republican members) has a predicted DW-NOMINATE score of 0.30. When that same Republican is placed in a heavily Republican district (two standard deviations above the average for Republican members), the DW-NOMINATE score rises to 0.41. The change for a Democrat is even greater, going

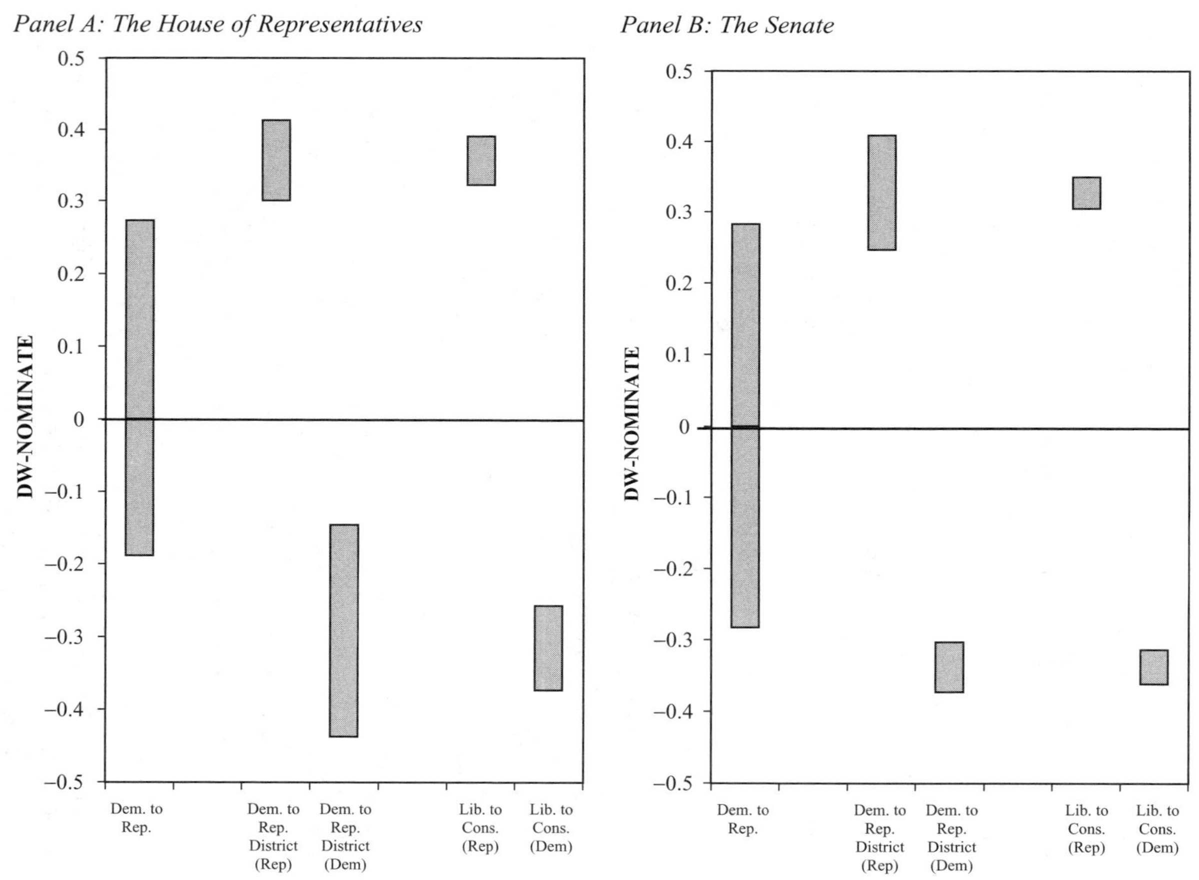

FIGURE 6.4. The Effect of Partisanship, Constituency, and Party Extremists on Members' DW-NOMINATE Scores.

from −0.44 to −0.19. Finally, the last set of bars show the effect of changing Republican and Democratic representatives, respectively, from party activists who are liberal to party activists who are conservative. The more conservative party activists led to a 0.07 change for Republicans and a 0.11 change for Democrats.[15] The Senate results, which nicely parallel the House results, are depicted in panel B.

The results presented in table 6.2 and depicted in figure 6.4 show that representatives and senators are responsive not only to their constituencies' preferences, but also to the ideology of their own party activists. The party activists' effect is about half as powerful as the effect of general election partisanship of the members' constituencies. For three reasons, the results for the party activists, although markedly lower than the general partisanship of the constituencies, should not be dismissed. First, the party activist variable was based on the self-reporting of ideological placement, which is subject to a variety of complications surrounding survey instruments generally and self-reported placements specifically. In contrast, the constituency partisanship is based on election outcomes, a far more reliable and generally more visible measure. Second, the party activist variable took the same value for all Republicans (or Democrats) in a particular region, whereas the constituency variable was based on votes cast within the actual jurisdiction of the member's district or state. Third, a long line of political science research with a multitude of verifications using different data and tests shows that members are responsive to their constituents. The literature of party activists is much smaller and, hence, less compelling. That my operationalization of party activists' ideology can even compete in the same regression model as the general election constituency's partisanship is surprising and a testament to the true effect of party activists.

The aggregate results for Democrats and Republicans in both the House and the Senate show that the influences of the constituency and party activists have not changed appreciably over the 32 years under examination in this study. How, then, can the increasing polarization

[15] The effect of party activists changes over time for both Republicans and Democrats in the House. Republicans become much more responsive to their party activists, whereas Democrats become much less responsive. The trends, though in reverse, are of similar magnitude. The use of the 101st Congress in this analysis shows the trends at about their midpoint.

be explained? The short answer is that the magnitude of the effect has not significantly changed, although the underlying values of the constituency and the party activists have significantly changed. Figures 5.3 and 6.1 show that, over time, members' constituencies have become more partisan and their party activists more extreme. As the values for these variables have become more extreme, the parties have increasingly separated in both the House and the Senate even though the strength of association (as revealed by the coefficient) has stayed roughly the same.

IV. Conclusion

According to evidence uncovered in this chapter, Mark Hatfield and Bob Packwood's replacements in the Senate are more ideological at least in part because the Democratic and Republican party activists in Oregon are more extreme. Two independent pieces of evidence show that the extremism of party activists has increasingly divided not only Oregon's delegation in the Senate but also more generally both parties in Congress. The first test, which compares senators from mixed party state delegations with senators from unified state delegations, suggests that party polarization is at least as much a consequence of party activist extremism as the increasing partisanship of members' constituencies. The second test uses convention delegates as proxies for party activists. Even though this variable's measurement is suspect for a variety of reasons, the results show an obvious impact caused by party activist extremism. Whether party extremists have caused as much party polarization as the growing partisanship of representatives' districts and senators' states as indicated by the first test or a relatively smaller portion as suggested by the second test, the overall impact is decisive and clear: party activist extremism increases the ideological voting of members in Congress.

As members' constituencies have sorted (either through redistricting or political migration), the ideology of the party activists has polarized. These concurrent trends have, in part, caused party polarization in the House and Senate. This causation has been direct and indirect. The part of the book concluded by this paragraph measured the direct effect. The next part of this book explores the indirect effect.

PART III

INSTITUTIONAL CHANGE

Part III of this book investigates institutional change in Congress, which is an intermediate step between constituency change (as analyzed in part II) and party polarization (as described in part 1). Although the changes taking place in members' constituencies have had a statistically significant and noticeable effect on party polarization, it alone does not explain all or even a majority of it. In part III of the book, I find that the lion's share of party polarization has come about as a consequence of the procedural divide between Democrats and Republicans in both the House and the Senate. To be sure, this procedural divide has roots in the growing partisanship of members' constituencies. These changes must interact with the legislative process for a clearer picture of party polarization to come into focus.

Chapter 7 examines the effect that increasing partisanship of members' constituencies has on the internal dynamics between members and their party leadership (arrow E in figure 3.2). As the party caucuses' constituencies have become more internally homogeneous, the rank and file members have been more willing to cede to their party leadership an increasing scope and use of powers so that they can entice, cajole, compel, or force party loyalty among the rank and file members. More polarized caucuses have led to more polarized party and committee leaderships in both chambers of Congress.

Chapter 8 investigates the consequence that the increased power exercised by party leadership has had initially on procedures in Congress and subsequently on party polarization in the House and Senate (arrow F in figure 3.2). It shows that almost the entirety of the increase in party polarization in the House and the Senate over the past three decades can be accounted for by an increase in the frequency of and polarization on procedural votes. The trend of increasingly polarized substantive votes is dominated and swamped by the growing divide between the party caucuses when they vote on procedural matters.

Chapter 9 explicitly links House polarization to Senate polarization (arrow G of figure 3.2). An increasing number of senators have House experience. These House veterans, especially Republicans, are much more ideological than House members who continue to serve in the House, senators who do not have House experience, and House veterans who moved to the Senate in years past. Almost the entire growth of party polarization in the Senate can be accounted for by this new breed of Republicans who came from the House since the 97th Congress (1979–80). Because their House and Senate careers overlapped with the most prominent congressional Republican of the last quarter of the twentieth century, I call these Republicans "Gingrich Senators."

7

Connecting Constituency Change to Institutional Change

The year 2001 was supposed to be the pinnacle of her congressional career. After Congresswoman Marge Roukema, a moderate Republican and dean of the New Jersey delegation, survived two tough primary challenges by Scott Garrett in 1998 and 2000, her sights were set firmly on increasing her prestige and power inside the House of Representatives. Roukema expected to become chair of the Banking Committee when the current chairman reached his three-term limit, which the Republicans imposed on full committee chairs when they took over the House in 1995. Her elevation would mark the first time in history that a woman would chair a major full committee in the House of Representatives.

Although she had not always been a loyal Republican team player, Roukema had burnished her banking and Republican credentials in leading up to the Banking Committee transition. Would-be Speaker Bill Livingston, in 1998, asked her to co-chair his transition team. Following his untimely demise in the wake of Clinton's impeachment, Roukema became an early and vociferous proponent of future Speaker Dennis Hastert. Additionally, Roukema – a former teacher – went back to school herself and amassed an impressive amount of knowledge about the financial sector of the American economy. She had long been an important member on the Banking Committee and played a crucial role in the 1999 law that overhauled the rules and regulations in the financial services industry.

Her clear path of ascendancy to the Banking Committee chair became clouded even before the 2000 election season was over. Richard Baker, the Republican with the third most seniority on the Banking Committee, was also actively trying to become its chair. He was a much more reliable Republican vote than Roukema and was a prodigious fundraiser for the party. In addition to Baker's challenge, proposals were being bandied about in Republican circles that would redefine the Banking Committee's jurisdiction, opening the door for a noncommittee member to step in and become its chair.

After the elections and before the new Congress convened, Speaker Hastert called all members who wanted to be committee chairs to interview with the Republican Steering Committee. During her half hour slot, Roukema campaigned on her "knowledge of the issues" facing the Banking Committee.[1] Nonetheless, on the first day of the 107th Congress, the House approved the new House Rules, which included changing the name and the jurisdiction of the Banking Committee. The move was largely interpreted as a sign that Mike Oxley of the Commerce Committee would become the new chair of the now-named Financial Services Committee. Oxley, like Baker, voted in line with the party leadership and campaigned vigorously for them (table 7.1 compares the three candidates' experience, ideologies, and fundraising records).

Hastert tried to mollify Roukema by seeking administration appointments for her. She reportedly turned down offers to become both the Treasurer of the United States and an undersecretary in the Department of Health and Human Services. Instead, she opted to retire from politics. In her November 8, 2001, retirement announcement, she noted her "grave disappointment" in being denied the Financial Services chair.[2]

The 107th Congress went from bad to worse for Roukema as the candidate she endorsed for her seat finished third in the Republican primary – well behind Garrett, her two-time primary competitor. On the heels of her protégé's loss, Roukema discovered that she had breast cancer, which required her to undergo debilitating chemotherapy.

[1] Quoted in Susan Crabtree, "Would-be Chairmen Prepare for Grilling," *Roll Call*, December 4, 2000, p. 1.

[2] Quoted in Laurence Arnold, "Veteran Moderate Voice in Congress to Retire after Current Term Ends," The Associated Press, November 8, 2001.

TABLE 7.1: *Factors of Consideration in the Race for the Banking Committee Chair, 2001*

	Marge Roukema	Richard Baker	Micheal Oxley
Committee Rank	3	5	n/a
Adjusted Committee Rank[a]	1	2	n/a
Years of Experience	20	14	19
Age	71	52	56
DW-NOMINATE	0.194	0.441	0.392
Party Unity Score	74	92	89
Party Money Raised	$40,000	$1,600,000	$420,000

[a] Adjusted Committee Rank takes into account only those "running" for the position. Chairman Leach had to step down. Second in line, Bill McCollum, chose to run for the Senate instead of seeking reelection to his House seat. Fourth in line, Doug Bereuter, was running for the chairmanship of International Relations.

Sources: Party unity, years of experience, and age from *CQ's Politics in America 2002*. Party money raised for Baker from *The Almanac of American Politics 2002*. Party money raised for Roukema and Oxley from an editorial in the *The Record* (Bergen County, NJ), January 8, 2001, "Sold to the Highest Bidder," p. L2.

In the fall elections, Roukema was silent as the Democratic candidate declared that she was the rightful recipient of Roukema's mantel of moderate and pragmatic politics. Even without Roukema's help and in spite of her implicit endorsement of his opponent, Garrett won her old seat.

Although the combination of institutional, personal, and political disappointments may have been unique to Roukema, a growing number of Republicans have been passed over for committee chairpersonships. Although Democrats violated seniority a number of times in the naming of their committee chairs back when they were the majority, they only did so when the most senior member was incapable of effectively running the committee. Few seniority violations had either ideology or party loyalty at their root. Following the 1994 elections, Republicans, at Speaker Gingrich's behest, explicitly used loyalty in lieu of seniority in the naming of committee chairs. This change advantaged the Republican party leadership in two ways. First, it put a premium on casting party-loyal votes for members who wished to become committee chairs. The threat of denying a chairpersonship became a powerful tool for the leadership in encouraging members to vote the party line. Second, increasingly loyal committee chairs more efficiently and more certainly enacted the party program. With tighter controls over who would wield committee gavels, the Republican leadership did not have to worry about rogue committee chairs who would enact their own personal agenda rather than the party's platform.

The political fate of Roukema and her fellow moderates was predicted by David Rohde (1991) and John Aldrich (1995) both individually and jointly (2001). They maintain that the leadership of political parties grows stronger when the parties become more internally homogeneous and externally heterogeneous. Under these conditions, rank and file majority party members recognize that they can achieve more politically and legislatively if they endow their leaders with more power to enact the party's agenda than if they use the individual discretion they received by virtue of their elections. Emboldened party leaders increasingly use the rewards and punishments at their disposal to enact their parties' agenda.

The two key prerequisites for party government are inter-party division and intra-party unity. The second chapter shows how the parties have separated over the past 32 years. The first section of this chapter explores the intra-party unity prerequisite. The second section shows how the ideology of the committee and party leaderships has mirrored the party separation presented in chapter 2. The third section examines how party government has been made manifest over the past 32 years in the U.S. Congress. The following chapter examines the ramification these inside-the-Capitol changes have had on party polarization.

I. The Growing Ideological Homogeneity of Political Parties

The constituencies of the respective party members have become almost twice as polarized over the past 32 years (see chapter 5). These more polarized constituencies have increasingly cast party-consistent votes in presidential and congressional contests. This sorting of districts and voters has resulted in fewer members who are cross-pressured between their parties and their districts. Members who cast partisan roll call votes are increasingly casting votes consistent with their constituents' preferences. The old dilemma forcing members to cast party-loyal votes or constituent-loyal votes is increasingly a false dichotomy (see figure 5.4).

The gradual reduction in cross-pressured members has had a significant effect on the make-up of the party caucuses. As demonstrated in chapter 2, the political parties have substantially polarized since the early 1970s. Aldrich and Rohde (2001) find that this polarization is one of the two conditions for party government, which gives rise to rank and file members ceding power to the party leadership in order to enact the party agenda. In addition to inter-party heterogeneity, they also suggest that the parties must be internally homogeneous for party government. Chapter 2 also contains the first hint that parties inside Congress have become more homogeneous. Figures 2.3 and 2.4 show that not only have the parties polarized, but also they have become more internally consistent, as depicted by the shrinkage of the standard deviation bars on either side of the mean. Figure 7.1 depicts this trend explicitly. The standard deviation of Democrats' and Republicans' DW-NOMINATE declined in the House (panel A) and Senate (panel B).

Combining the differences between the parties with the unity within the parties shows how much more the conditions for party government are satisfied in the 108th Congress than they were in the 1970s (see figure 7.2). The number of standard deviations (a measure of intra-party homogeneity) between one party's average ideology and the other party's average ideology (a measure of inter-party heterogeneity) has grown precipitously over the last 32 years. The average House Democrat was just shy of three standard deviations away from the average Republican in the 93rd Congress. By the 108th Congress, more than five standard deviations separated the average House Democrat from the average Republican. The smallest increase was 60 percent for the Democrats from the Republicans in the Senate. The largest increase was 133 percent for the Republicans from the Democrats in the Senate.

The combination of figures 2.3, 2.4, 7.1, and 7.2 shows how the party caucuses have become externally separated and internally consistent over time. If Aldrich and Rohde are correct, the satisfaction of these two conditions should result in more powerful party leaders. The next section examines the impact that the party caucus divide has had on committee and party leadership.

II. The Polarization of Congressional Leaders

The effect of the polarizing and sorting of members' constituencies has paralleled – or even caused – the growing polarization of

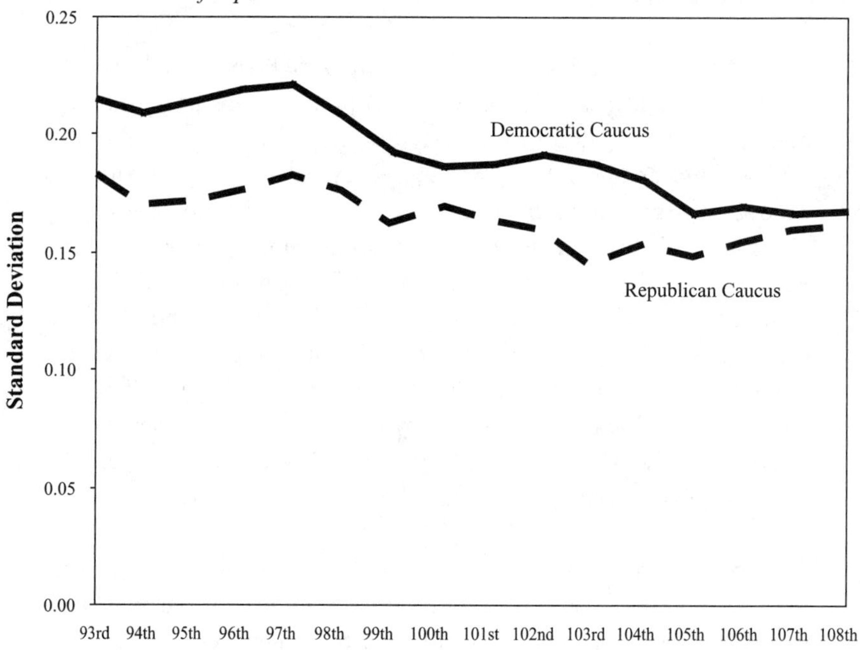

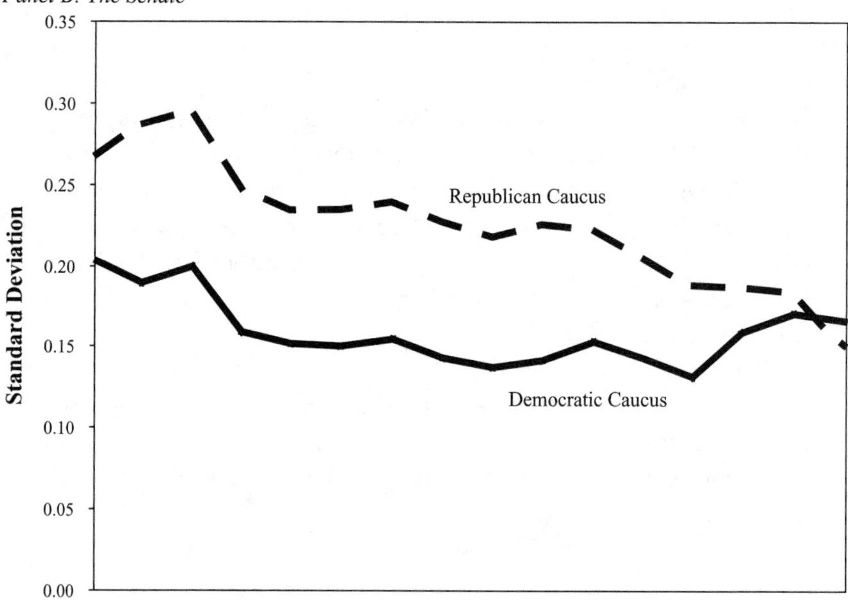

FIGURE 7.1. The Standard Deviations of the DW-NOMINATE Scores for the Republican and Democratic Caucuses, 93rd to 108th Congresses.

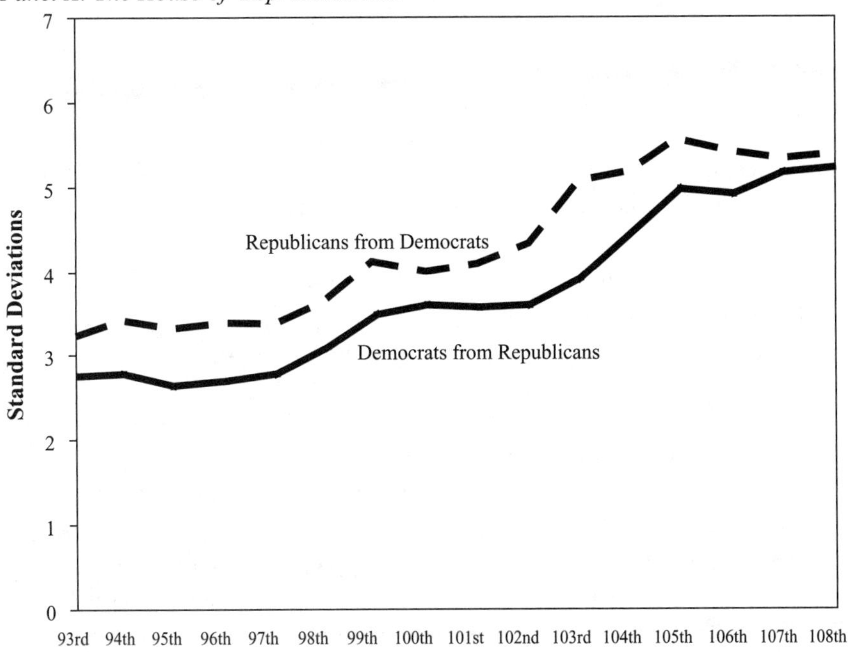

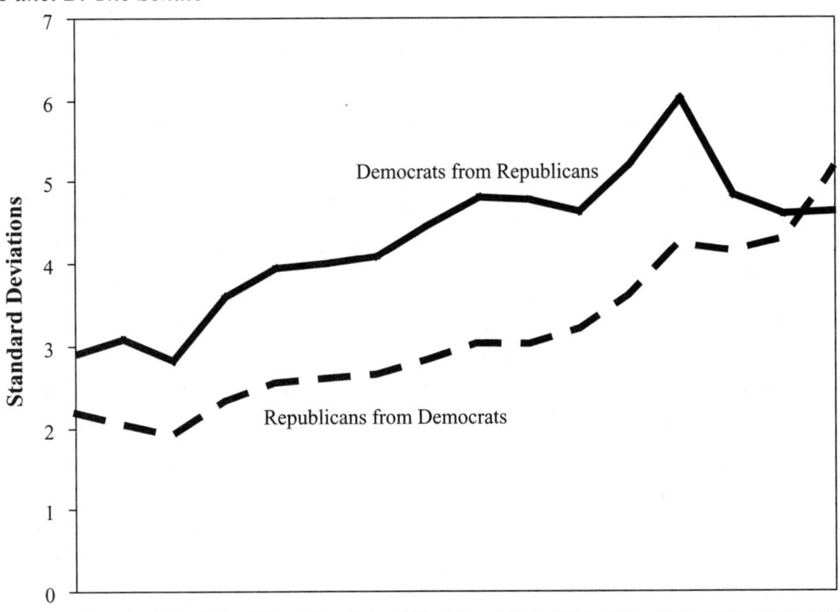

FIGURE 7.2. The Number of Standard Deviations from One Party's Average Ideology to the Other Party's Average Ideology, 93rd to 108th Congresses.

DW-NOMINATE scores between the parties' committee leadership and between the parties' floor leaders. Figure 7.3 shows how the average polarization of these three groups has changed from the 93rd Congress to the 108th Congress (1973–2004). The thin line is the caucus average polarization. The slightly thicker line is the polarization between the committee chairs (for the majority party) and the ranking members (of the minority party). The thickest line is the polarization between the Speaker, Floor Leader, and Whip for the majority party and the Floor Leader and Whip for the minority party.

While the House party caucuses have become 47 percent more polarized over the 32 years, the committee leadership has become 39 percent more polarized, and the party leadership has become 21 percent more polarized. The respective numbers for the Senate are 33 percent (party caucuses), 38 percent (committee leaders), and 32 percent (party leaders). The correlation between any two of the House (likewise, *Senate*) trends is never less than 0.92 (*0.82*). These data show that as the party caucuses have polarized, they have chosen more polarizing leaders – both for committee and party positions. The next section examines the resources that these party leaders have at their disposal.

III. The Growing Power of More Polarized Leaders

David Rohde (1991) shows how tied members are to their districts. In taking that argument a step further, John Aldrich (1995) smartly traces the development of the political parties in the United States. Particularly helpful for this chapter is his analysis on parties in the government (his chapter 7). His argument that the contemporary parties are best thought of as a service organization for the members confounds the relationship between political parties and members of Congress. Put simply, his argument suggests that the parties in Congress are strong today because members want them that way; and tomorrow, if they wanted them weaker, they would make them so. The invisible hands guiding these decisions, of course, are the members' constituencies, which have also become more externally polarized.

A series of reforms begun more than 30 years ago have, at every turn, bolstered party leaders. Not always at the same time or in the same manner, both Democrats and Republicans in both chambers have

Panel A: The House of Representatives

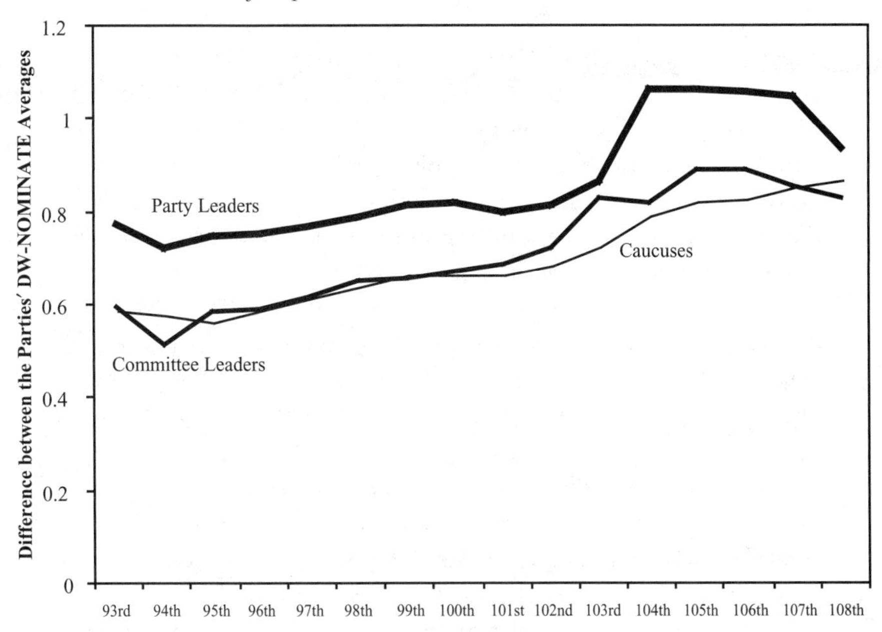

Panel B: The Senate

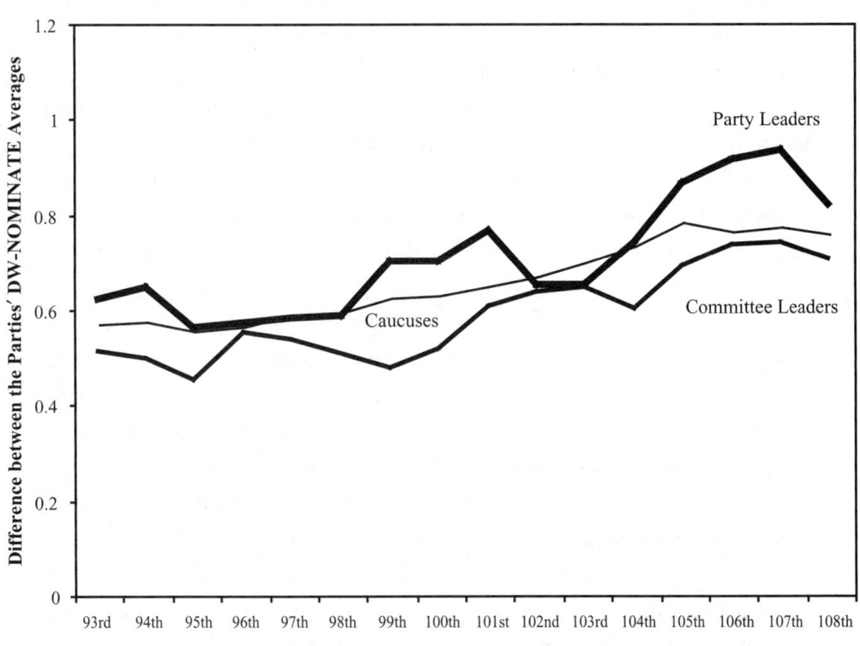

FIGURE 7.3. The Polarization of the Party Caucuses, Committee Leadership, and Party Leadership in Congress, 93rd to 108th Congresses (1973–2004).

endowed their leaders with more power so they could more forcefully encourage party discipline. These reforms, which came via legislation, changes in the chamber's rules, and modifications in party procedures, include: the Budget Act of 1974, which centralized fiscal decision-making in Congress; the establishment of multiple referrals; the increasing use of special rules on the House floor; the centralization of the committee assignment process; the increased inventiveness of Senate rules and procedures employed by party leaders during floor deliberations; the decreased autonomy of the Rules Committee; the creation of task forces to bypass committees; and the revitalization of the speaker's powers (Schickler 2001, Aldrich 1995, and Sinclair 2000).

Although most of these reforms can be pinpointed to specific dates, for a couple of different reasons party leaders accumulated and exercised their new powers only in fits and starts. First, various factions, acting upon different goals, pushed these reforms into enactment (Schickler 2001). The legislators and their leaders frequently interpreted these new powers differently. Second, even when these new powers were granted to leaders, they frequently would not be fully utilized until a new generation of leaders came into power (Cooper and Brady 1981). For example, powers that were given to Speakers Carl Albert in 1974 and Newt Gingrich in 1995 were used more vigorously by their successors, Jim Wright and Dennis Hastert.

Given the complication of when members instituted and leaders exercised these new grants of power, I do not try to match up increases in party divergence with individual reforms. I choose to paint the picture of accumulated party leadership power with broad strokes, which can most easily be seen in the resources that party leaders have at their disposal. As a proxy for these resources, consider the huge growth in the number of employees that the party leaders have (see figure 7.4). Frances Lee (forthcoming) also has nicely shown how much the leaders' resources beyond number of employees have grown.

Party leaders can use two different strategies to influence floor voting. First, leaders can encourage member compliance through various rewards and punishments (APSA 1950, Ranney 1951). Second, leaders can induce members' compliance by aggressively structuring the legislative agenda on the floors (Cox and McCubbins 2005, Van

Panel A: The House of Representatives

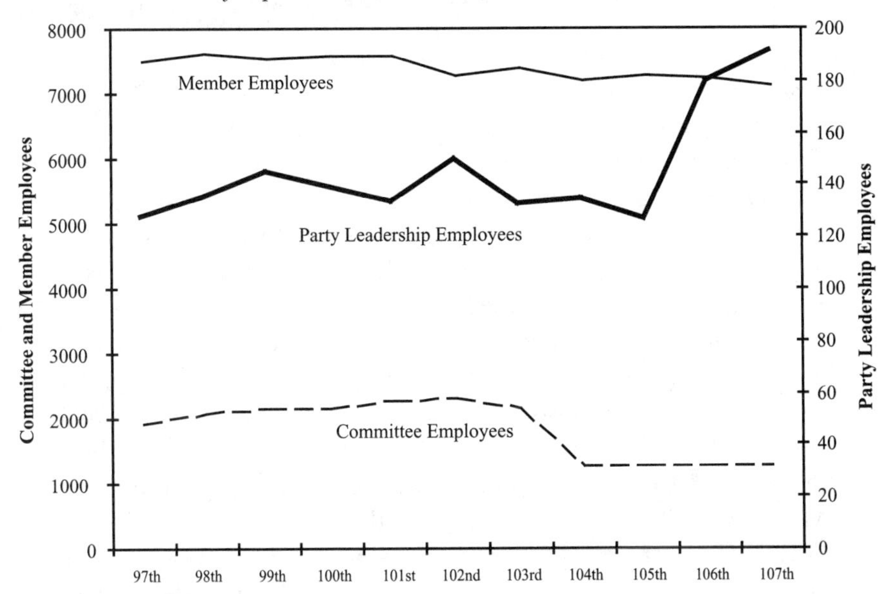

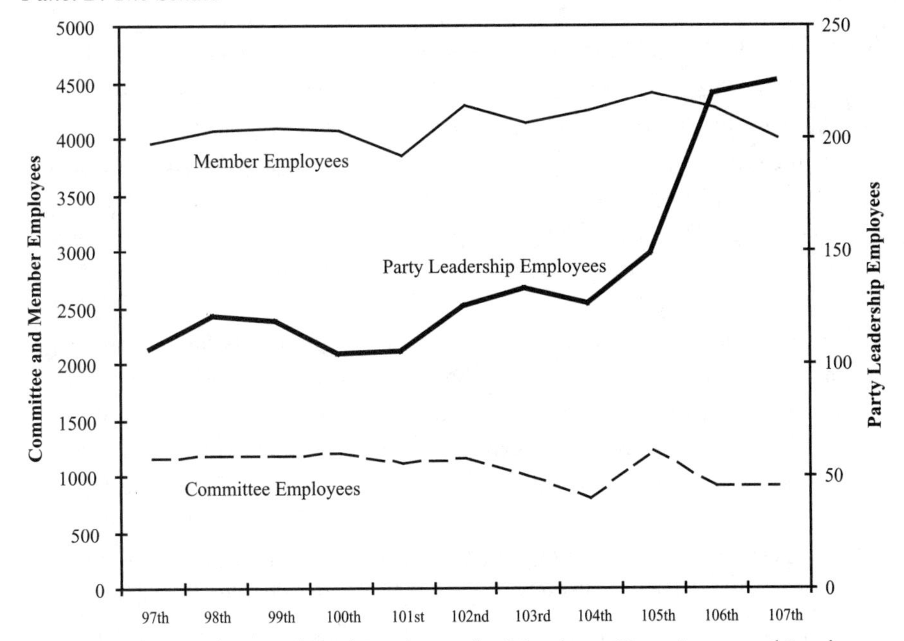

FIGURE 7.4. The Number of Employees for Members, Committees, and Leadership, 93rd to 108th Congresses (1973–2004).

Houweling 2003). Party leaders' reliance upon these differing strategies has varied over time. I examine each strategy in turn

Rewards and Punishment

Party leaders have an arsenal of weapons to cajole recalcitrant members into casting party-loyal votes on the floors of the House and Senate. Two episodes on the floor of the House provide an indication of the extent to which party leaders will go to get their way. On August 5, 1993, Clinton's presidency hung in the balance. His economic stimulus package was defunct, his health care initiative was in need of emergency care, and his tax and deficit reduction package was close to default. Time was expiring on the final passage vote in the House and the roll call was tied. After initialing announcing her opposition to the legislation because her wealthy constituents would bear the brunt of Clinton's proposed tax increases, Marjorie Margolies-Mezvinsky, a first-term Democrat from the wealthy Philadelphia suburbs, broke the tie by switching her vote from nay to yea after being beaten down by senior Democrats. Although she won the day for Clinton and the Democrats in the House, the Republicans were gleeful at her now much-diminished prospects for reelection in 1994. On the floor, they chanted "Good-bye Marjorie" as she signed the green card that officially changed her vote.[3] In exchange for her vote on the Clinton budget, the administration held an entitlement conference in Margolies-Mezvinsky's district. Nonetheless, true to the Republican prediction, Margolies-Mezvinsky lost in 1994. As she recounted more than 10 years later, "[The package] raised taxes on 1.2 percent of the population and they all lived in my district... I would have loved to run the campaign against me."[4]

More than 10 years later and after the Republicans had captured all the federal levers of power, the party leadership again attempted to ensure loyalty, though this time the majority party's behavior went from unseemly to borderline unlawful. On November 22, 2003, Republicans were fretting that the Bush Administration's prescription

[3] Quoted in Kevin Merida, "A Day of Tension, Cajoling – and Relief; Campaign-Rally Atmosphere Gripped Capitol Hill Before Vote," *The Washington Post*, August 6, 1993, p. A1.

[4] Quoted in Bree Hocking, "Victims, Beneficiaries Reflect on GOP Takeover," *Roll Call*, September 12, 2005, p. B-12.

drug plan was going to be defeated on the House floor. One Republican skeptic of the plan was Nick Smith, who at the time was hoping to pass his House seat on to his son in the 2004 elections. In lobbying Smith, Republicans questioned whether the party would support the son of someone who refused to cast a loyal vote on this major piece of legislation. The extent to which the threat was veiled is open to interpretation.[5] Smith, disgusted by the tactic, was not swayed from voting no. The following year, his son lost in the Republican primary.[6]

Although these two cases may be so noteworthy because they are relatively rare, party leaders have more weapons in their arsenal than promises of entitlement conferences and threats to defeat disloyal members' children. Two of the more systematic weapons that leaders have at their disposal to reward loyalty and punish betrayal are campaign contributions and committee assignments. In total, the party leaders of both parties in both chambers had more than three times as much cash in the 2003–4 cycle as they had had in the 1987–8 cycle even though the actual amount they could contribute to any one campaign stayed the same (see figure 7.5 for the breakdown by chamber, party, and election cycle). While the aggregated campaign contributions have grown, the standard deviations of the amount given in particular races have grown even more. In fact, leaders have even been exercising more discretion by picking and choosing particular races in which to spend lavishly. They have been using these campaign contributions to entice loyalty among their members or to help members who have cast loyal votes fend off aggressive challengers.

In addition to having more cash at their disposal, party leaders also have more discretion in the naming of not only committee members (a power they have exercised back to Henry Clay's days in the House in the early nineteenth century), but also committee leaders. Through a series of reforms begun by the Democrats in the early 1970s and continued by the Republicans in the 1990s, committee leadership positions are now more a function of how the members are viewed by the party

[5] See http://www.house.gov/ethics/Medicare_Report_Cover.pdf and http://www.house.gov/ethics/Medicare_Report.pdf for the official report from the House Ethics Committee.

[6] For more, see R. Jeffrey Smith, "GOP's Pressing Question on Medicare Vote: Did Some Go Too Far to Change a No to a Yes?" *The Washington Post*, December 23, 2003, p. A1.

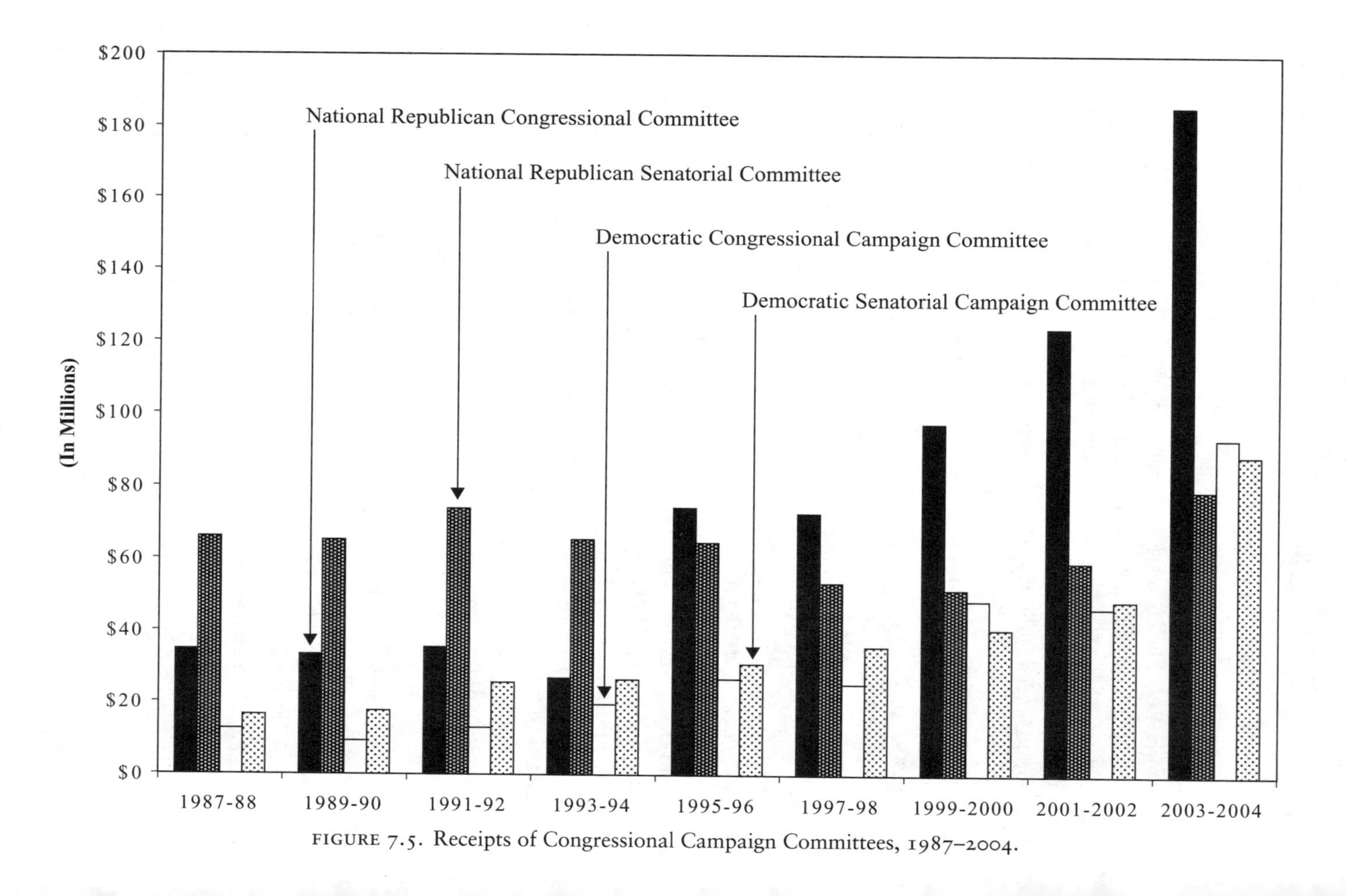

FIGURE 7.5. Receipts of Congressional Campaign Committees, 1987–2004.

leadership rather than of the age-old seniority system. The Republican party leaders have refused to give the committee chair job to the most senior Republican on the committees 14 times (including Roukema in 2001) since they became the majority in 1995, instead naming a more loyal Republican to the position (Pearson 2005). Ten of these seniority violations alone occurred in the 107th and 108th Congresses.

A third strategy for party leaders to cajole recalcitrant members is to give their favored legislation either a privileged or detrimental position on the calendar (Jenkins, Crespin, and Carson 2005; Pearson 2005). Votes members take contrary to their constituents' position can be quickly followed by positive action on a constituency-related bill that, otherwise, would languish on the Calendar.

Structuring the Legislative Agenda

During the "Textbook Congress" that reigned in the mid-twentieth century, committee decisions were typically rubber stamped on the floor by the entire chamber. Beginning in the early 1970s, however, committee decisions were increasingly subject to scrutiny and to amendments from legislators who did not serve on the respective committee (Shepsle 1989, Smith 1989). As the norms of reciprocity, specialization, and committee division of labor began to weaken, committees continued to exercise their power through the use of the ex post veto – e.g., their membership on conference committees – and by fighting fire with fire – e.g., their ability to offer second degree amendments (Shepsle and Weingast 1987, Weingast 1992). Nonetheless, the floor became an important place to get the work of the House done. As more internally homogeneous rank and file representatives and senators gradually ceded more authority to their party leaders, the majority party began to assert not only structure, but also, more importantly, its will on the floor. The powers the individual members took away from the committees were seized by party leaders.

One obvious manipulation of the House floor's agenda occurred between the important votes cast by Representatives Margolies-Mezvinsky and Smith. After the Republicans lost seats and their speaker in the 1998 midterm elections, most pundits thought that the House's pursuit of Clinton's impeachment would putter out, perhaps with a censure resolution, a popular legislative move with wide support in the House. Not wanting the Democrats to have an easy vote, however, Tom DeLay and the other Republican leaders forbade that option from coming up on the House floor. They wanted Democrats to go on record as either condoning or supremely punishing the president's behavior. By forcing Democrats and Republicans alike into a position of impeachment or acquittal, the leadership transformed an issue where members had moderate preferences into a highly polarizing vote. At the end of the day, only five Republicans voted to acquit Clinton and only five Democrats voted to impeach him. The final vote was much more polarized than the underlying sentiment in the House.[7]

Figure 7.6 is a rough stylized depiction of member opinion on Clinton's impeachment. Almost all members thought that Clinton acted inappropriately, but many of those thought that his offenses did not rise to the level of impeachment. The appropriate punishment endorsed by the members varied between the two end points of acquittal and conviction. The underlying preferences of members may have looked something like the light shaded region in the figure. The moderate, Roukema, might have been toward the middle of the distribution, whereas Oxley, who is more conservative, might be closer to the endpoint on the right. The Republican leadership, however, did not permit members to show such gradation on impeachment; rather, they forced members to align with one of the two end points on the continuum. From the impeachment votes, there was no way to differentiate the viewpoints between the moderates and the extremists, as those like Roukema voted exactly the same way as those like Oxley.

Although this example comes from the House, the party leaders in the Senate also have weapons in their arsenal to encourage party discipline. True, the senate party leadership cannot as easily manipulate the legislative agenda on the senate floor due to the filibuster's supermajoritarian requirement and the absence of the previous question motion. Furthermore, the seniority system for naming committee chairs is still highly prized and rarely violated in the Senate. In spite of these institutional factors, senate party leaders today have more power and responsibility than their predecessors. The parties fill committee vacancies more deliberately. Additionally, unanimous consent

[7] For more, see Ethan Wallison, "Democrats Stick to Plan, Stage Walkout on Censure," *Roll Call*, December 21, 1998, p. xx. See also, *Congressional Quarterly Almanac 1998*, pp. 12–3 to 12–53.

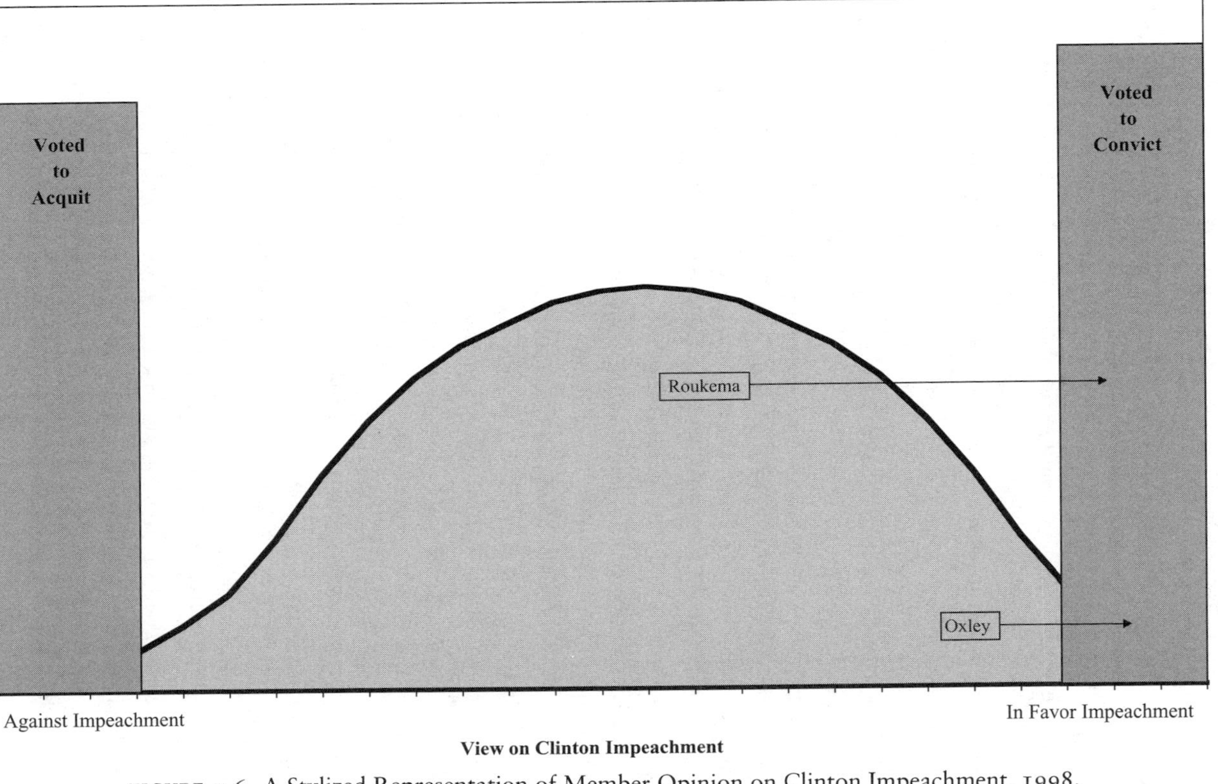

FIGURE 7.6. A Stylized Representation of Member Opinion on Clinton Impeachment, 1998.

agreements have become much more difficult to negotiate and, as a result, more complex (Smith 1989).

In all fairness to the majority party leaders, their responsibility to organize a growing and changing legislative agenda has made their job more difficult. Furthermore, after the Supreme Court opinions in the 1960s that forced equal-population districts, members' constituencies became more heterogeneous. As a result, members were less willing to abide by the division of labor norm that had granted committees wide discretion in developing legislation (Shepsle 1989). Committee proposals were increasingly subject to a greater number of amendments during floor proceedings, which heightened the importance of the House and Senate floors in the legislative process (Smith 1989). As floor-amending activity increased and as the majority party's margin decreased, the party leaders were under pressure to exert more control over the rampant floor deliberations (Binder 1997, Dion 1997, and Schickler 2001). Through different legislative means, the majority party leadership in both chambers restricted floor deliberation.

In the House, the Democratic leadership increasingly relied upon restrictive rules. As late as the 97th Congress (1981–2), more than three-quarters of the bills in the House making it to the floor were debated under an open rule and less than one-quarter had a restrictive rule (see panel A of figure 7.7). Over the next six congresses, the proportions almost reversed as 70 percent of House legislation was debated under a restrictive rule (Davidson and Oleszek 2006). The trend on the most important pieces of legislation was even more dramatic. In the early 1970s, at least four out of five bills were debated under an open rule (see panel B of figure 7.7). In the 103rd Congress (1993–4), the last of the Democratic-controlled congresses, only 2 of the 20 major pieces of legislation debated on the House floor had an open rule.

In leading up to their takeover in the 1994 elections, the Republicans vowed to bring democracy back and deliberation to the floor of the House. They pointed to the increasing number of closed and restricted rules as a sign of the Democratic leadership's arrogant use of power. True to their word, the percentage of bills that received an open rule almost doubled from 30 percent in the 103rd Congress (1993–4), the last one in Democratic hands, to 57 percent in the 104th Congress (1995–6), the first one in Republican hands. Since then,

Panel A: Based on All House Rules

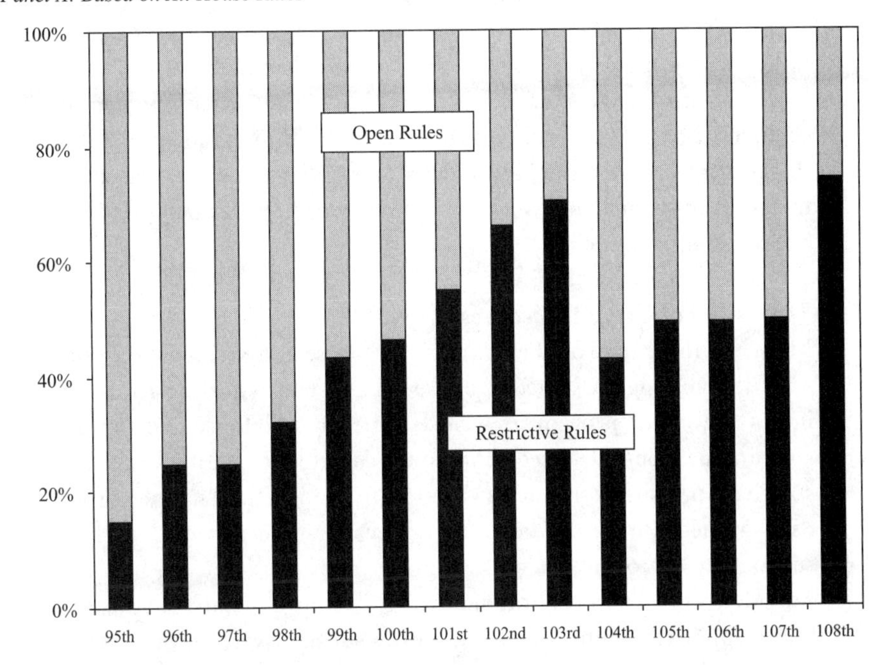

Panel B: Based on House Rules for Most Important Pieces of Legislation

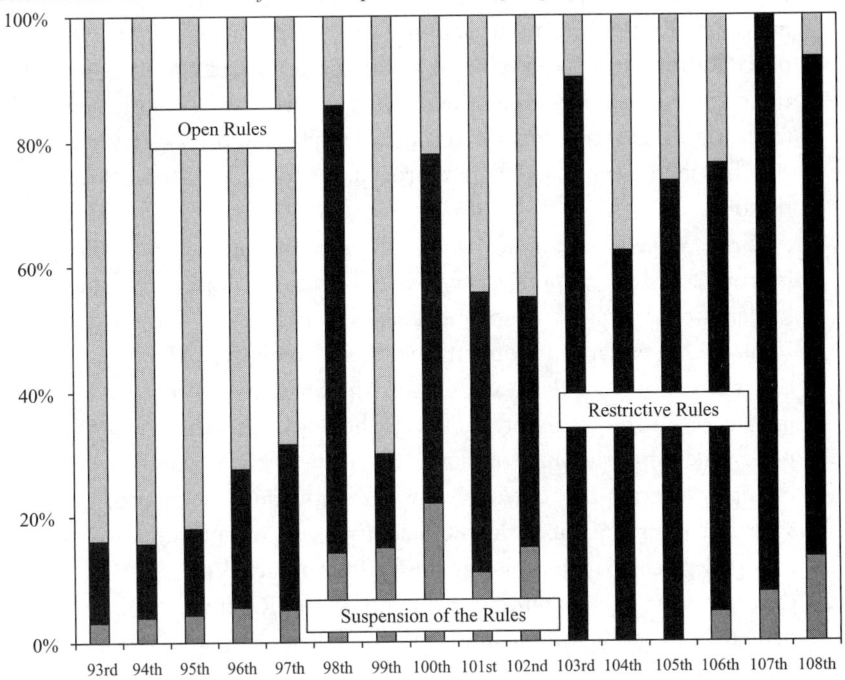

FIGURE 7.7. Open and Restricted Rules on the House Floor, 93rd to 108th Congresses.

however, the percentage of restrictive rules has climbed, such that by the 108th Congress (2003–4), the Republicans used a higher percentage of restricted or closed rules than the Democrats ever did. In the 107th (2001–2), the House debated no major piece of legislation under an open rule, and only one major piece had an open rule in the 108th Congress (2003–4).

The Utility of Using Procedures

More and more time on the floors of the House and Senate is consumed with determining the structure of the debate. The majority parties have increasingly used procedures – closed rules in the House and complex Unanimous Consent Agreements in the Senate – to hardwire the substantive outcomes of policies debated in Congress. As Jones (1968, 618) argued almost 40 years ago, "Leaders are expected to build substantive majorities – employing the many bargaining advantages provided by their procedural majorities." In turn, members, who have fewer opportunities to amend legislation substantively, have sought to use procedures to make substantive arguments – or at the very least to express their disapproval with the majority party leaderships' increasing reliance on procedure to organize their respective chambers. These procedural votes make it clear that the minority party only turned to these various motions when the majority party starting implementing more rigorous structures on the debate. The majority party leadership has increasingly relied upon procedures for at least three different reasons.

First, procedures can streamline decision making. Even if the legislators could reach preference-induced decisions on every issue, the leadership may want to implement rigid procedures so that those decisions could be reached more efficiently. The majority party may claim that the restrictive rules do not affect the final substance. By consulting various members before a bill hits the floor, the majority party can determine what the final outcome would be if the debate were truly open. By offering that option versus the status quo, the majority party saves the entire chamber the inefficient process of figuring it out with an open rule. For example, in the Help America Vote Act (HAVA) example from the beginning of this book, the Republicans may have denied Conyers the opportunity to offer his amendment because they knew that it would be defeated. In this sense, the majority party may claim that the vote is "merely procedural."

Second, the majority party leadership may implement procedures to protect their fellow partisans from casting substantively difficult votes or to force their political opponents to cast difficult votes (Van Houweling 2003, Cox and McCubbins 2005). Arnold (1990, 100) explains: "The aim of procedural strategies is to structure the legislative situation in a way that either increases or decreases the ability of an instigator to rouse inattentive publics or of a challenger to make a good campaign issue our of a specific roll call vote." The Republicans may have implemented a closed rule in the HAVA debate because they wanted to spare their vulnerable members from casting a vote that future opponents could spin in a negative light.

Third, the majority party may implement procedures to alter the outcome reached on the floor. Riker (1986) has shown how a proper structure of the procedures used can elicit the right substantive outcome. Without recognition of the political science behind these results, Dingell's quote demonstrates that the politicians are fully aware of the advantage in writing the procedures to achieve the preferred substantive outcome. Finally, Republicans may have implemented a closed rule for HAVA because they knew that the Conyers Amendment would pass and they preferred their bill to the amended bill.

The Frequency of Procedural Votes

Majority party members are not the only members who have increasingly used procedures on the floors of the House and Senate. As a consequence of the majority party's use of procedures, the minority party may only have one avenue of recourse: more procedure! When the minority party is shut out of the opportunity to offer an amendment during floor consideration, its only recourse may be to force a vote on the adoption of the restrictive rule or to offer a motion to recommit the bill to the committee with instructions to report forthwith. Such was the case when Conyers transformed his amendment to a motion to recommit the HAVA bill to committee. If the bill eventually goes to conference committee, the minority party may also make a motion to instruct the conferees to adopt or reject particular language. Transforming these seemingly procedural motions into substantive issues is

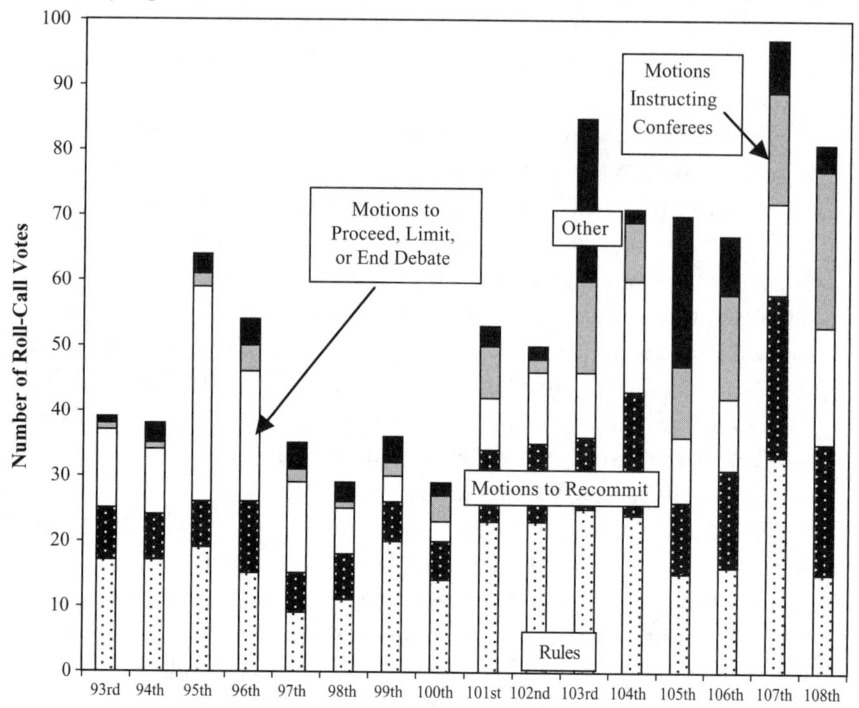

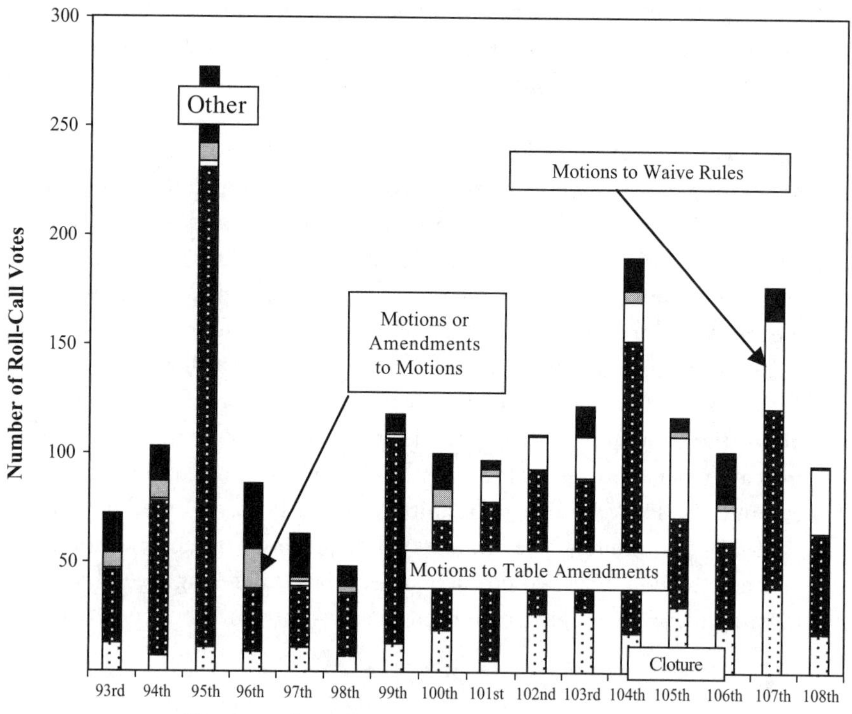

FIGURE 7.8. The Growth in Procedural Voting, 93rd to 108th Congresses.

exceedingly difficult for the minority party as the majority party leadership can offer legitimate reasons, quite independent of the substance, for their members to reject them. Nonetheless, it is frequently the only way that the minority party can offer substantive alternatives during the normal debate on the chamber floor. To offer these substantive arguments, even as procedural motions that result in procedural votes, is better from their perspective than not offering them at all. Beyond making substantive pitches with procedural motions, minority party leaders can also use procedures to delay congressional action or simply out of retaliation for the majority party's use of procedure.

Figure 7.8 shows how the various categories of procedural votes on the most important pieces of legislation have grown in the House (panel A) and Senate (panel B). As the House leadership has proposed more restrictive rules, the members have taken more votes on those rules. Additionally, as they have been shut out of the formal amending process, members have increasingly turned to motions to recommit and motions to instruct conferees, either to assert their will on the House floor (infrequent) or to lodge a protest against the restrictions imposed by the majority party leadership (frequent). In retaliation, the majority party, typically, has offered more motions to structure the debate by forcing the House to proceed, limit, or end debate.

Senators have also turned to making more procedural motions on the floor. The number of cloture votes has risen over the past 30 years. Additionally, they have also taken more votes on motion to table amendments, where individual members are trying to affect how they can debate as they have been shut out from determining what they can debate. The Senate also frequently takes votes on waiving its rules or motions or amendments to motions. Both chambers have had more procedural votes since the majority parties have more explicitly exerted their wills on the chamber floors.

IV. Conclusion

As the members' constituencies have become more polarized and have sorted themselves, they have increasingly elected members to Congress who share their partisanship (chapter 5). As the parties' respective constituencies have become more homogeneous, the majority party has been less dependent upon cross-pressured members. This trend, when coupled with the growing divergence between the parties (chapter 2), has led to party leadership organizations that are more powerful than they have been since the heyday of the strong speakers Thomas Reed and Joe Cannon.

More powerful party leaders have resulted in more seniority violations in the naming of committee chairs, like Roukema in the Banking Committee; more party-leadership-directed campaign cash (figure 7.5); and fewer opportunities to influence debate on the floor. As such, the arrow that links constituency change to institutional change is well placed.[8] The ramification of these trends is explored in the following chapter.

As floor deliberations became increasingly complex in the 1970s, party leaders used their newfound powers to streamline the process both directly and indirectly. First, to combat directly the number of amendments being offered on the floor, party leaders increasingly structured the floor debate. Second, leaders indirectly used the carrots and sticks of campaign support and committee assignments to ensure that the party backbenchers would support their decisions on the floor. Leaders had to exercise carefully these rewards and punishments. From the leaders' perspective, mavericks in their own party may be bad, but maverick losses to the other party in the next election are much worse. For example, Representative Silvio Conte, the ranking Republican member on the Appropriations Committee in the 1980s, famously remarked that his party would frequently tell him on which votes he should shun the party to maintain electoral viability in his liberal Massachusetts district (Edwards 2003). If Democrats had extended the same courtesy to Marjorie Margolies-Mezvinsky, she might now be serving in her second decade as a member of Congress. As the number of cross-pressured members has declined, stories like Conte's have, in turn, declined.

Wanting party discipline on roll call votes and yet wanting her members to be as electorally secure as possible in their reelection efforts complicates a party leader's strategy. Leaders have increasingly

[8] The only real dispute with the arrow may be that it is pointing in the wrong direction (Fleisher and Bond 2001). Even if the initial step in polarization came from the elites, the reinforcing step of the constituencies sorting themselves certainly enforced the polarization that may have already begun in the legislature.

resolved this complication by requiring discipline on procedural votes but allowing members more discretion on substantive votes (Cox and McCubbins 2005). Leaders may have chosen to focus on procedural votes for a variety of reasons. First, through an adequate use of procedures, leaders can either make the floor more efficient or hardwire votes on substance (Farquharson 1969, Riker 1986, Denzau, Riker, and Shepsle 1985). Additionally, constituents are more likely to examine their members' votes on substantive matters rather than procedural matters. Building on Froman and Ripley (1965) and Wilkerson (1991), I show in earlier work (Theriault 2004, 2005) that the electorate is more likely to punish members for their substantive votes than their procedural votes. In examining votes on congressional pay raises – the challengers' favorite vote to bring up in campaign literature and during candidate debates – members who vote against their constituents' interests on explicit pay raise votes face a more certain and substantively larger electoral punishment than members who vote for pay raises through a series of procedural votes. The difference between procedural and substantive voting is the subject of the next chapter.

Admittedly, the votes on impeachment were only a small percentage of the votes cast during the 105th Congress. If members with moderate preferences are forced time and again to cast their lot with the extremists, the polarization apparent in Congress might be nothing more than the artifact of casting roll call votes in debates in which the two positions are at the ideological extremes. The only way that a moderate voting record could develop with such rigid voting rules is if members sometimes voted with the extremes on one end and at other times voted with the extremists on the other end. In addition to determining the structure of debate on the floor for major bills, party leaders can also reward or punish a rank and file member by giving her bill a privileged position in the House calendar (Pearson 2005).

8

The Interaction in the Legislative Process

In 1977, the Democratic party was as dominant as it had been since the heyday of the Johnson administration. In addition to Jimmy Carter's capture of the White House in 1976, Democrats held a 149-seat advantage in the House and a 24-seat advantage in the Senate. Although the minimum wage had just been raised to $2.30 an hour in 1974, economic liberals in Congress and labor unions were again hoping to boost workers' pay. After months of negotiations, labor unions and President Carter agreed on a legislative proposal, which they then sent to Congress. The proposal not only increased the wage to $3.15 but also indexed the wage to 50 percent of the average manufacturing wage. The House Education and Labor Committee quickly reported, on a 29–7 vote, the compromise bill on July 22, 1977.[1]

A week later, the House overwhelmingly adopted, 331–44, the rule for floor consideration of the minimum wage bill. Typical of legislation in the 1970s, the rule allowed any member to amend any part of the bill. When Republicans successfully delayed the bill's debate until after the summer recess, the Chamber of Commerce and other business groups organized a massive grassroots campaign to pressure members of Congress to scale back the minimum wage proposal. Upon reconvening after the Labor Day recess, the full House took up the bill. The Republican efforts to scale back the bill won on the first vote

[1] Details on the 1977 minimum wage bill can be found in *CQ Almanac 1977*, p. 138.

of the debate. By a 223–193 vote, the House deleted the indexing provision and replaced the proposed $3.15 wage with three annual incremental increases, the last of which would raise the wage to $3.05. The House adopted a number of other amendments, some of which were pro-business and others were pro-labor. Under the open rule, the House took roll call votes on nine amendments and decided a number of others by voice votes and standing votes. In the end, the House overwhelmingly passed the bill, 309–96.

The Senate also gave the bill a thorough review. After voting on 16 amendments, the Senate passed a more pro-labor bill with four yearly incremental raises topping out at $3.40. The conference committee split most of the difference between the pro-business House-passed bill and the pro-labor Senate-passed bill. At the end of the minimum wage's legislative journey, the president signed the bill raising the wage to $3.35 through four yearly incremental increases (see panel A of table 8.1 for the party breakdown on all of the roll call votes in the House and Senate).

In 1996, the Democrats and the minimum wage faced a very different set of circumstances. Although a Democrat, Bill Clinton, resided in the White House, the Republicans controlled both chambers of Congress. After their 1994 midterm election victory, they enjoyed a 21-seat advantage in the House and a 10-seat advantage in the Senate. Because Presidents Reagan and Bush opposed raising the wage during their 12 years in office, the minimum wage had increased only once since 1977, to $4.25 in 1989.[2]

Shortly after the Republican takeover of the U.S. Capitol in 1995, Clinton called for a minimum wage increase. Unsurprisingly, his words fell on deaf ears in Congress. During the 1996 State of the Union Address, Clinton reiterated his call for an increase in the minimum wage. Again, his plea fell on deaf ears. It was not until Pat Buchanan's triumphant New Hampshire presidential primary win over Senator Bob Dole in early 1996 that blue-collar economic issues, including the minimum wage, received any attention on Capitol Hill. Nonetheless, Republicans were eager neither to debate nor to raise the minimum wage.

[2] Details of the 1996 minimum wage increase can be found in *CQ Almanac 1996*, p. 7–3.

TABLE 8.1. *Votes on Minimum Wage Legislation*

Panel A: 1977

Votes in the House of Representatives		Republican Yes	Republican No	Democrat Yes	Democrat No	Party Disparity
Jul 30	Adoption of the Rule	87	36	244	8	0.261
Sep 16	Erlenborn Amendment	126	15	97	178	0.541
Sep 16	Perkins-Tucker Amendment	68	73	233	45	0.356
Sep 16	Burton Amendment	14	127	175	100	0.537
Sep 16	Quie Amendment	132	11	132	150	0.455
Sep 16	Milford Amendment	128	13	113	170	0.509
Sep 16	Cornell Amendment	130	12	80	199	0.629
Sep 16	Meeds Amendment	122	17	160	115	0.296
Sep 16	Ashbrook Amdt to Blouin Amdt	83	54	35	235	0.476
Sep 16	Pickle Amdt to Blouin Amdt	127	10	94	173	0.575
Sep 16	Final Passage	61	76	248	20	0.480
Oct 13	Erlenborn motion to Perkins motion	118	20	20	246	0.780
Oct 21	Adopt Conference Committee Report	17	124	219	63	0.656
	House Total Party Disparity					0.504
	House Party Disparity on Procedures					0.520
	House Party Disparity on Amendments					0.486
	House Party Disparity on Final Passage					0.568

Panel B: 1996

Votes in the House of Representatives		Republican Yes	Republican No	Democrat Yes	Democrat No	Party Disparity
May 22	Adoption of the Rule	219	14	0	196	0.940
May 22	Final Passage of HR 3448	227	0	186	10	0.051
May 23	Portman question to reconsider vote	76	156	190	5	0.647
May 23	Riggs' Minimum Wage Amendment	77	156	188	6	0.639
May 23	Goodling Amendment	212	20	27	167	0.775
May 23	Goodling Amendment	189	43	7	185	0.778
May 23	Final Passage	93	138	187	6	0.566
Aug 02	Adopt Conference Committee Report	160	70	193	2	0.294
	House Total Party Disparity					0.586
	House Party Disparity on Procedures					0.793
	House Party Disparity on Amendments					0.730
	House Party Disparity on Final Passage					0.304

Votes in the Senate						
Oct 07	Bartlett Amdt to Williams Amdt	15	19	2	53	0.405
Oct 07	Tower Amendment	20	15	12	45	0.361
Oct 07	Domenici Amendment	21	13	11	45	0.421
Oct 07	Williams Amendment	24	9	52	5	0.185
Oct 07	Stone Amendment	21	13	21	33	0.229
Oct 07	Allen Amendment	21	13	21	34	0.236
Oct 07	Stafford Amendment	33	1	48	6	0.082
Oct 08	McClure Amendment	18	19	5	55	0.403
Oct 08	Stevenson Amendment	25	11	13	44	0.466
Oct 08	Schweiker Amendment	26	10	12	45	0.512
Oct 08	Domenici Amendment	28	8	16	41	0.497
Oct 08	Scott Amendment	12	24	2	53	0.297
Oct 08	Williams motion to Deconcini Amdt	8	28	35	20	0.414
Oct 08	Tower motion to Bumpers Amdt	24	10	14	41	0.451
Oct 08	Chiles Substitute Amendment	18	15	11	44	0.345
Oct 08	Final Passage	16	17	47	7	0.386
	Senate Total Party Disparity					0.356
	Senate Total Party Disparity on Amendments					0.354
	Senate Total Party Disparity on Final Passage					0.386

Votes in the Senate						
Jul 09	Bond Amendment	46	5	0	47	0.902
Jul 09	Kennedy Amendment	2	49	44	3	0.897
Jul 09	Roth Amendment	51	0	45	2	0.043
Jul 09	Final Passage	27	24	47	0	0.471
Aug 02	Adopt Conference Committee Report	31	22	45	0	0.415
	Senate Total Party Disparity					0.545
	Senate Total Party Disparity on Amendments					0.614
	Senate Total Party Disparity on Final Passage					0.443

When the pressure finally became too great to ignore, the Republican leaders of both chambers presented their own plans to raise the wage. The Ways and Means Committee quickly reported the House Republican leadership plan on a 33–3 vote. The Rules Committee only permitted the proposed wage increase on the House floor as an amendment to legislation that, through the same rule, would, after the House passed them individually, combine two business tax break bills prior to sending them to the Senate. In a last-minute move, the Rules Committee Chairman, Gerald Solomon, decided to allow a number of amendments to the minimum wage amendment that would, if adopted, further insulate small businesses from the economic consequences of the sure-to-pass minimum wage increase. Even though 14 Republicans voted with every Democrat in opposing it, the House adopted the two-bills-plus-a-minimum-wage-amendment rule.

The first tax cut bill passed 414–10. The minimum wage amendment was attached to the second bill by a 267–161 vote (33 percent of Republicans joined with 97 percent of Democrats to pass the minimum wage amendment). The House also approved one of the two amendments to assuage the economic impact of the increased minimum wage on small businesses. When the second tax bill passed (281–144), in accordance with the complicated rule, it was combined with the first tax cut bill and sent to the Senate. After weeks of negotiations, Majority Leader Trent Lott and Minority Leader Tom Daschle agreed on a unanimous consent agreement that would permit three amendments during the Senate's floor consideration. The first, offered by Lott and Daschle and approved by the chamber on a voice vote, broadened the business tax breaks of the House bill. The second amendment, offered by Senator Kit Bond, sought to weaken the minimum wage increase by increasing the number of exemptions to it. The third amendment, offered by Senator Ted Kennedy, sought to increase the wage an additional $0.90 and to decrease the small business exemptions from the bill. Most Democrats and a few Republicans defeated, 46–52, the Bond Amendment and most Republicans with a few Democrats defeated, 46–52, the Kennedy Amendment. During the conference committee, Republicans tacked on a few more tax and trade provisions that had languished on their legislative agenda before both chambers adopted the conference committee report and sent it to Clinton for his signature (see panel B of table 5.1 for a party breakdown on all of the 1996 roll call votes in the House and Senate).

The legislative histories for these two bills highlight several important trends taking place in the lawmaking process between the 1970s and the 1990s. First, the floor has become a less important arena in the lawmaking process. In retaliation for an explosion of amendments being offered on the House floor, party leaders used restrictive rules to protect favored legislation from torture at the hands of the minority party and majority party backbenchers. In 1977, members in the House were afforded essentially unlimited opportunities to amend the bill. In 1996, they were only given three opportunities to amend the minimum wage amendment prior to deciding whether the amendment should be attached to the business tax break bills. In 1977, senators took roll call votes on 16 amendments prior to passing the minimum wage. In 1996, because of Lott and Daschle's unanimous consent agreement, they were given only three chances to amend the legislation. To use an analogy from the education world, members in both chambers took very different "tests" in 1996 than they did in 1977. Whereas the tests in 1977 were made up of questions submitted by the entire membership, the party leadership almost exclusively designed the 1996 tests.

Second, members in 1996 cast more partisan votes than they did when raising the minimum wage in the Carter Administration. In 1977, 75 percent of Democrats voted against 75 percent of Republicans on only one vote in the House and none in the Senate. In 1996, four of the eight House votes and two of the five Senate votes achieved this level of party separation. Overall, the House party difference score for the 1977 minimum wage legislation was 0.50, which implies that, on average, 25 percent of Republicans voted with 75 percent of Democrats on the minimum wage roll calls. In 1996, the party disparity increased to 0.59. Senate party disparity on the minimum wage legislation rose from 0.36 to 0.55. To continue the analogy, the members "scored" very differently on the tests in 1977 and 1996.

Third, the final passage votes were less polarizing than voting on procedures in the more recent congresses. Procedure had slightly less conflict than substance in 1977. Procedural votes in the House had a 0.52 party difference score, which was 0.05 less than the party disparity score on substantive votes. By 1996, procedure was more than twice as divisive as final passage. In 1996, the party difference on final passage votes (which include the vote on adopting the conference committee report) in the House was 0.30, but 0.79 on procedural matters. The Senate did not cast any procedural votes during either minimum wage bill. In essence, the different tests yielded very different scores. Because the 1977 test, which contained mostly substantive questions, and the 1996 tests, which contained mostly procedural questions, were so very different, we cannot be certain how the 1977 students would have done 19 years later or how the 1996 students would have done 19 years earlier.

What we do know is that the roll call votes, mostly as a consequence of procedures, were more polarizing in the more recent minimum wage debate. These dual legislative histories underscore the importance of dissecting the legislative process in analyzing party polarization in the U.S. Congress. This chapter analyzes the extent to which these and other evolving floor practices polarized the parties in Congress. The first half performs this dissection by separating votes into three categories: procedural votes, amendment votes, and final passage votes. Almost the entirety of the increase in party polarization since the early 1970s can be accounted for by the increasing frequency of and increasing polarization on procedural votes. The second half examines the underlying motivations members face when casting roll call votes. It finds that a member's constituency is increasingly dominated by their party affiliation on procedural votes.

I. Categorizing the Votes

The voting history of the 1977 and 1996 minimum wage legislation starkly shows that all votes are neither equivalent nor equally important. Understanding party polarization in Congress requires a dissection of the legislative process. I divide the 7,028 House and Senate votes on the 609 most important pieces of legislation from 1973 to 2004 into three categories. First, procedural votes are those votes (described in chapter 7) that set up and govern the debate on the floors of the House and Senate. Second, the amendment category includes straightforward votes on amendments as well as second-degree amendments. Third, final passage votes decide the final resolution of policies and include votes on final passage, votes on the adoption of conference committee reports, votes in which one chamber agrees to the changes made by the other chamber, and votes to override presidential vetoes.[3]

Some scholars would reject the very notion of dividing up the votes into procedural, amendment, and final passage categories. They would argue that any procedural vote is simply a mask for "substance" and, as such, is no different from amendment or final passage votes. The political science literature shows the mixing of procedure and substance both empirically and theoretically. More than 40 years ago, Froman and Ripley (1965, 56) argued, "Most votes, of course, involve both procedural and substantive questions. Even a motion to adjourn can sometimes be partly a substantive issue, if the motion is directed at postponing action on a bill." Put more simply and contemporarily, Arnold (1990, 105) claims: "Conflict over substance can quickly evolve into conflict over procedures."

Robin Farquharson (1969), in his seminal book, *Theory of Voting*, shows how the procedures surrounding a sequence of votes affect the voters' ultimate decisions. Using this logic, Riker (1986, ix) developed his "heresthetic" argument to describe the practice of "structuring the world so you can win." "Agenda control," which procedures establish, is, according to Riker (1986, 130), "a concentration of the opportunity for heresthetical manipulation." But, Riker (1986, 140) warns, "Heresthetical resources of parliamentary leaders are entirely dependent on a supportive majority." Denzau, Riker, and Shepsle (1985, 1118) show how heresthetics work in the legislature: "Result- or outcome-oriented legislators should regard the alternatives on the floor at any stage of the voting process (but the last) not as objects of choice per se, but rather as vehicles that carry the process into the next stage of the sequence." For example, even the procedural move to recommit a bill, according

[3] Because of their overall importance, various scholars examine only final passage votes in testing their arguments about the process (see Jenkins, Crespin, and Carson 2003, Thorson 1998, Cox and McCubbins 2005, and Krehbiel, Meirowitz, and Woon 2005). Krehbiel and Woon (2005) criticize this approach because, as a summary of member behavior, it both excludes other important votes and includes largely irrelevant votes. My approach is subject to this criticism, but less so because I am more interested in the difference in voting on substantive votes (largely composed of final passage vote) and procedural votes. Additionally, I test the argument on all substantive votes as well as the substantive votes on only the most important pieces of legislation, which reduces the errors associated with the inclusion of irrelevant votes.

to Krehbiel and Meirowitz (2002), provides the minority party a substantive check on the majority party at the penultimate stage of the legislative process in the House. These arguments assume, of course, that members are forward looking and sophisticated enough to understand that by adopting certain procedures in a bill's debate, they are significantly affecting their ability to alter substantively the bill's language in the future. As Dingell's quip about procedures suggests, this assumption is not particularly heroic.

Although this literature suggests that procedural votes are fraught with substantive effects, none of the aforementioned would deny that procedural votes are generally more invisible than either amendment votes or final passage votes. Again, Froman and Ripley (1965, 59) explain, "The only fully visible kind of voting is roll-call voting on final passage of measures." Den Hartog and Monroe (2008) make the same conclusion more than 40 years later when they argue that votes on motions to table are not equivalent to final passage votes because a votes on tabling motions are much less visible to the public. Procedural votes may be substantive votes in hiding, though because of their less visible nature, members may treat them differently. The point at which members treat them differently, the tests that members take, change in a fundamental way.

While the number of procedural votes has increased over the past 32 years, the number of amendment and final passage votes members face on the most important pieces of legislation has actually decreased. The frequency trend of the vote types is visually represented in figure 8.1 and is characterized in panel A of table 8.2. Although figure 8.1 shows a certain amount of instability in the frequency of different kinds of votes on the most important pieces of legislation in the House (panel A) and the Senate (panel B), its characterization by a time trend in the regression results in table 8.2 more easily shows the trends over the 16 congresses from the 93rd to the 108th (1973–2004). Each of the coefficients in panel A of table 8.2 comes from a different regression in which a time trend is regressed on the frequency of the different types of votes. According to the regression results, the number of procedural votes has increased on average by three votes per congress in the House and one vote per congress in the Senate. In contrast, the number of amendment and final passage votes has decreased by as little as one vote per six congresses or as much as five votes per congress.

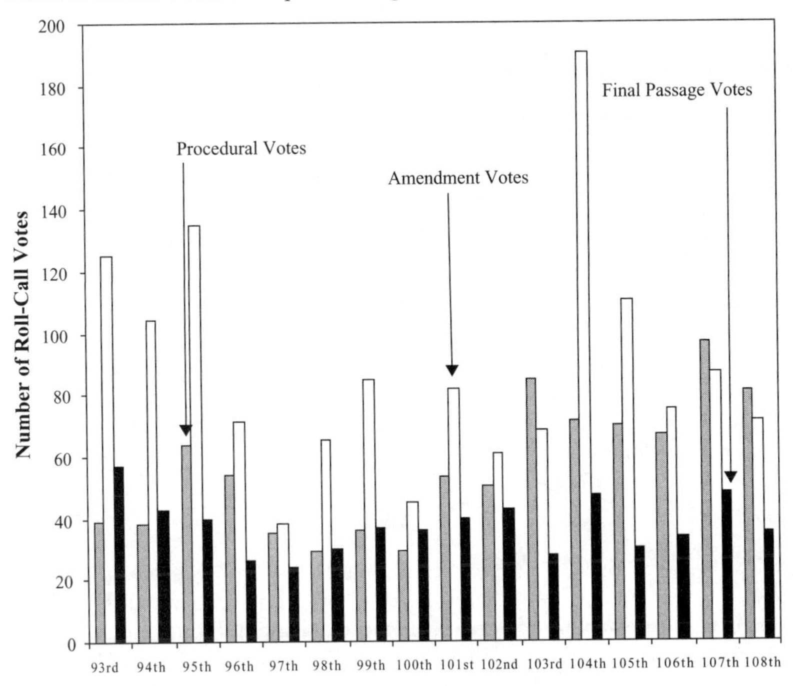

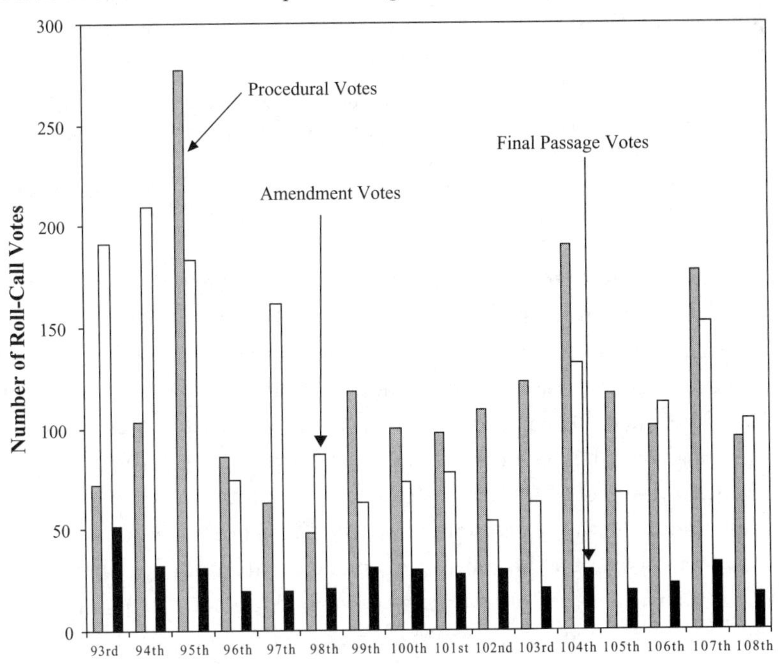

FIGURE 8.1. Frequency of Vote Types, 93rd to 108th Congresses (1973–2004).

TABLE 8.2. *The Effect of Time on the Vote Type Categories, 93rd to 108th Congresses*

	House Votes on Important Legislation	Senate Votes on Important Legislation
Panel A: Frequency of...		
Procedural Votes	3.194**	1.293
	(0.83)	(3.12)
Amendment Votes	−0.435	−4.800
	(2.12)	(2.61)
Final Passage Votes	−0.179	−0.756
	(0.50)	(0.42)
Panel B: Party Difference on...		
Procedural Votes	0.036***	0.034***
	(0.005)	(0.004)
Amendment Votes	0.017***	0.016***
	(0.003)	(0.003)
Final Passage Votes	0.022***	0.014**
	(0.002)	(0.005)
Panel C: Responsibility of Party Polarization Resulting From...		
Procedural Votes	0.018***	0.021***
	(0.003)	(0.004)
Amendment Votes	0.004	0.003
	(0.003)	(0.003)
Final Passage Votes	0.003*	0.001
	(0.001)	(0.001)

Note: The numbers in the table are the coefficients of the time trend variable with the various dependent variables as indicated (the numbers in parantheses are the standard errors of the coefficients).
*Statistically significant at 0.05; **statistically significant at 0.01; ***statistically significant at 0.001.

The mere differences in frequencies do not suggest that procedural votes are different from final passage votes. If members perceive them to be different, they should vote differently on them even if that perception difference is based on the extent to which the vote is visible to their constituents. The polarization on all three categories of votes has risen, though its rise has been most dramatic on procedural votes (see figure 8.2 and panel B of table 8.2). Among the House votes on the most important pieces of legislation, the party difference scores on procedural votes, on average, became 4 percentage points more polarizing each congress, whereas the polarizing trend of amendment and final passage votes increased around 2 percentage points each congress. These same

Panel A: House Votes on Important Legislation

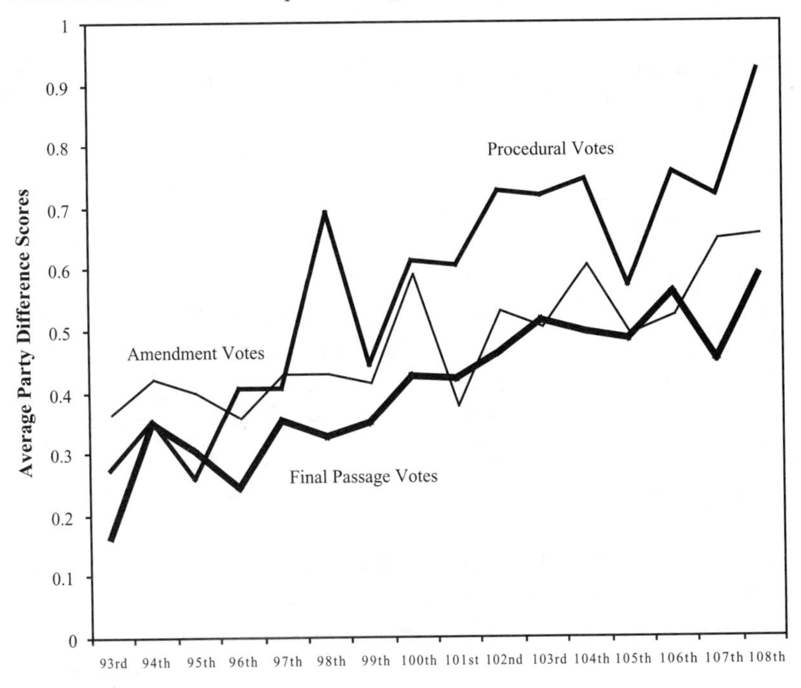

Panel B: Senate Votes on Important Legislation

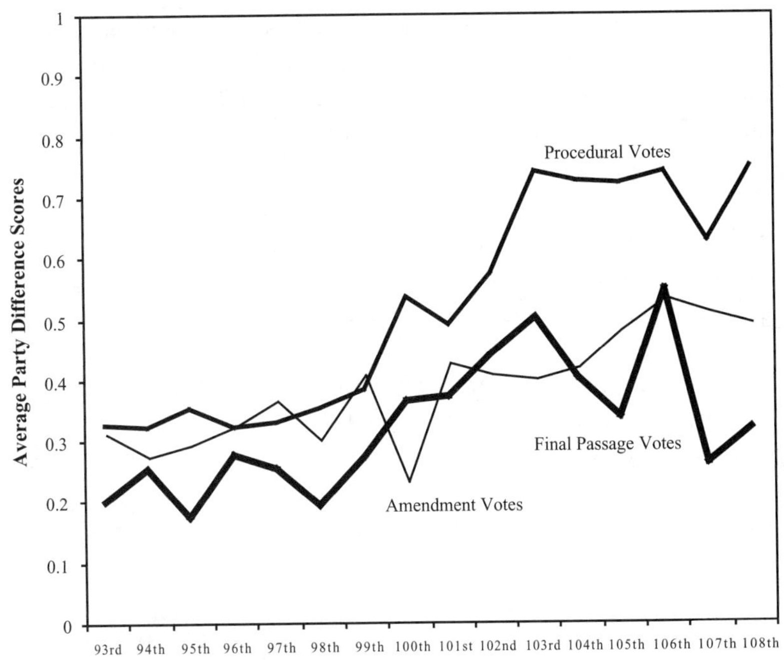

FIGURE 8.2. Average Party Difference Score by Vote Category, 93rd to 108th Congresses (1973–2004).

relationships are played out in the Senate, though in each category, the party difference scores increased slightly less each congress than they did in the House.[4]

In the 93rd Congress (1973–4), the procedural votes were less than 10 percentage points more divisive than final passage votes in the House. By the 108th Congress (2003–4), that difference more than doubled. In the Senate, the difference went from just over 10 percentage points to more than 45 percentage points. Whereas the members may have voted similarly on procedural and final passage in the early 1970s, by the 108th Congress, they voted much differently on them.

Figure 8.3, which combines the two trends depicted in figures 8.1 and 8.2, reveals how much each of the vote categories contributes to party polarization in the U.S. Congress. The top line shows the increase is the party difference score since the early 1970s (it is the same line that would exist if the dots – data points – were connected in figure 2.6). That entire party difference score, of course, is composed of votes in the three different categories. The shaded regions show how much each of the vote categories contributes to the overall party difference score, taking into consideration both the frequency of and the polarization on the different kinds of votes. Panel C of table 8.2 characterizes the trend. With each passing congress, the House became 1.8 percent more polarized as a consequence of the increasing frequency of and polarization on procedural votes. In comparison, amendment and substantive votes increased the polarization about 2 percent for all three congresses. In the Senate, procedural votes increased polarization by 2.1 percent each congress, whereas the impact of amendment and final passage votes was a total of 0.4 percent for each congress. The overall increase in party difference scores appears to be simply a reflection of the increasing polarization on and frequency of procedural votes.

These results demonstrate that the lion's share of party polarization in Congress can be accounted for by the changing dynamics of voting on procedures. That is, members in the House and Senate in the 108th Congress were taking fundamentally different tests than their counterparts in the 93rd Congress. To say that procedural change has *caused*

[4] Rohde (1991), Ansolabehere, Snyder, and Stewart (2001), and Cox and Poole (2002) find the same results in their exploration of procedural and final passage votes.

Panel A: House Votes on Important Legislation

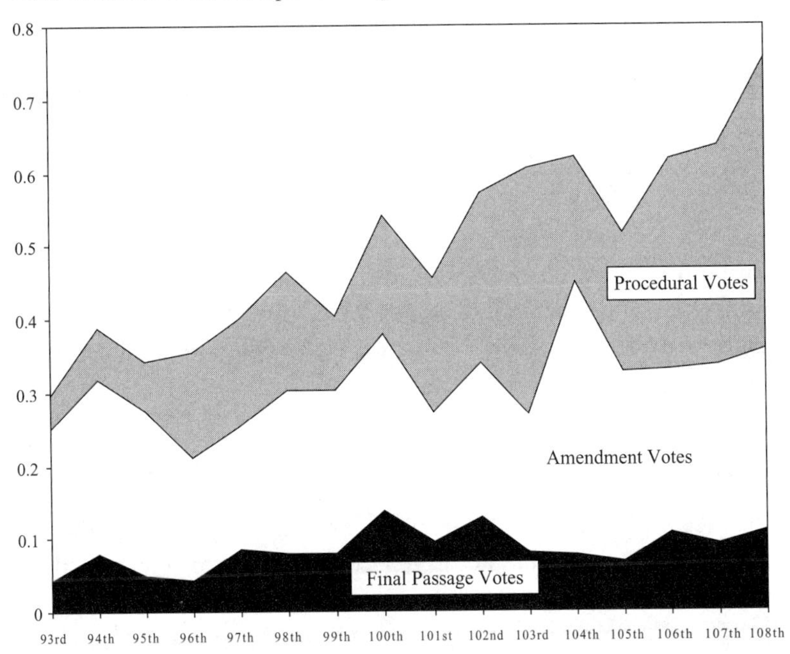

Panel B: Senate Votes on Important Legislation

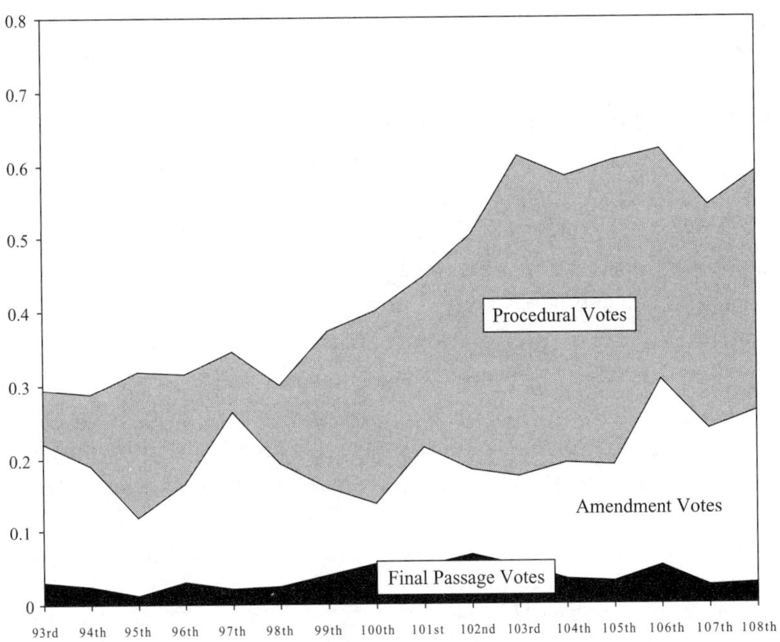

FIGURE 8.3. Responsibility of Polarization by Vote Types, 93rd to 108th Congresses.

party polarization is accurate only if party polarization is defined as the overall growth in party difference scores. If a more substantive definition for party polarization is used, it may only be more accurate to say that procedural polarization is symptomatic of and correlated with – not necessarily the cause of – party polarization. Regardless of the particular interpretation, the increasing frequency of and polarization on procedural votes account for nearly all of the increase in party polarization in Congress since the early 1970s. The next section sheds more light on how members view procedural and final passage votes.

II. The Interaction of Constituency Change and Institutional Change

The electoral changes in members' constituencies, which were discussed in chapter 5, interact in important ways with the procedural innovations described in chapter 7. This interaction shows up most obviously in members' voting behavior on the floors of the House and Senate. Members' parties and their constituencies are two critical factors affecting their roll call votes.[5] This section examines both procedural votes and final passage votes in both the early 1970s and early to mid-2000s to reveal how these two factors influence members' votes.[6]

If the electoral explanation were, by itself, sufficient to explain party polarization, we should see members being similarly affected by their constituencies on both procedural and final passage votes. In fact, we might expect the electorate to influence procedural votes more given that almost the entire increase in party polarization over the past 32 years can be accounted for in procedural votes. To test these conclusions, the two factors – party identification and partisanship of the members' constituencies – compete against one another in the same regression model. Members of the Republican party are coded "1" and members of the Democratic party are coded "0." As with party identification, the members' constituencies are coded in the direction

[5] Of course, members also rely on their personal preferences, but these are exceedingly difficult to measure (see Herrera and Shafer 2003 for one effective way).

[6] Amendment votes in the House of Representatives on the most important legislation act about halfway between procedural votes and final passage votes. To simplify the analysis, I only include the results for the procedural and final passage votes.

of the Republican party. The measure for the members' constituency is the Republican presidential vote advantage (RPVA) as introduced in chapter 5.[7]

The dependent variable is the percentage of time that a member agreed with the majority of the Republican party on votes dividing the majority of Democrats from the majority of Republicans.[8] To get at the differences between procedural and final passage voting, I calculate dual Republican party support scores (RPSS) for procedural and final passage votes. The high correlation (0.91; $p < 0.001$) between these votes is mostly a function of high scores for Republicans and low scores for Democrats. The correlation falls when the parties are analyzed separately: among Republicans the scores are correlated at 0.72 ($p < 0.001$) and among Democrats they are correlated at 0.69 ($p < 0.001$).[9]

Panel A of table 8.3 shows the regression results for the procedural (columns A and B) and final passage (columns C and D) RPSS during the 93rd and 108th Congresses. The interesting results in this table are not attached to any one coefficient, but rather the changes in the coefficients from the 93rd to the 108th Congress. For example, on procedural votes, the party identification coefficient more than doubles; on final passage votes, the party coefficient also increases, though not nearly as much. Additionally, the coefficient on the constituencies' partisanship increases on final passage votes, but falls on procedural votes.

Ordinary Least Squares regression may not be the proper statistical tool for these data. The dependent variable, because it is a percentage, has a lower limit of 0 and an upper limit of 1. When the dependent variable is bounded, the proper regression procedure is tobit. The parallel results for the tobit model are presented in panel B. Although

[7] Different specifications of this variable act almost identically. If I do not average the results across all elections in a decade, neither the variables' coefficients nor the coefficients on any other variable change appreciably. Likewise, if the vote is not normalized, the results are nearly identical so long as the election year is explicitly modeled in the regressions.

[8] *Congressional Quarterly* calls the votes when the majority of the parties vote against one another's "party votes." The results in this chapter vary only slightly if all of the votes – instead of the party votes – are analyzed. In these analyses, I calculate Majority Party Support Scores, which correspond to the percentage of time that a member votes with the majority of the majority party.

[9] The conclusions reached in these analyses are not at all dependent upon the use of party votes. Parallel analyses that take into consideration all of the important votes yield conclusions with the exact same flavor.

TABLE 8.3. *The Effect of Constituency and Member Partisanship on Party Support Scores in the House*

	(A)	(B)	(C)	(D)
	Procedural Votes		Final Passage Votes	
	93rd Congress	108th Congress	93rd Congress	108th Congress
Panel A: Ordinary Least Squares Analysis				
Republican Presidential Vote Advantage	0.586**	0.265**	0.687**	1.004**
	(0.10)	(0.02)	(0.11)	(0.07)
Republican Party Indicator	0.425**	0.884**	0.296**	0.516**
	(0.02)	(0.01)	(0.02)	(0.02)
Constant	0.257**	0.069**	0.316**	0.331**
	(0.01)	(0.003)	(0.01)	(0.01)
N	434	439	432	437
R^2	0.630	0.991	0.455	0.863
Panel B: Tobit Analysis				
Republican Presidential Vote Advantage	0.660**	0.419**	0.756**	1.281**
	(0.11)	(0.03)	(0.12)	(0.09)
Republican Party Indicator	0.437**	0.896**	0.308**	0.560**
	(0.02)	(0.01)	(0.02)	(0.03)
Constant	0.247**	0.062**	0.309**	0.327**
	(0.01)	(0.01)	(0.02)	(0.02)
N	434	439	432	437
Pseudo-R^2	1.095	1.631	0.878	0.922

Note: The dependent variable is the member's Republican party support scores.
*Statistically significant at 0.01; **statistically significant at 0.001.

some of the coefficients change, neither the overall thrust of the results nor the conclusions summarized in the previous paragraph change as a result of using tobit.[10]

Figure 8.4 shows the impact of changing the members' partisanship or the partisanship of their constituencies. The first set of bars

[10] Only one of the results changes beyond the 95% confidence interval established by the regression results. The constituencies' partisanship goes from 0.265 to 0.419 in the 108th RPSS for procedural votes. Although this is a rather large increase, the tobit estimate on constituencies' partisanship for the 108th Congress is still less than two-thirds of the tobit estimate for the 93rd Congress.

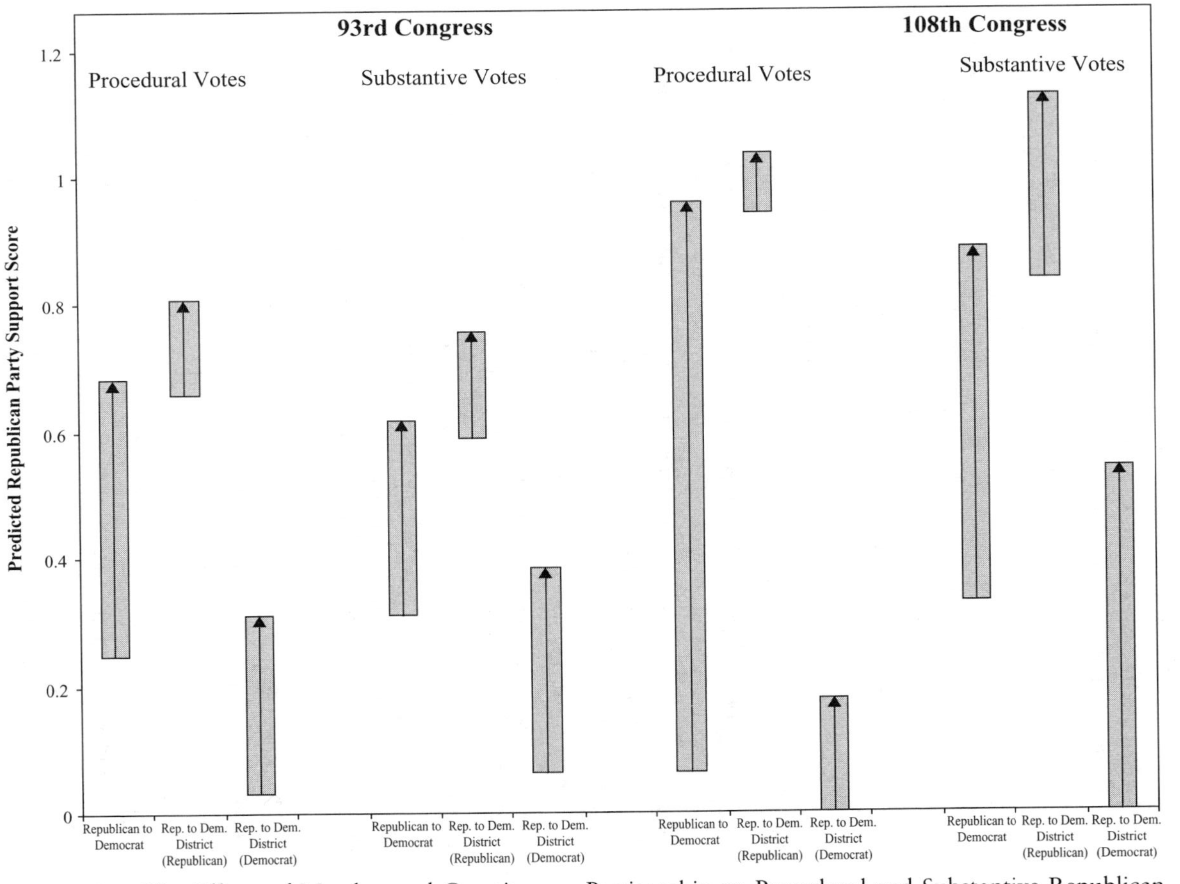

FIGURE 8.4. The Effects of Member and Constituency Partisanship on Procedural and Substantive Republican Party Support Scores in the House of Representatives, 93rd (1973–4) and 108th (2003–4) Congresses.

corresponds to the procedural RPSS during the 93rd Congress. The first bar shows the impact caused by changing a Democrat into a Republican (holding all other variables constant). The second bar shows the impact of changing a Republican's district from a poor-performing Republican district to a Republican-friendly district.[11] The third bar shows the same impact from changing a Democrat's district from a poor-performing Republican district to a Republican-friendly district.

In the 93rd Congress, the effect of the members' party identification was 42 percent greater on procedural votes than it was on final passage votes. In the 108th Congress, that percentage rose to 60 percent. In the 108th Congress, the effect of their constituencies' partisanship was 13 percent greater on final passage votes than it was on procedural votes. In the 108th Congress, the constituency effect was more than three times greater on final passage votes. Slicing the data a different way shows that the influence of the members' party more than doubled on procedural votes and increased 82 percent on final passage. Their constituencies' influence grew by 70 percent on final passage votes, but shrank by more than a third on procedural votes.

The same story, though to a varying degree, exists in the Senate (table 8.4 and figure 8.5 present the parallel numbers for the Senate).[12] Party identification's effect in the 107th Congress was 82 percent greater than it was in the 93rd Congress on procedural votes and 63 percent greater on substantive votes. Although the constituencies' effect was 12 percent greater during the 107th Congress than it was in the 93rd Congress on substantive votes, its effect was almost halved on procedural votes.

The appendix presents two separate analyses ensuring that any potential idiosyncrasies with the 93rd and 107th/108th Congresses do not drive the trends apparent in tables 8.3 and 8.4 and

[11] The district effects are measured for a district at the 5th and 95th percentile of district partisanship for the respective party. The 5th percentile best performing Republican district had a Republican disadvantage of 0.038; the 95th best performing Republican district had a Republican advantage of 0.186. The 5th percentile best performing Democratic district had a Republican disadvantage of 0.326; the 95th best performing Republican district had a Republican advantage of .097.

[12] The analysis is parallel to the House except that the ending congress is the 107th (2001–2). As the appendix clearly shows, the estimates for the 108th Congress are atypical.

TABLE 8.4. *The Effect of Constituency and Member Partisanship on Party Support Scores in the Senate*

	(A)	(B)	(C)	(D)
	Procedural Votes		Final Passage Votes	
	93rd Congress	108th Congress	93rd Congress	108th Congress
Panel A: Ordinary Least Squares Analysis				
Republican Presidential Vote Advantage	1.483* (0.50)	0.813** (0.17)	1.362* (0.43)	2.061** (0.33)
Republican Party Indicator	0.375** (0.05)	0.778** (0.02)	0.373** (0.05)	0.563** (0.05)
Constant	0.256** (0.03)	0.146** (0.020)	0.239** (0.03)	0.292** (0.03)
N	99	99	98	97
R^2	0.416	0.938	0.480	0.769
Panel B: Tobit Analysis				
Republican Presidential Vote Advantage	1.736** (0.52)	0.937** (0.19)	1.498* (0.47)	5.122** (1.03)
Republican Party Indicator	0.388** (0.06)	0.793** (0.03)	0.399** (0.05)	1.026** (0.14)
Constant	0.255** (0.04)	0.144** (0.02)	0.229** (0.03)	0.187 (0.08)
N	99	99	98	97
Pseudo-R^2	0.668	1.710	0.713	0.522

Note: The dependent variable is the member's Republican party support scores.
*Statistically significant at 0.01; **statistically significant at 0.001.

figures 8.4 and 8.5 These analyses show the robustness of the results. Using different assumptions on the statistical models yield the exact same conclusions. Party identification matters more on procedural votes and final passage votes and the constituency matters more only on final passage votes; on procedural votes, the constituency effect is significantly reduced.

These results highlight the problem with scholars and pundits who claim that changes in the constituency *explain* party polarization. As these regressions (and those in the appendix) show, changes in the constituency would show up in polarization of only the final

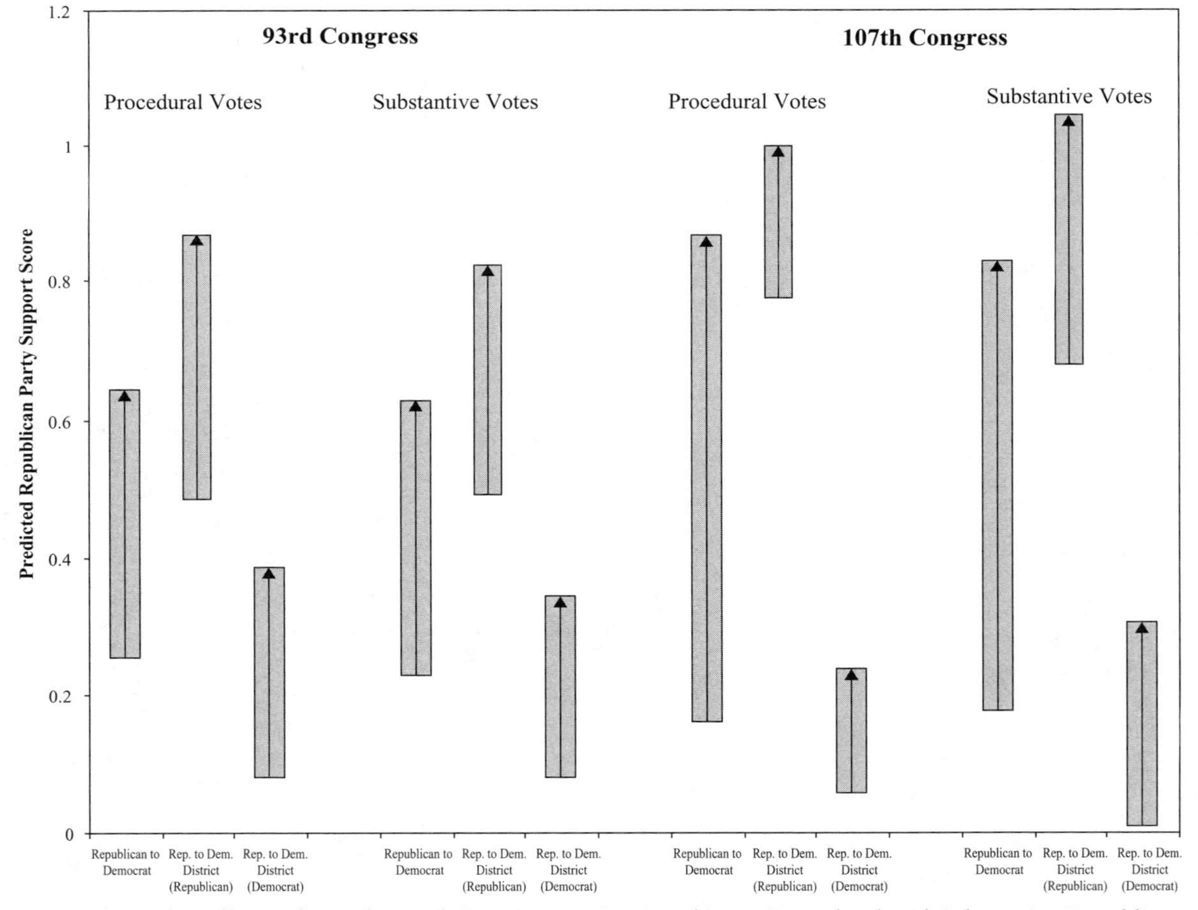

FIGURE 8.5. The Effects of Member and Constituency Partisanship on Procedural and Substantive Republican Party Support Scores in the Senate, 93rd (1973–4) and 107th (2001–2) Congresses.

passage votes, and yet from figure 8.3 we know that procedural votes account for almost the entirety of the increasing divide between the parties. These electorally based explanations must be interacted with the legislative process in order to arrive at an accurate picture of party polarization.

A Reality Check between Data and Theory

A combination of the conditional party government argument and these statistical results would suggest that members are exceedingly pressured to follow their party on procedural votes. They are given considerably more latitude to deviate from their parties' position on final passage votes. The members most in need of the freedom to deviate from their party are those whose constituency preferences do not necessarily align with their partisan identification – or in the language of chapter 5, "members from weak districts." Furthermore, the logic of using procedural votes suggests that majority parties try to structure easy votes for their members and hard votes for the opposition party.[13]

If these arguments, which stand individually, can be combined, the distinction between procedural and final passage voting should be small for either strong or weak majority party members because it is their party leaders who are structuring the voting agenda. The distinction between procedural and final passage voting for electorally safe minority members should also be small – their partisan identification is reinforced by their constituencies' partisanship. Alas, if party leaders – even minority party leaders – are gaining power and if the parties are procedurally polarized, the distinction between voting on procedures and final passage votes for weak minority party members should be growing as minority party members stick with their party on procedures – when their constituents are not attentive – and with the majority party on final passage when their constituents are attentive.

Figure 8.6 shows the data points and trend lines for these data series. For example, the solid circle for the 93rd Congress in panel A tells us that the majority party support score for electorally weak House

[13] Because the important distinction is between majority versus minority party members and not between Democrats and Republican, the Republican party support scores (RPSS) analyzed earlier in the chapter are transformed into majority party support scores (MPSS). For Republican-controlled chambers, the RPSS equals the MPSS. For Democratic-controlled chambers, the MPSS is equal to one minus the RPSS.

Panel A: The House of Representatives

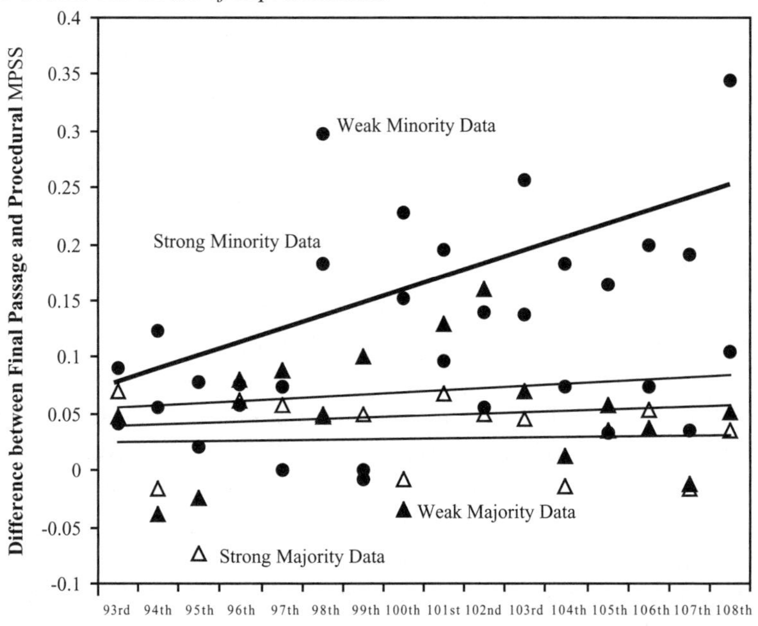

Panel B: The Senate

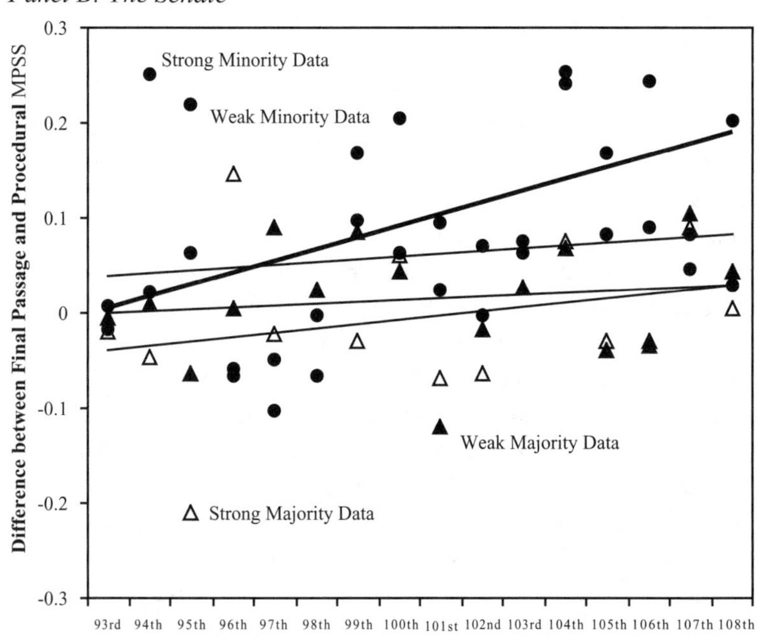

FIGURE 8.6. The Difference between Final Passage and Procedural Majority Party Support Scores by Electoral Security and Majority Party Status.

members of the minority party is 9 percent higher on final passage votes than it is for procedural votes. The differences between final passage and procedural voting for the other three types of members (weak majority party members and safe and weak minority party members) vary between 4 and 9 percent. In the 108th Congress, the differences for three types of members – safe minority party members and safe and weak majority party members – did not change much, but the difference between procedural and final passage voting for weak minority members increased to 34 percent. The same pattern, though a bit less systematic, is present in the Senate (panel B).[14]

These data show that the increase in party voting can be isolated even beyond procedural voting as suggested earlier in the chapter. In particular, it is the procedural voting by minority party members from weak districts that accounts for much of the increase in the divide between the parties in Congress. In the early 1970s, strong Democrats and strong Republicans voted very differently from each other on both procedural and final passage voting. That trend has continued into the twenty-first century. Weak majority party members, in part because their party leadership structured the vote, frequently vote similarly on procedural and final passage votes and the overwhelming percentage of time it is with their strong party colleagues. Weak minority party members are the only kind of member who vote schizophrenically and they have done so at an increasingly higher rate (presumably, as their party leadership has become more powerful). On final passage votes, they have and consistently do vote with the majority party just as they did in the early 1970s. On the procedural votes leading up to the final passage votes, however, they have increasingly voted with their own party leadership. This shift in party voting accounts for much of the increasing divide between the parties on Capitol Hill.

IV. Conclusion

This chapter explicitly tests the effect that a changing legislative process has had on party polarization in Congress over the past 32 years.

[14] The trend for weak minority members is statistically significant in both the House ($b = 0.011$, s.e. $= 0.004$) and the Senate ($b = 0.012$, s.e. $= 0.005$). None of the other six trends nears statistical significance.

While substantive debates in both the House and the Senate have become more partisan over this time period, the increasing partisanship on procedural votes and the increasing frequency of procedural votes account for almost the entire growth in party polarization since 1973. Members of Congress take more procedural votes in which their party leadership is given more latitude in compelling recalcitrant party members to vote in accord with their partisan affiliation. Members' constituencies play a much more important role in determining members' votes on substantive votes than they do on procedural votes.

As the parties increasingly rely upon procedures, they are pushing themselves further apart above and beyond the substance of their policy proposals. The substantive decisions that members make are exceedingly homogeneous within their parties, but not nearly as much as the procedural somersaults that have been increasingly frequent in the legislative process. The structuring, meaning, and voting on these procedural matters have drastically changed since the early 1970s. These drastic changes account for the overwhelming majority of the party polarization that has occurred in the U.S. Congress from 1973 to 2004.

Appendix: Verifying the Results with Different Statistical Models

Tables 8.3 and 8.4 show that both parties and constituencies are important on final passage votes and that parties are more important on procedural votes. In contrast, they demonstrate that constituencies are increasingly less important on procedural votes. The results from tables 8.3 and 8.4 may be an artifact of unique qualities of or circumstances in the 93rd and 107th/108th Congresses. To be sure that the trends are real, in this appendix I test the trends on all the congresses from the 93rd to the 108th in two different analyses. Both suggest that the trends described in the main part of the chapter are real and accurate.

Time Trends in One Regression Model

To test for the trends over the 16 congresses, in the first set of results in the appendix, I include a time variable as well as time interactions with the partisanship and constituency variables.[15] Because we have

[15] When this time trend is replaced with specific congress fixed effects, the increased power of the model is insufficient to reject the time trend simplification.

over time observations from the same member, ordinary least squares regression is insufficient. I must correct for the dependence of the error terms on these observations. I can employ two different corrections: member random effects and member fixed effects. The Hausman Test reveals which of the two is the proper correction. In both instances, the Hausman Test points to the fixed effects model. Unfortunately, there are two additional problems with the fixed effects model. First, whereas tobit can incorporate random effects as a canned statistical procedure, it cannot incorporate fixed effects.

Second, the fixed effects model, in essence, estimates 1470 separate coefficients (and one constant) on the 1471 members who served in the House between 1973 and 2004 and 282 separate coefficients for the 283 different senators. These separate coefficients dummy out the otherwise interesting effects from the two key independent variables. The model is only able to estimate coefficients for party identification because of the 17 House members and three senators who switched parties during the 16 congresses under consideration. The only reason it can estimate coefficients on the constituencies' partisanship is because of mandatory redistricting changes that force members to run in slightly different districts and the changing presidential votes cast by the constituencies. Only the variation within the individual members permit the estimation of the coefficients on these two variables. In other words, it does not consider the overall differences among all the members. As such, fixed effects bleed the interesting aspects of the independent variables from them. Nonetheless, I present the results from all three models in tables 8A.1 (for the House) and 8A.2 (for the Senate): random effects in columns A and B, fixed effects in columns C and D, and tobit random effects in columns E and F. I restrict my discussion of the House results in columns E and F, though in footnotes indicate when the results are dependent upon the particular model.

The number of observations in the procedural models are 6938 and 6917 in the final passage model (corresponding to 6960 observations – the 435 members' unity scores in 16 congresses – plus members elected in special elections and minus vacancies and members with insufficient data).[16] The regressions perform well. In every case, the overall R^2 is

[16] If a member did not cast at least five votes in the forming of his or her support scores, the observation was deleted from the analysis so that the relationships are not tested on unreliable data.

TABLE 8A.1. *The Effect of Strength of Constituency Partisanship on Republican Party Support Scores in the House*

	(A)	(B)	(C)	(D)	(E)	(F)
	OLS (Random Effects)		OLS (Fixed Effects)		Tobit (Random Effects)	
	Procedural	Substantive	Procedural	Substantive	Procedural	Substantive
Time Trend	−0.012**	0.0001	−0.011**	0.0004	−0.012**	0.0005
	(0.001)	(0.001)	(0.001)	(0.001)	(0.001)	(0.001)
Republican Presidential Vote Advantage	0.630**	0.462**	0.206*	−0.103	0.780**	0.503**
	(0.06)	(0.07)	(0.08)	(0.10)	(0.06)	(0.08)
Time Trend* Republican Presidential Vote Advantage	−0.029**	0.004	−0.022**	0.010	−0.030**	0.011
	(0.004)	(0.01)	(0.005)	(0.01)	(0.004)	(0.01)
Republican Party Indicator	0.382**	0.330**	0.173**	0.164**	0.372**	0.327**
	(0.01)	(0.02)	(0.04)	(0.05)	(0.01)	(0.02)
Time Trend* Republican Party Indicator	0.025**	0.015**	0.023**	0.015**	0.026**	0.017**
	(0.001)	(0.001)	(0.001)	(0.002)	(0.001)	(0.002)
Constant	0.300**	0.254**	0.391**	0.320**	0.303**	0.241**
	(0.01)	(0.01)	(0.02)	(0.02)	(0.01)	(0.01)
N	6938	6917	6938	6917	6938	6941
R^2 Within	0.087	0.048	0.095	0.057		
R^2 Between	0.899	0.782	0.884	0.738		
R^2 Overall	0.870	0.731	0.851	0.689	0.582	0.815

Note: The dependent variable is the members' Republican party support scores.
*Statistically significant at 0.01; **statistically significant at 0.001.

TABLE 8A.2. *The Effect of Strength of Constituency Partisanship on Republican Party Support Scores in the Senate*

	(A)	(B)	(C)	(D)	(E)	(F)
	OLS (Random Effects)		OLS (Fixed Effects)		Tobit (Random Effects)	
	Procedural	**Substantive**	**Procedural**	**Substantive**	**Procedural**	**Substantive**
Time Trend	−0.011**	−0.002	−0.011**	−0.001	−0.012**	−0.006
	(0.001)	(0.002)	(0.001)	(0.002)	(0.001)	(0.003)
Republican Presidential Vote Advantage	1.094**	0.975**	0.493*	−0.648	0.979**	0.997**
	(0.18)	(0.26)	(0.24)	(0.44)	(0.19)	(0.37)
Time Trend* Republican Presidential Vote Advantage	−0.053**	−0.011	−0.040**	0.024	−0.045**	0.027
	(0.01)	(0.02)	(0.02)	(0.03)	(0.02)	(0.03)
Republican Party Indicator	0.411**	0.405**	201**	0.199**	0.409**	0.406**
	(0.02)	(0.03)	(0.11)	(0.19)	(0.02)	(0.04)
Time Trend* Republican Party Indicator	0.025**	0.016**	0.023**	0.013**	0.026**	0.027**
	(0.001)	(0.003)	(0.002)	(0.004)	(0.002)	(0.004)
Constant	0.289**	0.246**	0.385**	0.349**	0.303**	0.252**
	(0.02)	(0.02)	(0.05)	(0.09)	(0.01)	(0.03)
N	1606	1506	1606	1506	1624	1524
R^2 Within	0.104	0.013	0.1105	0.023		
R^2 Between	0.827	0.780	0.813	0.661		
R^2 Overall	0.830	0.695	0.816	0.590		

Note: The dependent variable is the members' Republican party support scores.
*Statistically significant at 0.01; **statistically significant at 0.001.

at least 0.69, with a multitude of statistically significant independent variables. In the six regression equations corresponding to the two types of votes and three different models, all but six of the variables are statistically significant and all the tests measuring the probability that all the coefficients are jointly zero are roundly rejected.

Because of the interaction of the time trends, it is difficult to see the substantive results contained in tables 8A.1 and 8A.2. Paralleling figures 8.4 and 8.5, the graphical depictions of the tobit random effects regression model are presented in figures 8A.1 and 8A.2. Although the results are based on all 16 congresses, I present only the starting and ending points to show how the coefficient's effect has changed over the 32 years. In the 93rd Congress, the change in partisan identification caused a 21 percent larger impact on procedural votes than on final passage votes in the House. In the 108th Congress, the difference in the impact jumped to 35 percent. In the 93rd Congress, the change in the constituency's impact procedural votes was 21 percent greater than it was on final passage votes. In the 108th Congress, the constituency's partisanship mattered more than three times as much on final passage votes as it did on procedural votes. Although the coefficients of the other models are different, the two general conclusions from figures 8.4 and 8.5 are consistent across models: parties matter much more on procedural votes in the later congresses than they did in the earlier congresses and, in the later congresses, constituencies matter much more on final passage votes than they do on procedural votes.

Separate Estimates for Each Congress

The second analysis estimates coefficients for each of the congresses from the 93rd to the 108th for the tobit regressions presented only for the 93rd and the 107th/108th Congresses in tables 8.3 and 8.4. Gelman (2006) has dubbed this type of analysis, "The Secret Weapon," because it is not done very frequently yet provides the most complete picture of the data.[17] The disadvantage of this analysis is that it does not provide point estimates that can be as readily discussed and depicted as those in figures 8A.1 and 8A.2. On the other hand, this analysis provides the most complete picture of the data without needing to jump through

[17] See the website: http://www.stat.columbia.edu/~cook/movabletype/archives/2005/03/the_secret_weap.html; accessed on August 10, 2006.

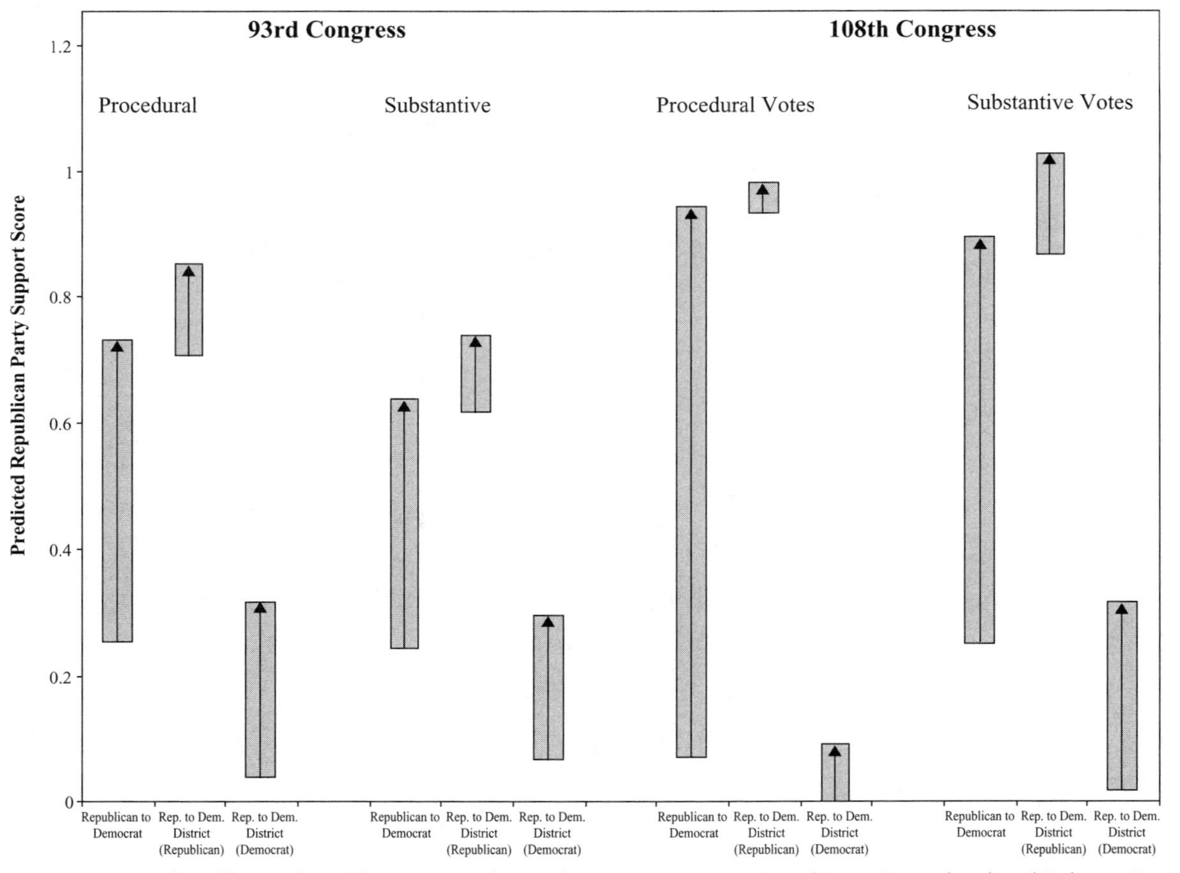

FIGURE 8A.1. The Effects of Member Partisanship and Constituency Partisanship on Procedural and Substantive Republican Party Support Scores in the House of Representatives 93rd and 108th Congresses (1973–2004).

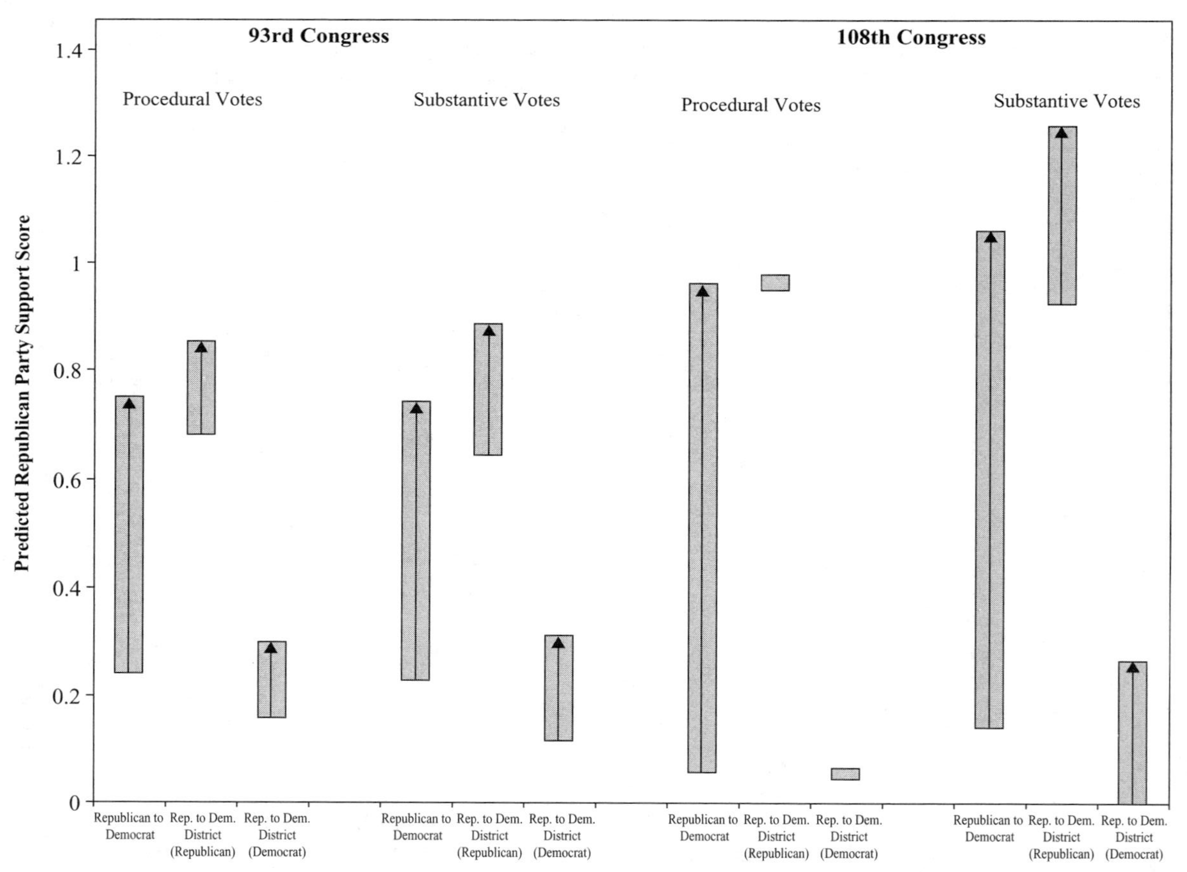

FIGURE 8A.2. The Effects of Member Partisanship and Constituency Partisanship on Procedural and Substantive Republican Party Support Scores in the Senate, 93rd and 108th Congresses (1973–2004).

TABLE 8A.3. *The Effect by Congress of Constituency Partisanship and Partisanship on Republican Party Support Scores in the House of Representatives*

Panel A: Procedural Votes								
	93rd	**94th**	**95th**	**96th**	**97th**	**98th**	**99th**	**100th**
Republican Presidential Vote Advantage	0.660	0.760	0.312	0.914	0.654	1.237	0.549	0.882
	(0.11)	(0.12)	(0.06)	(0.11)	(0.11)	(0.11)	(0.09)	(0.09)
Republican Party Indicator	0.437	0.524	0.421	0.547	0.614	0.777	0.612	0.708
	(0.02)	(0.03)	(0.01)	(0.02)	(0.02)	(0.02)	(0.02)	(0.02)
Constant	0.247	0.280	0.315	0.218	0.173	0.072	0.094	0.139
	(0.01)	(0.01)	(0.01)	(0.01)	(0.01)	(0.01)	(0.01)	(0.01)
Pseudo R^2	1.095	1.032	30.121	1.129	1.014	0.938	1.102	1.144
	101st	**102nd**	**103rd**	**104th**	**105th**	**106th**	**107th**	**108th**
Republican Presidential Vote Advantage	0.616	0.501	0.395	0.302	0.502	0.525	0.240	0.419
	(0.06)	(0.06)	(0.04)	(0.03)	(0.04)	(0.05)	(0.03)	(0.03)
Republican Party Indicator	0.797	0.829	0.747	0.537	0.735	0.804	0.807	0.896
	(0.01)	(0.01)	(0.01)	(0.01)	(0.01)	(0.01)	(0.01)	(0.01)
Constant	0.056	0.040	0.127	0.259	0.182	0.120	0.126	0.062
	(0.01)	(0.01)	(0.01)	(0.01)	(0.01)	(0.01)	(0.01)	(0.01)
Pseudo R^2	1.401	1.475	3.066	5.572	2.190	1.653	3.198	1.631

(continued)

TABLE 8A.3 *Continued*

Panel B: Final Passage Votes

	93rd	94th	95th	96th	97th	98th	99th	100th
Republican Presidential Vote Advantage	0.756	0.789	0.666	1.151	0.981	0.838	0.857	0.968
	(0.12)	(0.12)	(0.09)	(0.21)	(0.15)	(0.10)	(0.09)	(0.11)
Republican Party Indicator	0.308	0.471	0.389	0.503	0.497	0.473	0.486	0.554
	(0.02)	(0.03)	(0.02)	(0.04)	(0.03)	(0.02)	(0.02)	(0.02)
Constant	0.309	0.232	0.284	0.249	0.264	0.150	0.203	0.094
	(0.02)	(0.01)	(0.01)	(0.02)	(0.02)	(0.01)	(0.01)	(0.01)
Pseudo R^2	0.878	0.944	3.452	0.312	0.601	1.053	1.235	0.867
	101st	**102nd**	**103rd**	**104th**	**105th**	**106th**	**107th**	**108th**
Republican Presidential Vote Advantage	0.854	0.984	0.659	0.698	1.126	0.974	0.893	1.281
	(0.09)	(0.09)	(0.06)	(0.05)	(0.08)	(0.08)	(0.08)	(0.09)
Republican Party Indicator	0.516	0.584	0.473	0.352	0.537	0.553	0.714	0.560
	(0.02)	(0.02)	(0.02)	(0.01)	(0.02)	(0.02)	(0.02)	(0.03)
Constant	0.187	0.188	0.198	0.416	0.305	0.287	0.280	0.327
	(0.01)	(0.01)	(0.01)	(0.01)	(0.01)	(0.01)	(0.01)	(0.02)
Pseudo R^2	1.195	1.003	2.379	8.617	1.144	1.402	1.080	0.922

TABLE 8A.4. *The Effect by Congress of Constituency Partisanship and Partisanship on Republican Party Support Scores in the Senate*

Panel A: Procedural Votes								
	93rd	**94th**	**95th**	**96th**	**97th**	**98th**	**99th**	**100th**
Republican Presidential Vote Advantage	1.736	1.285	2.066	1.550	0.578	1.183	1.390	1.039
	(0.52)	(0.45)	(0.47)	(0.27)	(0.18)	(0.27)	(0.24)	(0.21)
Republican Party Indicator	0.388	0.380	0.404	0.515	0.602	0.483	0.527	0.648
	(0.06)	(0.05)	(0.05)	(0.03)	(0.02)	(0.03)	(0.03)	(0.02)
Constant	0.255	0.302	0.311	0.204	0.194	0.303	0.241	0.103
	(0.04)	(0.03)	(0.03)	(0.02)	(0.01)	(0.02)	(0.02)	(0.02)
Pseudo R^2	0.668	1.162	0.970	2.755	3.753	3.335	3.193	2.661
	101st	**102nd**	**103rd**	**104th**	**105th**	**106th**	**107th**	**108th**
Republican Presidential Vote Advantage	1.083	1.244	1.010	0.695	0.955	0.550	1.023	0.937
	(0.20)	(0.20)	(0.12)	(0.15)	(0.16)	(0.11)	(0.16)	(0.19)
Republican Party Indicator	0.559	0.651	0.792	0.765	0.759	0.835	0.707	0.793
	(0.02)	(0.02)	(0.02)	(0.02)	(0.02)	(0.02)	(0.02)	(0.03)
Constant	0.177	0.174	0.092	0.170	0.147	0.092	0.161	0.144
	(0.01)	(0.01)	(0.01)	(0.02)	(0.02)	(0.01)	(0.02)	(0.02)
Pseudo R^2	4.058	2.242	2.242	2.265	1.909	2.576	2.503	1.710

(continued)

TABLE 8A.4 *Continued*

Panel B: Final Passage Votes

	93rd	94th	95th	96th	97th	98th	99th	100th
Republican Presidential Vote Advantage	1.498	1.134	3.482	3.492	1.200	2.680	1.394	1.648
	(0.47)	(0.39)	(1.24)	(1.31)	(0.50)	(0.75)	(0.33)	(0.35)
Republican Party Indicator	0.399	0.291	0.514	0.773	0.666	0.511	0.463	0.593
	(0.05)	(0.04)	(0.14)	(0.16)	(0.06)	(0.08)	(0.04)	(0.04)
Constant	0.229	0.331	0.086	0.012	0.227	0.323	0.262	0.086
	(0.03)	(0.03)	(0.08)	(0.10)	(0.04)	(0.06)	(0.03)	(0.03)
Pseudo R^2	0.713	3.289	0.259	0.238	0.649	0.336	1.558	1.112
	101st	**102nd**	**103rd**	**104th**	**105th**	**106th**	**107th**	**108th**
Republican Presidential Vote Advantage	1.838	2.165	1.439	0.612	3.577	1.998	1.674	5.123
	(0.37)	(0.46)	(0.27)	(0.24)	(0.77)	(0.39)	(0.39)	(1.03)
Republican Party Indicator	0.662	0.905	0.688	0.465	1.048	0.873	0.652	1.026
	(0.04)	(0.05)	(0.04)	(0.03)	(0.11)	(0.06)	(0.05)	(0.14)
Constant	0.068	−0.072	0.114	0.388	0.240	0.174	0.177	0.187
	(0.03)	(0.04)	(0.03)	(0.02)	(0.06)	(0.04)	(0.04)	(0.08)
Pseudo R^2	0.955	0.843	1.000	2.520	0.634	0.765	0.710	0.522

Panel A: Procedural Republican Party Support Scores

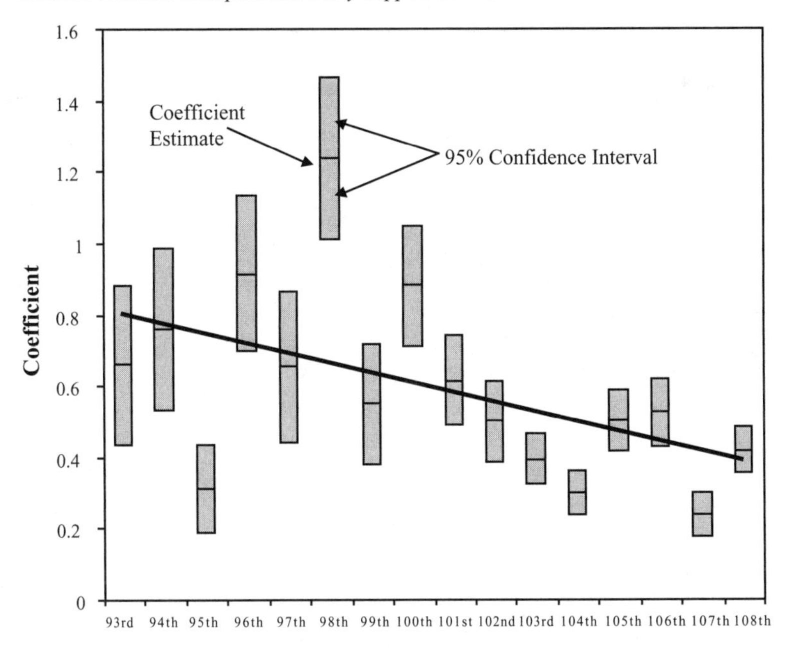

Panel B: Final Passage Republican Party Support Scores

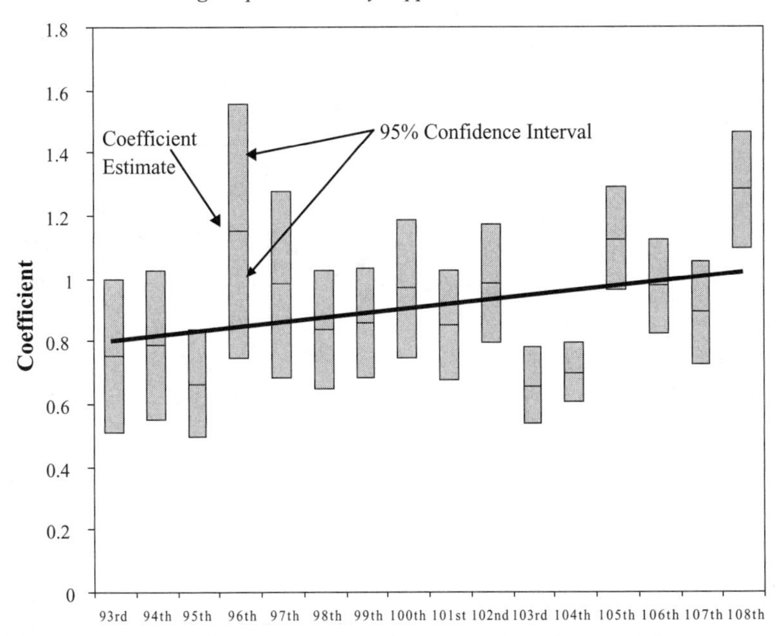

FIGURE 8A.3. Coefficients on Republican Presidential Vote Advantage on Republican Party Support Scores in the House, 93rd to 108th Congresses.

Panel A: Procedural Republican Party Support Scores

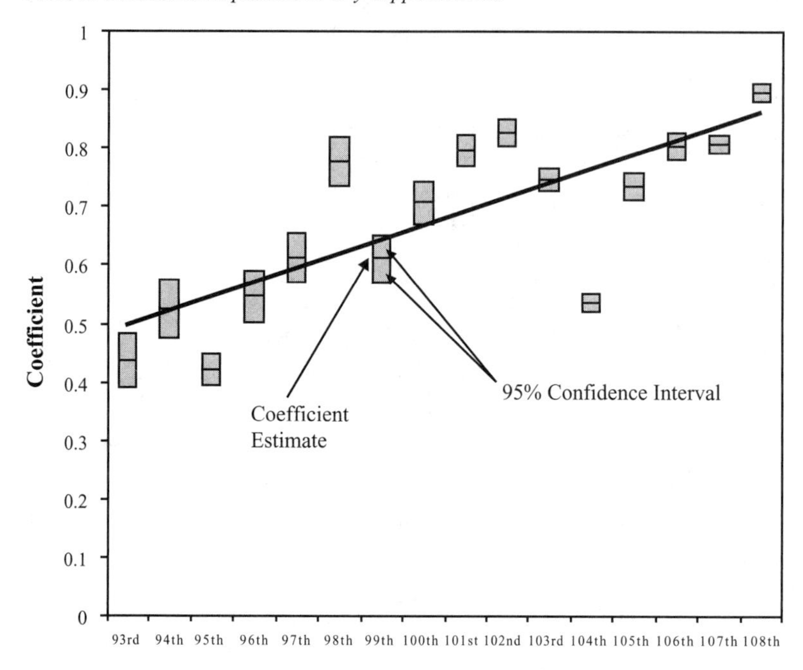

Panel B: Final Passage Republican Party Support Scores

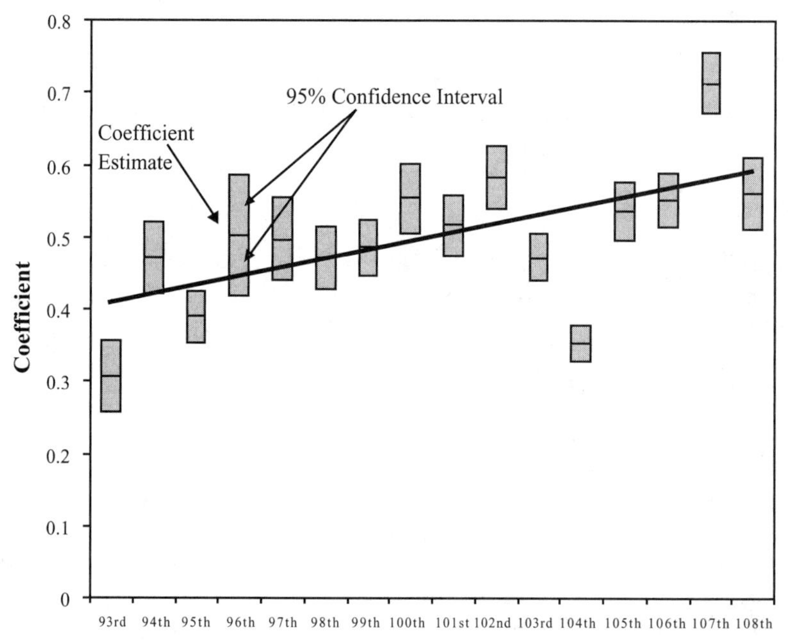

FIGURE 8A.4. Coefficients on Republican Identification on Republican Party Support Scores in the House, 93rd to 108th Congresses.

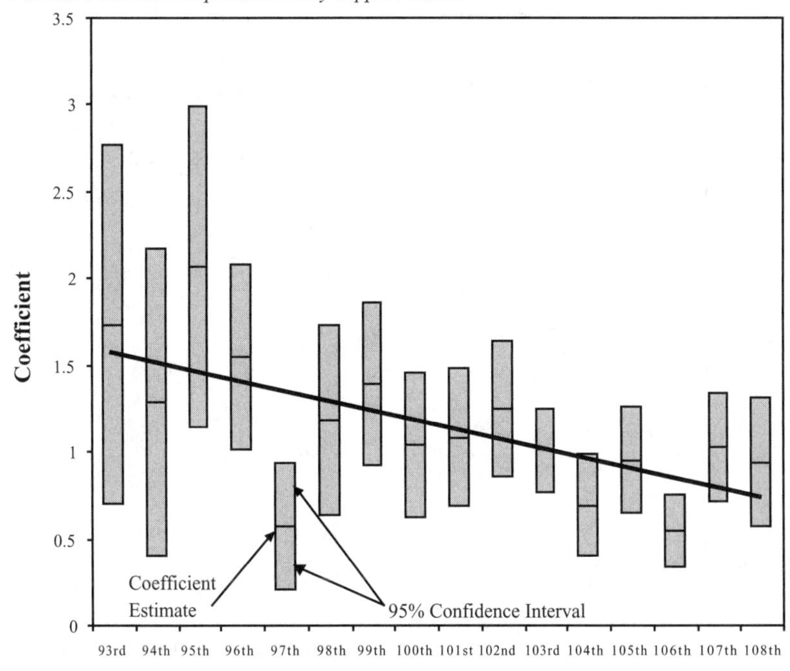

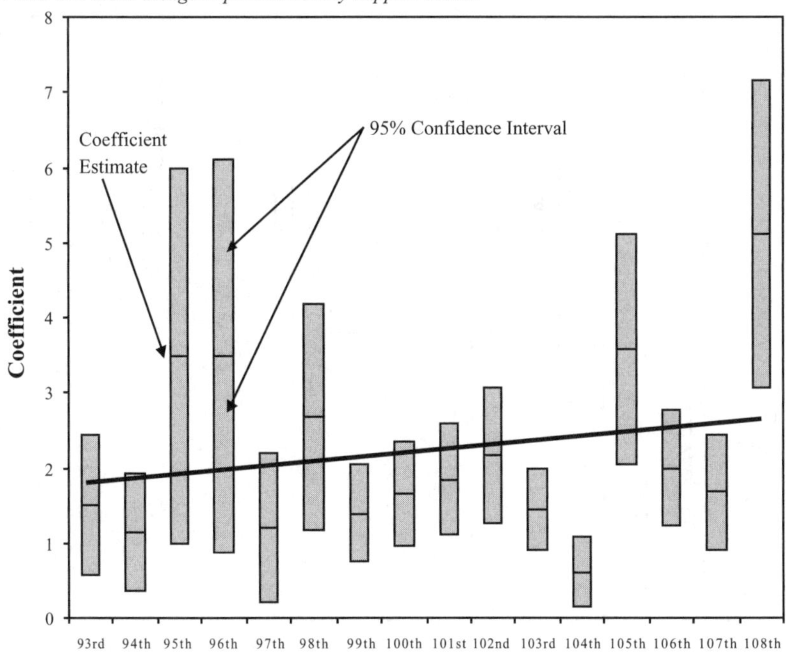

FIGURE 8A.5. Coefficients on Republican Presidential Vote Advantage on Republican Party Support Scores in the Senate, 93rd to 108th Congresses.

Panel A: Procedural Republican Party Support Scores

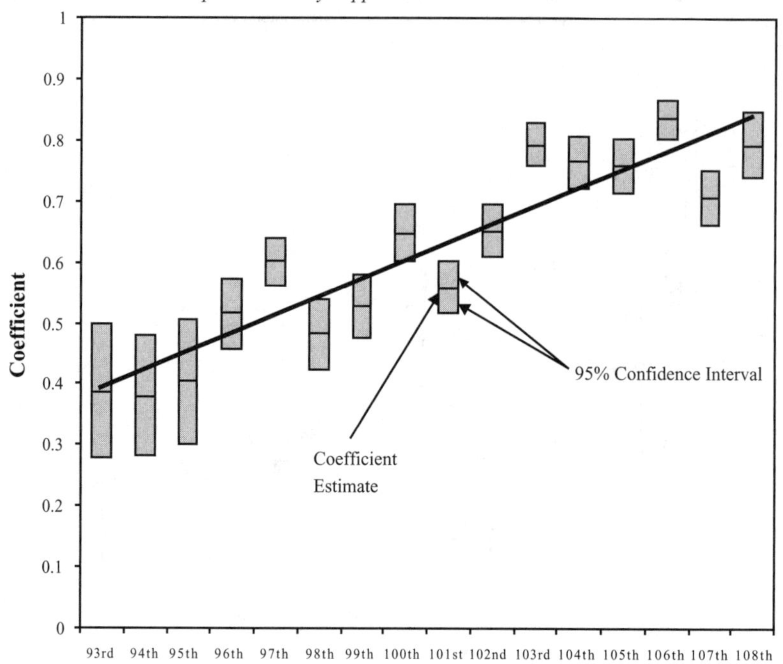

Panel B: Final Passage Republican Party Support Scores

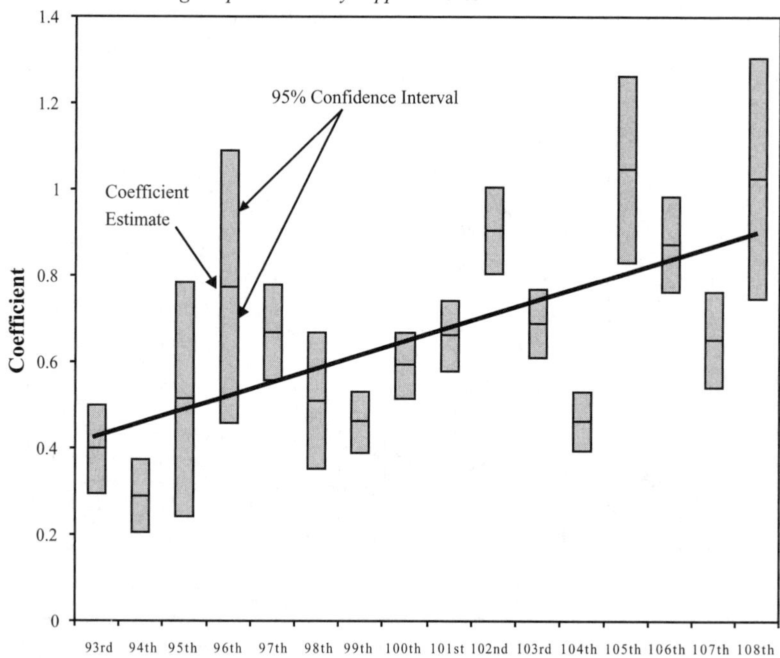

FIGURE 8A.6. Coefficients on Republican Identification on Republican Party Support Scores in the Senate, 93rd to 108th Congresses.

all the statistical hoops that are required when working with pooled data. Not only is the picture complete, but it is transparent, as the specifications are kept to a minimum.

The results for the congress-by-congress tobit regressions are presented in tables 8A.3 and 8A.4 and the graphic depiction of the effect of constituencies' partisanship and the members' party identification are presented in figures 8A.3–8A.6 The mark running through the shaded region is the coefficient estimate and the shaded region on either side is the 95 percent confidence interval of the coefficient estimate. The bold straight line running through the data is the trendline of the coefficients, which is implicitly estimated in table 8A.1.

The conclusions reached from the congress-by-congress regression results are the same reached in the main part of the chapter. Party has become more important on procedural and final passage votes and the constituencies' partisanship has become more important on final passage votes. The voice of the people on procedural votes, however, is almost completely silent.

Conclusion

The analyses in this appendix show that the conclusions presented in the main part of the paper are robust to various specifications and to the inclusion of all the intervening congresses between the 93rd and the 108th. In total, this chapter presents evidence that both members' parties and their constituencies' partisanship have become more important in final passage voting. On procedural voting, however, only party has become more important – the voice of the constituents is now almost completely silent even though in the 93rd Congress, its impact on procedural votes rivaled its impact on final passage votes.

9

The Link between the House and the Senate

Upon his return to the United States, Thomas Jefferson, who missed the constitutional convention because he was in Paris serving as an ambassador, queried George Washington about why he ever accepted the aristocratic characteristics of the U.S. Senate. Washington was to have famously remarked: "We pour legislation into the senatorial saucer to cool it."[1] The framers, wary to draw too direct a line between the impulse of the people and public policy, created a complex law-making system to dampen the people's demands. Chief among these was the Senate. As Madison explains in Federalist 63, "Such an institution [as the Senate] may be sometimes necessary as a defense to the people against their own temporary errors and delusions."[2] Only the persistent and enduring demands from the people would enjoy a hearing and successful disposition in the Senate. By virtue of its design and practice over the past 220 years, the Senate has been less likely to be captured by the trends of the day than the House. As I show repeatedly throughout this book, however, even the Senate's tradition of comity and supermajoritarian requirements have not been able to preclude party polarization from pervading it.

[1] Quoted in http://www.senate.gov/legislative/common/briefing/Senate_legislative_process.htm, accessed on March 21, 2006.

[2] Quoted in Garry Wills, ed., 1982, *The Federalist Papers by Alexander Hamilton, James Madison, and John Jay*, New York: Bantam Books, p. 320.

Since the early 1970s, the Senate has polarized about 80 percent as much as the House. That the Senate has polarized almost as much as the House is surprising given that at both the electoral and the institutional levels, the House is more easily manipulated than the Senate. First, unlike the fixed nature of states' borders, the lines for House districts can be manipulated through redistricting. Furthermore, constituents move more easily across district lines than they do across state borders. Second, unlike the egalitarian Senate, where work can only be accomplished through unanimous consent agreements, the House floor and the issues subject to roll call votes are subject to only a bare majority approval.

This chapter explains how the Senate could be almost as polarized as the House in light of the fact that both the constituencies and the institutions of the House can be more easily manipulated. The short answer is that the divisiveness of the House has been transported to the Senate by former House members upon their election to the Senate. Not all former House members have equally contributed to this transformation; rather it is former Republican House members elected to the House after 1978 who have played the greatest role in polarizing the Senate. I call these senators "Gingrich Senators" (see the appendix for a list of these senators).

This chapter proceeds as follows. First, I explicitly test whether party polarization in the House is directly comparable to party polarization in the Senate. It is. Second, I present evidence showing the uniquely polarizing voting behavior of the Gingrich Senators. Third, I conclude that almost the entire increase in party polarization in the Senate can be accounted for by post-1978 former Republican House members who were elected to the Senate.

I. Comparing Senate Polarization to House Polarization

Most of the evidence in this book suggests that the House is between 10 and 25 percent more polarized than the Senate (see figures 2.1, 2.3, 2.4, 2.5, 2.6, 8.4, and 8.5 and table 2.1). Not only is the extent of the polarization similar, but so, too, is the timing of the polarization. From the 93rd (1973–4) to the 108th (2003–4) Congress, the correlation between the House and Senate polarization scores is 0.970 ($p < 0.01$). In fact, over the entire post-Reconstruction time period, the correlation between House polarization and Senate polarization is 0.901 ($p < 0.01$). Additionally, the House has polarized roughly the same as the Senate from its low point to its high point.[3]

The potential problem with these data is that they may be comparing apples and oranges. Both fruit will grow with the proper amount of sunshine and rain, but at the end of the day, the apple is still an apple and the orange is still an orange. Such may be the case with party polarization in the respective chambers. Both House and Senate polarization may have grown as a result of the contentiousness of the Washington environment, the gamespersonship between the political parties, and the discourse of American politics in the electorate. Suggesting that their growth has been equal may be the equivalent of saying that an apple is an orange. Different floor procedures, different leadership structures, and different legislative agendas could result in apples in the House and oranges in the Senate. This section provides two tests measuring the equivalence of House and Senate party polarization. Both analyses substantiate the general conclusion that Senate polarization, for all intents and purposes, is very similar to the House polarization; rather than comparing apples to oranges, a more accurate metaphor may be comparing Red Delicious apples in the Senate to Macintosh apples in the House.

The first test examines two types of votes occurring in the legislative process that are exactly the same in the House as they are in the Senate: votes to adopt conference committee reports and votes to override presidential vetoes. If the House passes a bill that is not identical to the bill passed by the Senate, the chambers must work out their differences before the bill is sent to the president. Congress normally follows one of two paths to iron out its differences. First, either chamber may hold a simple vote to accept the changes made by the other chamber. If this vote passes, the bill, being exactly the same in both chambers, goes to the president. When neither chamber can completely agree to the other's changes or when negotiations between the entire chambers cannot be completed through floor action, the bill goes to a conference committee. When a majority of both chambers' conferees

[3] The House has polarized 0.173, from a low of 0.261 (in the 83rd Congress, 1953–4) to a high of 0.434 (in the 108th Congress, 2003–4). The Senate has polarized 0.166, from a low of 0.226 (in the 83rd Congress, 1953–4) to a high of 0.392 in the 105th Congress (1997–8).

agree on the bill's provisions, the bill faces the same up or down vote in the House and Senate. At this point (normally), representatives in neither chamber can offer amendments to the conference committee report. Because the votes are still, nonetheless, part of the legislative process, a determined opposition may still try to thwart the conference committee's compromise.

The second vote that is identical in both chambers is an attempt to override a presidential veto. As with votes to adopt the conference committee reports, both chambers vote on exactly the same legislative maneuver covering exactly the same piece of legislation (usually around the same date). By comparing party disparity on these two types of votes, we can determine whether party polarization in both chambers is comparing apples and oranges or whether, in fact, it is comparing Red Delicious to Macintosh.

From the 93rd Congress to the 108th Congress (1973–2004), both chambers voted on the same conference committee report 98 times (averaging 6 votes per congress; ranging from 3 votes in the 98th and 106th Congresses to 11 votes in the 93rd Congress). Over the same time period, there were 12 votes to override the same presidential veto (averaging less than 1 vote per congress, ranging from 0 votes in 10 congresses to 3 in the 102nd Congress). The party difference scores vary in the House and Senate depending upon the congress, but the 16-congress average is remarkably similar (see figure 9.1). For these 110 votes, the party difference score in the House was 0.34. In the Senate it was 0.32. Consequently, the House's polarization score on these common votes was 0.02 greater than the Senate's polarization score. On this measure, the House is 6.3 percent more polarized than the Senate. Although the congress-to-congress chamber difference fluctuates between 0.3 and 16.6 percent, the scores over the entire time period are highly correlated (0.91; statistically significant at the 0.001 level).[4]

The second test examines individual-level data from senators with experience in the House. If House and Senate party polarization are roughly equivalent and if former House members have the same

[4] The difference in party polarization between the House and Senate on these common conference committee report and presidential override votes is slightly larger than the overall DW-NOMINATE polarization scores as analyzed in chapter 2. Over the same 32-year period, the House's average polarization score is 0.346 and the Senate's score is 0.332. This difference is 0.014, which suggests that the House is 4.3 percent more polarized than the Senate.

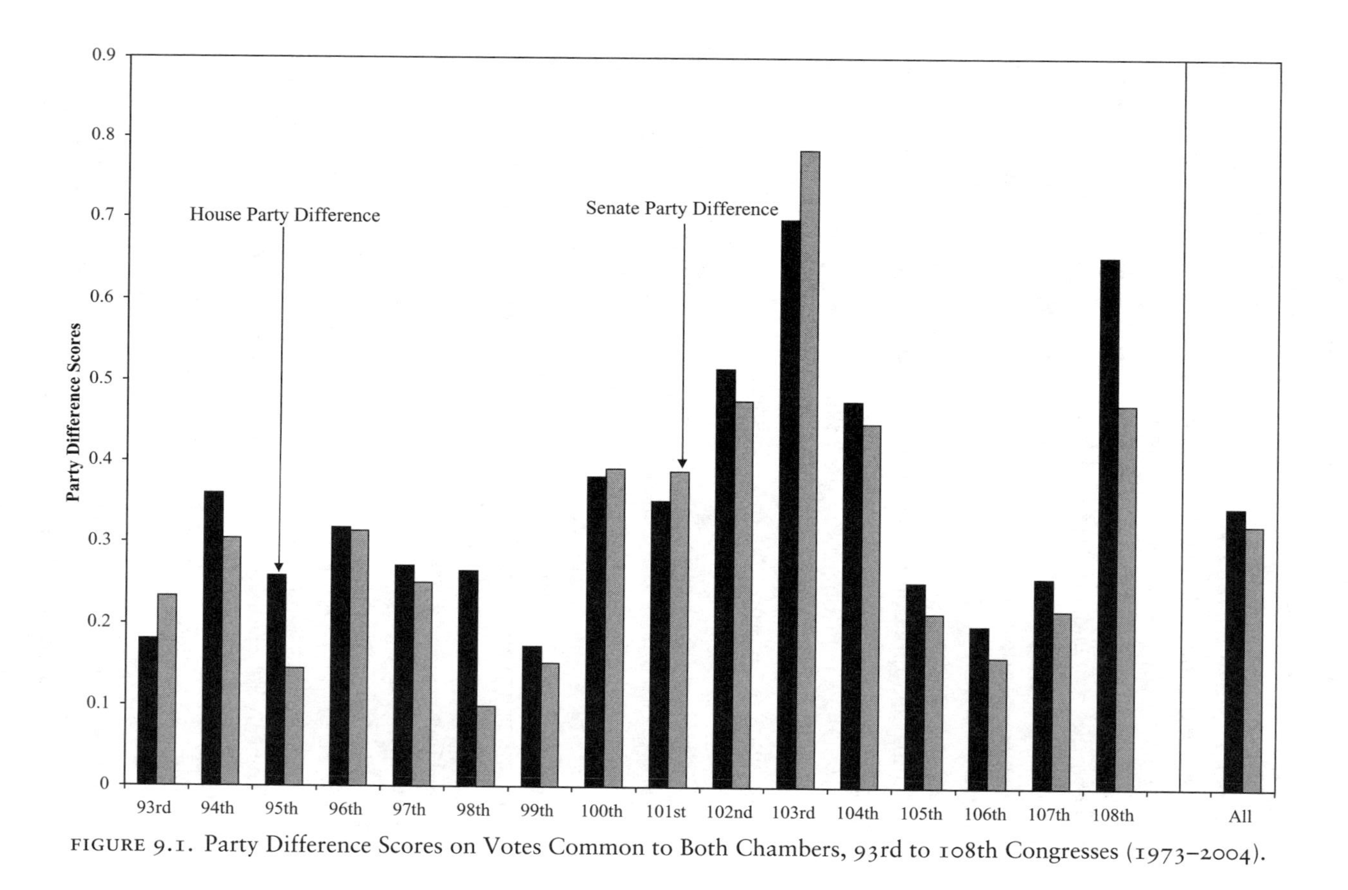

FIGURE 9.1. Party Difference Scores on Votes Common to Both Chambers, 93rd to 108th Congresses (1973–2004).

ideology in the Senate, senators who had previously served in the House should have similar ideology scores in both chambers.[5] Over the past 16 congresses, 82 former House members entered the Senate, ranging from only one in the 94th and 98th Congresses (1975–6, 1983–4) to nine in the 100th (1987–8) Congress. Sixty-seven of these former House members began their Senate careers in the congress after their House career ended. Two additional members began their Senate careers during the same congress that their House careers ended.[6]

Of these 82 senators, only 8 had a different DW-NOMINATE greater than 0.20, a standard equivalent to a polarization score change of 10 percent on the total DW-NOMINATE scale. Those members probably voted like apples in the House and oranges in the Senate. On the other hand, the overwhelming majority (90.2 percent) of the senators who served in the House voted similarly in both chambers. The 74 senators who had similar ideology scores in both the House and Senate were, on average, 0.019 more polarized in their first congress in the Senate than they were in their last congress in the House. This tiny difference is reduced further when we take into consideration that over this time period the House and Senate polarized 0.008 and 0.007, respectively, each successive congress.

Inasmuch as we can generalize from 112 votes over 32 years in the House and Senate and over 74 former House members who served in the Senate, party polarization in the House and Senate is really a comparison between the same fruit. This finding, satisfactory as it may be, nonetheless underscores the question of *why* the Senate is almost as polarized as the House.

II. The Effect of House Experience on Senator Ideology

The Senate has prided itself on not being the House. Collegiality, deference, and civility have long characterized the Senate (Matthews

[5] Poole and Rosenthal (1997) develop common-space scores, which they claim are comparable across chambers. In lieu of using these scores, which have not been updated to the 108th Congress, I continue to use DW-NOMINATE scores.

[6] James Broyhill (R-NC), while he was a sitting House member, was appointed to the 99th Congress. Ron Wyden (D-OR), another sitting House member, won a special election to the Senate in the 104th Congress. The longest gap between House and Senate service was that of Bob Krueger (D-TX), who left the House at the end of the 95th Congress and was appointed to the Senate in the 103rd Congress.

1960). Perhaps because of these folkways, the Senate considers itself the greatest deliberative body in the world. As stories of rancor, partisanship, and legislative gamespersonship in their beloved Senate began making the news, senators were quick to blame the House. Senator Alan Simpson commented, "The rancor, the dissension, the disgusting harsh level came from those House members who came to the Senate. They brought it with 'em. That's where it began."[7] Thad Cochran, who lost the majority leader's race to a former House member, Trent Lott, claims, "It's just a matter of age. I'm not going to use the word 'maturity.'"[8] As George Voinovich, a former governor of Ohio, added, there are "too many" former House members and not enough "other people."[9]

Political scientists have added their voices to the senators' anti-House refrain. Evans and Oleszek (2001, 107) argue that both Democrats and Republicans "increasingly have sought to structure floor action to publicize partisan messages" in the Senate and that many of these legislative tacticians worked closely with Gingrich and Gephardt prior to being elected to the Senate. Sinclair (2001, 75) maintains, "The 1990s saw an influx of ideologically committed conservatives into the Senate, with many of them being veterans of the highly partisan House." Finally, Rae and Campbell (2001, 8) add, "Many came to the House, after having been baptized by former minority whip Newt Gingrich (R-Ga) into relentless and combative partisanship. Most of them saw the Senate as another forum to advance the cause of the Republican party and their conservative philosophy on a national scale."

The primary culprit, according to even his fellow partisans, was a House member who never even served in the Senate: Newt Gingrich. The highly charged partisan atmosphere that Gingrich helped create in the House, so the story goes, poisoned the House members who served with him before they came to the Senate. The link is usually tied directly to two of Gingrich's chief lieutenants in the House, Trent Lott and Rick Santorum, who were elected not only to the Senate, but also to party leadership positions in the majority party. Lott, who was Republican Leader from the 104th Congress until his admittedly

[7] Quoted in CQ *Weekly*, December 13, 2003, 3069.
[8] Quoted in CQ *Weekly*, December 13, 2003, 3070.
[9] Quoted in CQ *Weekly*, December 13, 2003, 3069.

inappropriate remarks about Strom Thurmond's 1948 presidential run in December 2002, was criticized for bringing a more aggressive partisanship to the Senate. After some unprecedented legislative maneuvers received harsh criticism, Lott responded on the Senate floor: "This is no desire at all to set up the Rules Committee in the House of Representatives sense, but there is a desire by this majority leader, as by every majority leader, to find a way to move the process and the legislation through the Senate."[10] Santorum, who eventually became chair of the Republican Conference in 2000, cast aside Matthews's apprenticeship folkway in his first year in the Senate when he challenged the right of Senator Mark Hatfield, a fellow Republican, to chair the Appropriations Committee after Hatfield cast the deciding vote against the Balanced Budget Amendment in 1995. Perhaps the reason that Democratic firebrands like Charles Schumer and Richard Durbin have escaped some of these same criticisms is because they have served mostly in the minority.

A potential problem with the former House member explanation is that the House has always sent a healthy number of its former members to the Senate. Figure 9.2 shows the number of senators since the 93rd Congress (1973–4) who previously served in the House. The figure shows that House veterans comprised the greatest share of the Senate at the beginning of the series, when polarization was the lowest, and at the end of the series, when polarization was the highest. Given that the prevalence of former House members in the Senate has occurred in the least and most polarized congresses since the early 1970s, the mere presence of former House members cannot solely be the cause of party polarization in the Senate. Furthermore, because the House has usually been more polarized than the Senate, it cannot necessarily be a new phenomenon for new senators with House experience to bring their "poison" over from the lower chamber. In fact, the Senate has been more polarized than the House in only 16 of 64 congresses since Reconstruction ended and only eight congresses since World War II ended.

Rather than the mere presence of former House members shaping the impressions, perhaps it is the type of House member being elected to the Senate that has changed. One way to test for the influence of former

[10] *Congressional Record*, July 26, 1999, S9202.

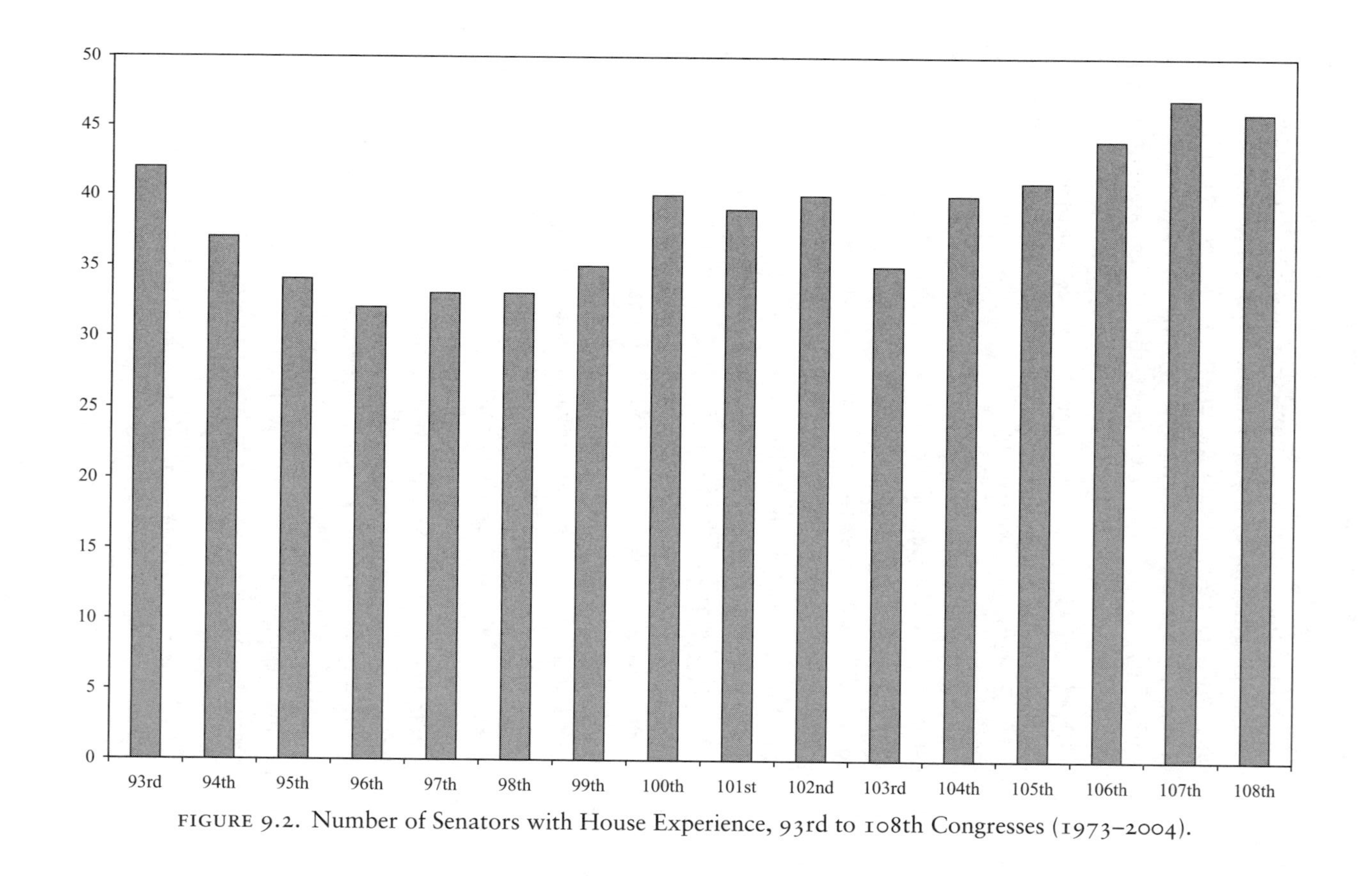

FIGURE 9.2. Number of Senators with House Experience, 93rd to 108th Congresses (1973–2004).

House members on Senate polarization is to compare the polarization scores of senators who served in the House to those of senators who did not serve in the House. Figure 9.3 shows this relationship broken down by party from the 93rd (1973–4) to the 108th Congress (2003–4). Democrats who had House experience were slightly more liberal than their non-House counterparts from the 94th (1975–6) to the 101st (1989–90) Congresses. Since the 102nd Congress, little has separated the two groups.

Until the 100th Congress (1987–8), Republicans who had served in the House were always less polarized than Republicans who had not served in the House. Beginning in the 100th Congress, however, the Republicans who came to the Senate from the House were much more polarizing than their non-House counterparts. The 100th Congress was Newt Gingrich's fifth term in the House. The Conservative Opportunity Society that he formed as a constant thorn in the side of the House Democratic leadership was, by that time, 4 years old. In the next congress, he would be elected minority whip. In four congresses, he would be elected Speaker of the House. Figure 9.4 shows the Republican polarization scores in the Senate if we disaggregate the line for Republicans with House experience into those who were elected to the House after Gingrich and those who were not. Since the 97th Congress, the first senate in which a former colleague of Gingrich could have served (though none did until the 99th Congress), Gingrich's former colleagues are, on average, 16.5 percentage points more polarized than the Republicans without House experience and 24.1 percentage points more polarized than Republicans elected to the House prior to Gingrich's election in 1978. In fact, only one Gingrich Senator – DeWine (0.236), a former House member who served one term as Ohio lieutenant governor prior to his Senate election – has a lower polarization score than the average Republican senator over this entire time period.

Because of the distinctive voice that these Republican senators, who had previously served with Gingrich in the House, brought to the Senate, I call them "Gingrich Senators." This name may be a bit unfair. After all, Gingrich would claim that he was only reacting to a House that had become increasingly partisan under Speaker Wright's tyrannical reign. The problem with labeling these former House members in the Senate as "Wright Senators" is that moniker would invoke the

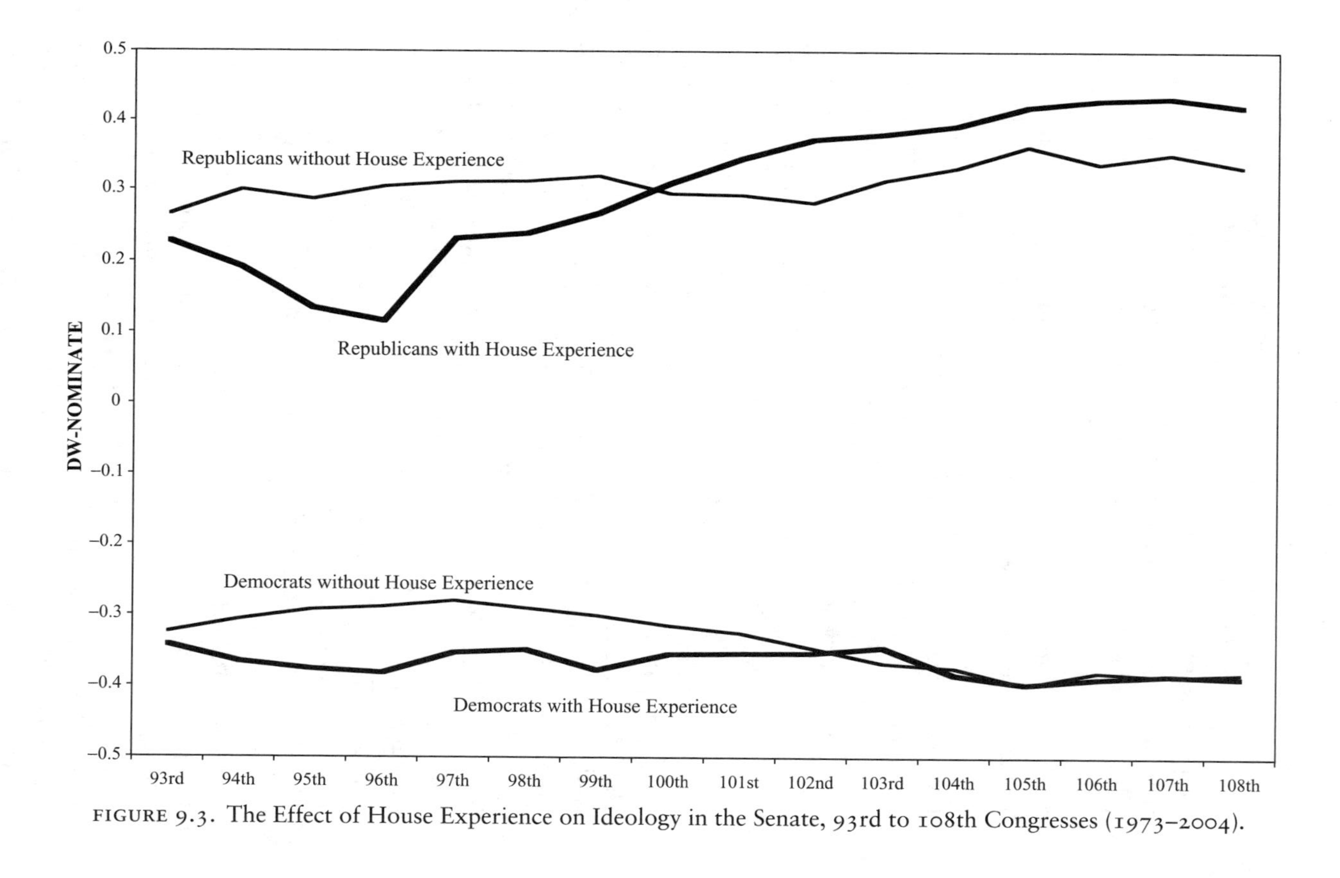

FIGURE 9.3. The Effect of House Experience on Ideology in the Senate, 93rd to 108th Congresses (1973–2004).

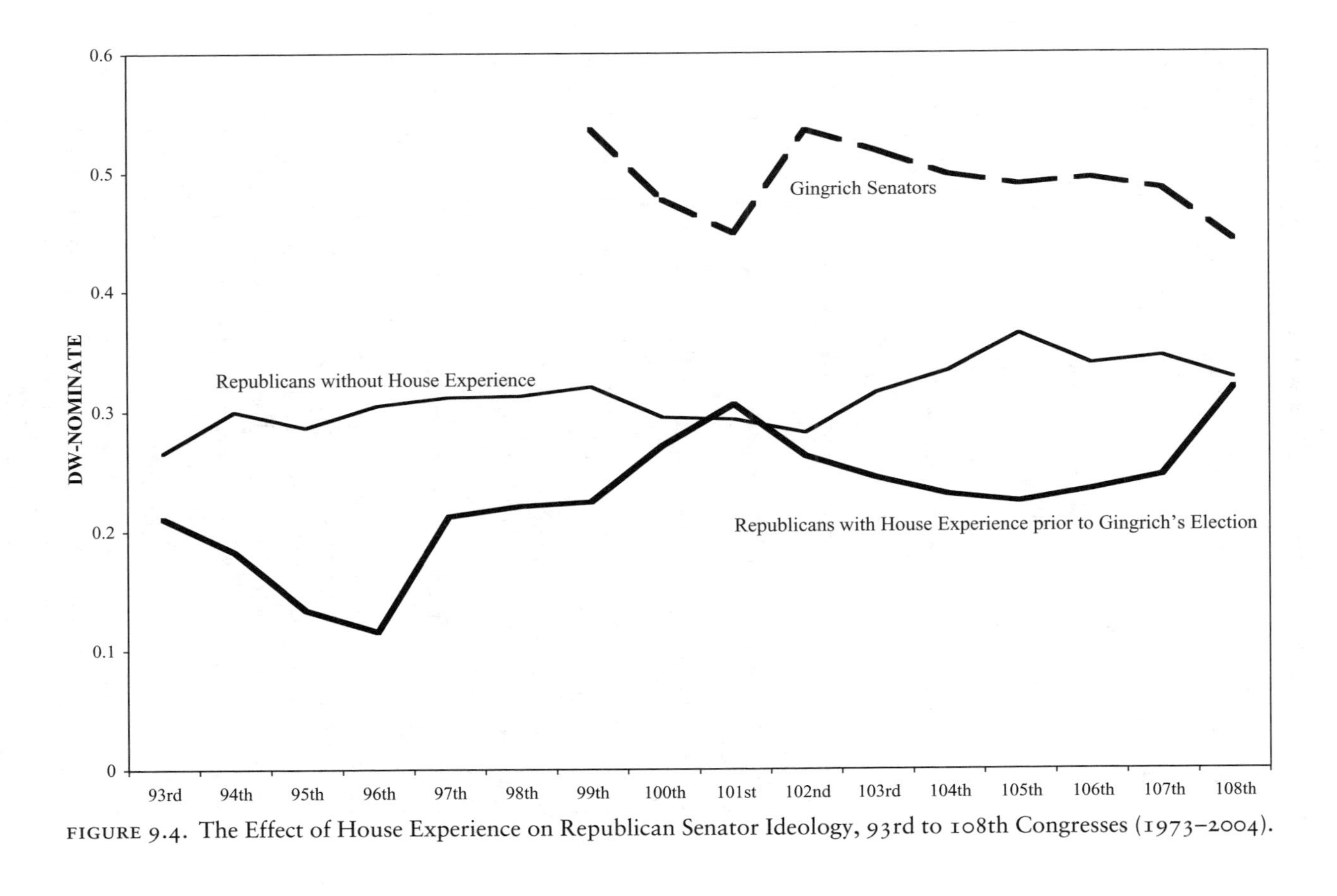

FIGURE 9.4. The Effect of House Experience on Republican Senator Ideology, 93rd to 108th Congresses (1973–2004).

image of Democratic senators instead of Republicans. Additionally, the effect lasted longer than Speaker Wright's reign in the House. It may also last longer than Gingrich's reign in the House, but as of the 108th Congress, there were no former House members in the Senate who served only in the House after Gingrich left in 1998.

To ensure that this effect is specific to Republicans in the House, I test to see whether those Democratic senators who served either with Representative Richard Gephardt or under Speaker Wright voted differently than those Democrats who came to the Senate before Gephardt's first election to the House. Gephardt was first elected in 1976, two years before Gingrich's election. There were three Democrats who were elected with Gingrich and after Gephardt. The inclusion or exclusion of these members – Senators Tom Daschle, Bill Nelson, and Richard Shelby – has no effect on the results.

As it turns out, Gephardt Senators vote no differently than non-House veterans and House veterans serving before Gephardt's election who subsequently served in the Senate. Since the 96th Congress, the first Senate that could have had a Gephardt Senator (the first actually served in the 100th Congress), Democratic senators who entered the House after Gephardt have slightly lower senate polarization scores, 0.367, than former Democratic House members who were elected prior to Gephardt, 0.372 ($p = 0.748$), and slightly higher than Democratic senators without House experience, 0.337 ($p = 0.162$).

Because of their uniquely polarizing presence in the Senate, I analyze Gingrich Senators' impact separately. Figure 9.5 isolates the Gingrich Senators, but for the other categories combines them across the two parties. It shows that the polarization resulting from senators who were elected to the House prior to Gingrich has remained flat throughout the 93rd to 108th Congresses (1973–2004). The polarization resulting from senators without House experience has risen 3 percent, from around 16 percent to 19 percent. Because Gingrich was not elected to the House until 1978, the Gingrich Senators necessarily had a zero polarization effect on the Senate until the 99th Congress (1984–5). From Reagan's second term through George W. Bush's first term, the Gingrich Senators' polarization score steadily increased. By the 108th Congress (2003–4), they contributed 8.5 percentage points to the Senate polarization score. Given that the Senate polarization score has only increased 7.8 percentage points since the 99th Congress and

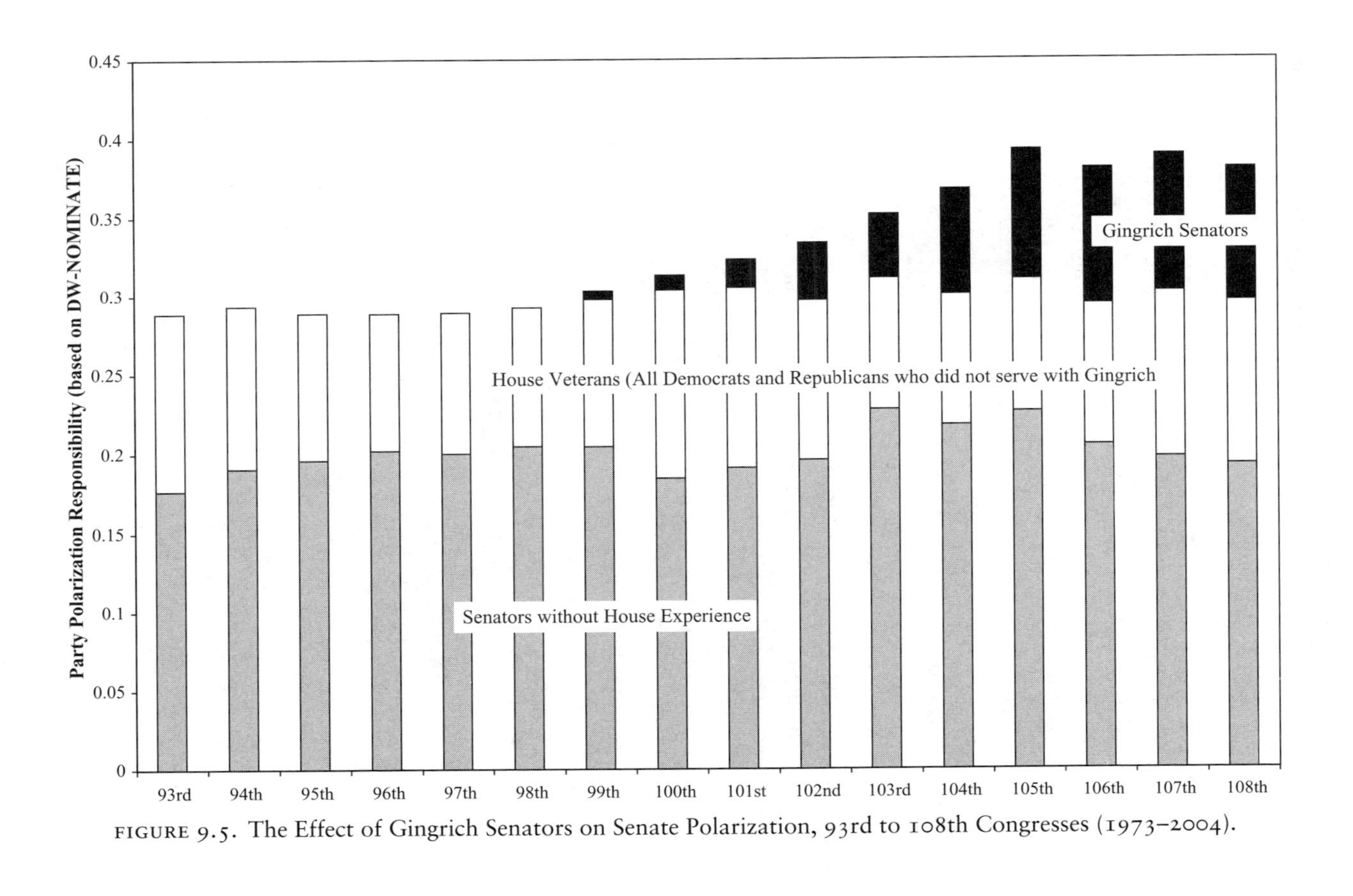

FIGURE 9.5. The Effect of Gingrich Senators on Senate Polarization, 93rd to 108th Congresses (1973–2004).

8.4 percentage points since the 93rd Congress, the Gingrich Senators alone can account for more than the entire Senate polarization under consideration in this book.

Another cut at the same data presented in figure 9.5 shows how clearly the Gingrich Senators have polarized the Senate. From the 99th Congress to the 108th Congress (1980–2004), the contribution of senators without House experience to the Senate polarization score actually fell an average of 0.12 percentage points each congress. The contribution of all Democrats who served in the House and those Republicans who served in the House prior to Gingrich averaged an increase of 0.15 each congress. The contribution attributed to Gingrich's former colleagues, however, rose on average 0.85 each congress. Again, with this measure, the Gingrich Senators account for all of the increase in Senate polarization over the past 32 years.

Early evidence from after the 108th Congress suggests that the trends in figure 9.5 will continue into the future. In the 2004 and 2006 congressional elections, seven new former House members were elected to the Senate. The five Republicans (all elected in 2004) all had House polarization scores above 0.35 in the last congress of their House tenure.[11] The two Democrats (both elected in 2006) were more polarized than the average Democrat, but less polarized than the five Republicans.[12]

III. The Gingrich Senators

As of the 108th Congress (2003–4), 26 Republican senators had previously served in the House of Representatives after Newt Gingrich's election in 1978. Another 10 served with Gingrich in the House, but were elected prior to or with Gingrich.[13] The appendix lists the

[11] The five Republicans (and their DW-NOMINATE in their last House term) were Richard Burr (0.355), David Vitter (0.487), Johnny Isakson (0.421), Jim DeMint (0.646), and Tom Coburn (0.787).

[12] The Democrats (and their DW-NOMINATE from the 108th Congress) were Sherrod Brown (−0.609) and Bob Menendez (−0.388), who was appointed to the Senate in the 109th Congress and won the right in the 2006 elections to continue serving.

[13] The 10 senators who were elected to the House prior to or in the same election as Gingrich's first election in 1978 are about as conservative as the average Republican senator (0.297 and 0.301, respectively), but both groups are more than one-third less polarized than the 26 senators who were elected to the House after Gingrich's election in 1978 (0.472).

senators, their states, the congresses they served in the House and Senate, and their DW-NOMINATE scores in the House and Senate. Although there was only one Gingrich Senator in the 99th Congress, their numbers grew steadily so that by the time Gingrich became Speaker of the House, 14 of his former House colleagues were in the Senate. In the 108th Congress, 19 Republican senators served in the House after Gingrich was first elected.

The higher polarization scores among Gingrich Senators may, in fact, have nothing to do with Gingrich; rather, they may simply be indicative of new senators entering a highly charged partisan atmosphere. We can use the other new senators who came to the Senate during the same period to help gauge the House's true influence on Senate polarization. The 26 Gingrich Senators had an average polarization score of 0.475 in their first term in the Senate. Their counterparts arriving in the Senate after the 97th Congress, who had not served in the House, had an average polarization score of 0.328 ($p = 0.001$).

Not only are the Gingrich Senators more conservative than their fellow Republican senators, but also they were more conservative than their fellow House members. On average, their polarization scores were 47.1 percent during their House careers. The Republican House members who never served in the Senate, during this same time period, averaged a 38.9 percent polarization score ($p = 0.002$). The Gingrich Senators, by the time they left the House, were not only leaving a more conservative Republican caucus, but they were the most conservative members of the conservative Republican caucus.

Representation among the Gingrich Senators

This analysis of Gingrich Senators creates tension between the results from the previous chapter and this chapter. At the end of chapter 8, I suggested that we need to understand party polarization within a representation framework. Indeed, senators have become more polarized, but almost all of that polarization has occurred on procedural votes. Substantive votes have also polarized, though constituencies temper senators' substantive polarization scores. In this chapter, I argue that knowing whether a Republican senator served in the House after Newt Gingrich's first election, irrespective of their constituents, is key to understanding Senate polarization. These results, when coupled, raise the question: Do senators' constituencies matter in explaining senate polarization?

The short answer is yes, a senator's constituency does matter. It matters at two different levels. First, the Gingrich Senators come from more reliably Republican states than the non-Gingrich Republican senators. Gingrich Senators come from states where Republican presidential candidates do, on average, 3.6 percent better than they do nationwide. In contrast, non-Gingrich Republican senators, since the 97th Congress, come from states where Republican presidential candidates do a statistically significant smaller 1.6 percent better than they do nationwide ($p = 0.017$). Although the difference between the two – 2 percentage points – is small, about 25 percent of all the states over all the presidential elections yield a result in which the winning presidential candidate in that state won by less than 2 percent.

In contrast to the Gingrich Senators, the Gephardt Senators come from less Democratic states than the non-Gephardt Democratic senators. Gephardt's former House colleagues come from states that, on average, give Democratic presidential candidates 1.2 percent more votes than their nationwide average. Those Democratic senators since the 96th Congress who did not serve in the House come from states that, on average, give Democratic presidential candidates 2 percent more votes than their nationwide average ($p = 0.271$).

The second level at which a senator's constituency matters builds on the results displayed in table 8.4. Constituencies matter above and beyond a senator's past with Gingrich (or Gephardt). In addition to the variables in table 8.4, table 9.1 also includes two new indicator variables to isolate the effect of serving with Gephardt or Gingrich in the House prior to starting a career in the Senate. The two new variables, which are fully interacted with each other and the Republican variable, indicate whether the members served in the House and whether they started their Senate career after the 98th Congress. The three-way interaction acts as an indicator for the Gingrich Senators, controlling for their primary effects and their three double interactions.

When these indicators are included in the regression model predicting senators' Republican party support scores (columns A and B) and DW-NOMINATE (column C), the coefficients on their states' partisanship still have a large impact on their voting behavior (see table 9.1). Taking a Gingrich Senator in a Democratic state (with a −0.09 RPVA) and placing her in a safe Republican state (with a 0.13 RPVA) increases her DW-NOMINATE from 0.41 to 0.50 (a percentage increase

TABLE 9.1. *The Effect of Gingrich Senators on RPSS Scores and DW-NOMINATE*

Independent Variables	(A) RPSS Procedural Votes	(B) RPSS Substantive Votes	(C) DW-NOMINATE
Republican Presidential Vote Advantage (RPVA)	−0.011** (0.001)	−0.002 (0.002)	−0.003** (0.0004)
Time Trend	1.073** (0.18)	0.979** (0.26)	0.412** (0.08)
Republican	0.424** (0.03)	0.394** (0.03)	0.595** (0.03)
Former House Member	−0.003 (0.03)	−0.041 (0.03)	−0.048 (0.03)
Time Trend* Republican	0.024** (0.002)	0.014** (0.003)	0.006** (0.001)
Time Trend* RPVA	−0.055** (0.01)	−0.021 (0.02)	−0.019** (0.01)
Republican* Former House Member	−0.052 (0.04)	−0.013 (0.05)	−0.027 (0.05)
Republican* Former House Member* Post 98th Congress (Gingrich Senators)	0.136** (0.06)	0.104* (0.07)	0.183** (0.05)
Post 98th Congress	0.025 (0.03)	−0.002 (0.04)	0.001 (0.01)
Republican* Post 98th Congress	−0.007 (0.04)	0.059 (0.05)	−0.004 (0.02)
Former House Member* Post 98th Congress	−0.040 (0.04)	−0.005 (0.05)	0.021 (0.02)
Constant	1.319** (0.12)	0.443** (0.20)	−0.059 (0.05)
Member Random Effects	Yes	Yes	Yes
N	1603	1598	1619
R^2 Within	0.098	0.009	0.071
R^2 Between	0.832	0.782	0.765
R^2 Overall	0.835	0.678	0.771

*Statistically significant at 0.10; **statistically significant at 0.05.

of 22 points).[14] But that large impact does not soak up the effect of the Gingrich Senator indicator variables. Because of the confusion brought about by all the interactions and multicollinearity, figure 9.6

[14] These RPVAs represent the 5th and 95th percentiles of the RPVA for Republican senators.

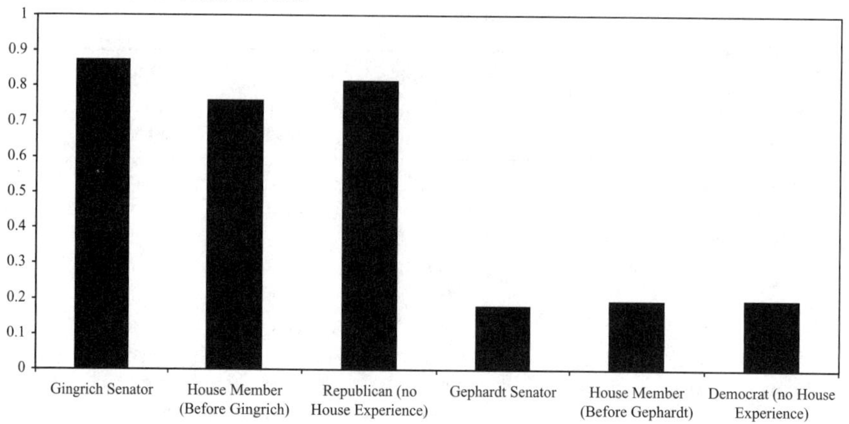

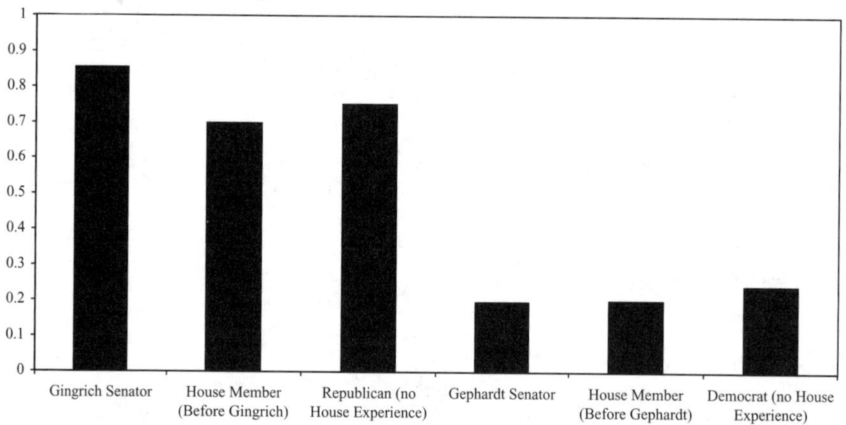

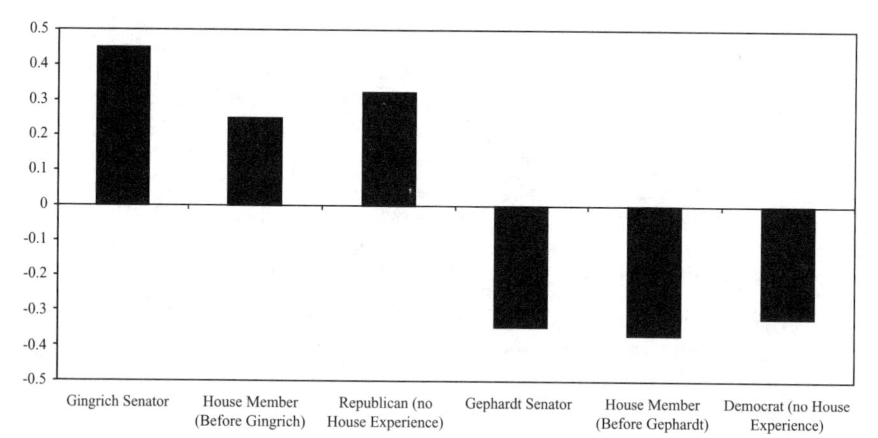

FIGURE 9.6. RPSS and DW-NOMINATE for Selected Types of Senators.

summarizes the substantive results. Serving with Gingrich in the House raised Republican Senators' RPSS 6 percentage points on procedural votes and 10 percentage points on final passage votes in comparison to Republican senators who were not former House members. The "Gephardt" effect on Democratic senators was less than 50 percent of the Gingrich effect. The results for the DW-NOMINATE scores are even clearer. The predicted DW-NOMINATE for a Gingrich Senator is 0.45; for a senator with House experience prior to Gingrich's election, it is 0.25; and for a non-House veteran Republican, it is 0.32. The parallel DW-NOMINATE scores for Democrats were −0.35, −0.37, and −0.32.

IV. Conclusion

The analysis in this chapter links Senate polarization to polarization in the House. The beginning of the chapter shows, through two different and independent tests, that for the most part, the polarization in the Senate is equivalent to the polarization in the House. The exact same votes in the House and Senate yield very similar party difference scores. Additionally, senators with House experience have similar ideological scores in both the House and Senate.

Having determined that, in fact, comparing Senate polarization to House polarization is like comparing apples to apples, the analysis in the middle of the chapter shows that all of the polarization that has occurred over the past 32 years in the Senate can be accounted for by a particular type of senator – namely, Republican senators who had previously served in the House of Representatives after the 98th Congress. Although it may be too easy (and a bit too cute) to lay the cause for Senate polarization at Newt Gingrich's feet, the multivariate analysis suggests that it is more than just serving in the House prior to the Senate and more than just serving in the House after the 98th Congress. It is the interaction of these variables that has so dramatically polarized the Senate. In the case of explaining Senate polarization, the conventional wisdom, as articulated by both politicians and political scientists, was absolutely correct – a new breed of intensely partisan Republicans began getting elected to the Senate in the 1990s. As the breed grew and advanced into leadership positions, the polarization in the Senate grew in concert with that in the House.

This new breed, however, has not served without regard for their constituencies. The Gingrich Senators are more likely to come from well-performing Republican states. Additionally, a senator's constituency matters above and beyond his or her designation as a Gingrich or a Gephardt Senator. The constituency effect, though, is half as important in determining a senator's ideology as is her designation as a Gingrich Senator. The evidence from this chapter only emboldens the conclusion that party polarization must be understood (1) procedurally and (2) in light of a member's constituency.

APPENDIX: *The 26 Gingrich Senators and 10 Former Gingrich Colleagues*

		Senate		House of Representatives	
Name	State	Tenure	Ideology[a]	Tenure	Ideology
Elected to the House after Gingrich's 1978 Election					
Allard	Colorado	105-present	0.596	102–104	0.601
Allen	Virginia	107–109	0.383	102	0.492
Brown	Colorado	102–104	0.568	97–101	0.495
Brownback	Kansas	105-present	0.473	104	0.499
Bunning	Kentucky	106-present	0.592	100–105	0.515
Chambliss	Georgia	108-present	0.423	104–107	0.419
Coats	Indiana	102–105	0.408	97–100	0.344
Craig	Idaho	102–110	0.554	97–101	0.535
Crapo	Idaho	106-present	0.462	103–105	0.505
DeWine	Ohio	104–109	0.236	98–101	0.383
Ensign	Nevada	107-present	0.372	104–105	0.544
Graham	South Carolina	108-present	0.396	104–107	0.443
Gramm[c]	Texas	99–107	0.591	98	0.612
Grams	Minnesota	104–106	0.535	103	0.529
Gregg	New Hampshire	103-present	0.402	97–100	0.450
Hutchinson	Arkansas	105–107	0.471	103–104	0.422
Inhofe	Oklahoma	104-present	0.649	100–103	0.491
Kyl	Arizona	104-present	0.602	100–103	0.548
Mack	Florida	101–106	0.420	98–100	0.557
McCain	Arizona	100-present	0.326	98–99	0.339
Roberts	Kansas	105-present	0.388	97–104	0.435
Santorum	Pennsylvania	104–109	0.380	102–103	0.306
Smith	New Hampshire	102–107	0.784	99–101	0.579
Sununu	New Hampshire	108-present	0.441	105–107	0.555
Talent	Missouri	108–109	0.324	103–106	0.434
Thomas	Wyoming	104-present	0.504	101–103	0.416
Elected to the House with or prior to Gingrich's 1978 Election					
Abdnor	South Dakota	97–99	0.266	93–96	0.268
Andrews	North Dakota	97–99	0.010	88–96	0.130
Broyhill	North Carolina	99	0.458	88–99	0.297
Grassley	Iowa	97-present	0.322	94–96	0.336
Jeffords[b]	Vermont	101–107	-0.087	94–100	0.025
Lott	Mississippi	101–110	0.477	93–100	0.376
Quayle	Indiana	97–100	0.476	95–96	0.484
Snowe	Maine	104-present	0.039	96–103	0.114
Symms	Idaho	97–102	0.705	93–96	0.745
Trible	Virginia	98–100	0.300	95–97	0.253

[a] Ideology is measured by the average DW-NOMINATE scores.

[b] In the 107th Congress, Jeffords switched his party affiliation from Republican to independent.

[c] Gramm was first elected as a Democrat to the 96th Congress. In January 1983, he resigned his seat, switched parties, and won re-election as a Republican. The data include only his service as a Republican.

10

Procedural Polarization in the U.S. Congress

On July 18, 2003, Chairman Bill Thomas substituted a bipartisan pension overhaul bill with a Republican-concocted plan less than 12 hours before the Ways and Means Committee mark-up. The Democrats, an already frustrated minority, vigorously retaliated. To stall committee action, all but one of the Democrats on the committee barricaded themselves in the committee library. Although Thomas called for the Capitol Police and the Sergeant at Arms to evict the Democrats, neither chose to get involved in the highly charged partisan fight. Representative Pete Stark, the only committee Democrat not in the library, continuously objected to Thomas's unanimous consent to dispense with the bill's reading. On one particular attempt, Thomas banged down the gavel before Stark could object. When Stark criticized Thomas's move, Representative Scott McInnis told him to "shut up." Stark retorted, "You think you are big enough to make me, you little wimp? Come on, come over here and make me, I dare you... You little fruitcake. You little fruitcake. I said you are a fruitcake." Overtly partisan games quickly deteriorated into playground taunts. After Democrats and the political pundits used the weekend political shows to ridicule him, Thomas offered a tearful apology on the House floor for his heavy-handed tactics.[1]

[1] See Juliet Eilperin and Albert B. Crenshaw, July 19, 2003, "The House that Roared," *Washington Post*, p. A1, and Juliet Eilperin, July 24, 2003, "Ways and Means Chairman Apologizes to House," *Washington Post*, p. A1, for the journalistic accounts of the episode.

Although a news story for less than a week, this event has come to typify the relationship between Democrats and Republicans on Capitol Hill. The majority party has a substantive goal (business-friendly reforms for the pension system). Most likely, they have the votes and loyalty to achieve their goal through normal legislative means. But, in the name of efficiency and expediency, they employ questionable legislative procedures. Democrats, who may or may not agree with the substantive end, strenuously object to the Republicans' means by creating a media circus around the abrogation of the normal legislative process. At the end of the day, the Democrats and Republicans both look petty: the real debate about pension legislation is lost in media-centered strategies and procedural games. What could have been a shining example of successful bipartisan lawmaking turned into another ugly episode of party polarization in Congress. Debate on the floor centered on whether Thomas abused his powers as chair of the committee or Stark used language unbecoming of a member of Congress. Because the overhaul bill had become such a political minefield, the Republicans abandoned their efforts – both bipartisan and purely partisan – to amend the pension laws in the 108th Congress.

Three summers later, the House and Senate overwhelmingly passed – and President Bush promptly signed – a pension overhaul bill. Its ride to enactment was less reminiscent of Jerry Springer than its legislative ancestor and more a model of the Schoolhouse Rock video, "A Bill on Capitol Hill." Forty percent of Democrats joined with 92 percent of Republicans to pass the bill in the House; in the Senate, only three Republicans joined two Democrats in opposing the 93 senators who voted for its final passage. Just prior to final passage in the House, however, only one Republican joined with all but four Democrats in agreeing to a motion to recommit the bill to the House Education and Workforce Committee. The substance of the legislation enjoyed bipartisan support only after a procedural vote almost perfectly divided the parties.

Even though the legislative processes on the pension overhaul bills in the 108th and 109th Congresses represent end points on the modern bipartisan to purely partisan continuum, both episodes underscore the importance of procedures in the legislative process. Thomas's heavy-handed use of procedures ultimately blew up and caused paralysis on the issue in the 108th Congress. In the following Congress, the House and the Senate passed, with ample support from both parties, pension overall but not before implementing procedures hardly seen even 20 years before. The unanimous consent agreement for debate on the Senate floor did not permit any amendments and the House adopted a closed rule. Being shut out of the amending process in both chambers, the Democrats used further procedures (a motion to recommit with instructions) to make their substantive arguments. In the end, the legislation was approved on largely bipartisan lines even though the procedures used could not have been more divisive.

Political observers, political scientists, and politicians have used the 2003 Ways and Means fiasco to showcase the destruction caused by partisan warfare. They have claimed that the episode, although a bit more dramatic than most, is symptomatic of an institution mired in party polarization. *The* causes they have offered for party polarization in the U.S. Congress are plentiful. Charlie Cook (2003, 1406) provides perhaps the simplest explanation: "I trace the extreme partisanship back to the 1984 fight over a contested race in Indiana's 8th District between Democratic incumbent Frank McCloskey and Republican Rick McIntyre." Others have pointed to various other causes, including redistricting, income inequality, changes in House procedure, political migration and segregation, the ideological sorting of voters, Newt Gingrich's combative style, Clinton's impeachment, the breakdown in social connections between members' families, and changes in the Washington community.

My investigation of party polarization finds that each of *the* causes may be, at some level, correct, but that each, in isolation of the others, seriously misunderstands the complexity underlying the phenomenon of the divergence between Republicans and Democrats in Congress. A comprehensive explanation of party polarization must include two steps. First, members' constituencies have become more polarized. Partisan gerrymandering, geographic and ideological sorting, and the extremism of party activists has each played a role in dividing Republican voters from Democratic voters. As constituents have sorted themselves or been sorted by the redistricting and nomination processes into more politically homogeneous districts and states, they have elected more ideologically charged members, who cast increasingly partisan votes. These trends, however, can explain neither the entirety of party polarization nor even a substantial portion of it.

Although it is true that more homogeneous constituencies have elected more partisan members to the House and Senate, it is not only the homogeneous constituencies. Heterogeneous constituencies – those who roughly divide their votes equally between Democrats and Republicans – have also been represented by members with more ideological voting records.

The second step of party polarization follows the first. As the constituencies have polarized and sorted, fewer and fewer members are cross-pressured between what their constituencies want them to do and what their parties want them to do. As these preferences become increasingly aligned, rank and file members have ceded more power to their party leaders. As their power has grown, so have the party leaderships' burdens to produce legislative victories. Implementing consequential procedures has been a favored strategy to get things done in both the House and the Senate. These procedural debates, which are more frequent these days, are especially divisive. Additionally, as the debates are more common and divisive, the minority party leaderships have been reduced to making their substantive arguments in the form of procedures, which, of course, exacerbates the frequency and divisiveness of the procedural debates. It is the increasing frequency of and polarization on these debates that account for the overwhelming growth in the voting disparity between Democrats and Republican in both the House and the Senate since the early 1970s.

These two steps must be taken together. The first step provides the cause; the second step accounts for the extent of the ensuing polarization. Without taking the first step, we have no underlying cause of why rank and file members have ceded power to their party leaders. Without taking the second step, we would have observed only a trivial amount of polarization – an amount probably not worthy of study. Both steps together provide an explanation for a trend worthy of explanation.

I. Mandates for Future Research

My examination of polarization uncovers several features that must become a part of any explanation for the divide between the parties. The penultimate section of this book outlines three of these features. The last section outlines several paths for future research.

More than Electoral Changes Have Caused Polarization

First, future polarization studies must go beyond electoral explanations. Members from increasingly homogeneous districts do cast more highly partisan votes. But, they are not the only members who have been casting more highly partisan votes. All members – even those from marginal districts – have been casting more highly partisan votes. In fact, when the frequency and polarization of members in these groups are evaluated, the evidence suggests that around 20 percent of the polarization in the U.S. Congress can be explained by the increasing partisanship of all members' constituencies. To explain the lion's share of polarization, scholars must move beyond members' constituencies.

To be sure, constituency changes are an important step in the process. Without the homogenization of the members' constituencies within the party caucuses, it is unlikely that back bench members would have ceded more power to their party leaders. Currently, congressional observers focus too much on the electoral side, though to ignore it would be equally imprudent.

Procedural Votes Must Be a Part of the Polarization Conversation

Second, future polarization studies must explain the increasing frequency of and polarization on procedural votes. The evidence suggests that very little of the increase in party polarization in the U.S. Congress since the early 1970s has come about as a consequence of amendment or final passage votes. In less partisan days, all members agreed that all members could amend all parts of a bill. They would then fight over all parts of the bill before most members would vote to pass the bill. Today, members vigorously fight about which members can amend which parts of a bill. Usually after the majority party implements a highly restrictive rule, the members vigorously fight about their substantive differences, not on amendments, but rather on procedural motions. Then, as before, most members vote for the bill's final passage. The underlying partisan breakdown of final passage votes has not changed much since the 1970s. The floor dynamics before final passage have undergone a revolution. Scholars must appreciate the relationship between these floor mechanics as they try to explain party polarization.

At various times and in a variety of circumstances, party leaders have dismissed procedural votes as being "merely procedural." The evidence from my examination of party polarization suggests that there is not a more inaccurate adjective for these votes than "merely." Although they are roundly dismissed, they account for nearly the entire growth in the divide between the parties since the early 1970s.

Not All Votes Are the Same

Third, future scholars must appreciate that members use one set of considerations when they are casting procedural votes and a different set of considerations when they are casting final passage votes. This delineation is relatively recent. In the 1970s, members used the same set of considerations when casting both sets of votes. Over time, the members' political party has become, for all intents and purposes, the only consideration when casting procedural votes. Although their party is still important on final passage votes, members are increasingly voting with their constituents on final passage votes. This roll call voting dynamic has three implications – one on the real world of politics, one on observing politics, and the last on the study of politics.

Over time, the votes on these procedures are not only more frequent and more polarizing, but also more consequential. And yet these votes are typically successfully pitched to the rank and file as party loyalty votes. The increasingly heavy hand of party leadership is felt no more firmly than on procedural votes. Even if the members do not view them as such, they vote on them as though they view them as being substantively neutral. As John Dingell is quick to point out, there is probably not a more inaccurate understanding of the legislative process than a dismissal of the importance of procedure on the final disposition of a bill.

In the 1970s, congressional observers could summarize a bill's debate by examining a few key amendment votes and then the final passage vote. As procedures have become more consequential, they have remained largely invisible not only to the public, but also to the most astute political observers. In the 108th Congress, when 43 percent of the House votes on important legislation were taken on procedures (in comparison to 38 percent amendment votes and 19 percent final passage votes), *Congressional Quarterly* did not designate one single procedural vote as "key." The 108th Congress is not atypical. So long as procedural votes are invisible, members will be free to cast party-loyal votes without facing electoral repercussions. As long as there are no electoral ramifications, majority parties will be able to manipulate procedures to fulfill their substantive goals.

Finally, from a political science perspective, studies cannot isolate final passage votes to the exclusion of all the other votes if they hope to say something important about the entire legislative process. And yet, the recent trend is to analyze only final passage votes when studying Congress.[2] Final passage votes are increasingly different from the rest of the votes that members cast, are an increasingly smaller part of the legislative agenda, and are increasingly less reflective of the underlying dynamics in Congress. In fact, the lessons from this book suggest that roll call summary scores (like DW-NOMINATE) that use nearly all of the roll call votes in devising a summary score are increasingly summarizing member voting behavior on procedural matters, which are increasingly becoming distinct from final disposition votes. By increasingly summarizing a greater proportion of divisive procedural votes, DW-NOMINATE scores may be exaggerating the real substantive polarization of the parties.

II. Avenues for Future Research

In clarifying some of the debates involving polarization, this comprehensive investigation highlights the need for further study in understanding the growing divide between the parties in the U.S. Congress. This book ends with four recommendations for future study.

Fleshing Out the Comprehensive Model

The first recommendation is to fill out the comprehensive model depicted in figure 3.2. Although the model more or less contains all the necessary parts, the relationships among the parts are probably less systematic and a bit more nuanced than the figure suggests. To summarize the figure: (1) districts became more partisan, (2) procedures changed, and (3) the parties inside Congress polarized. This sequence of events is overly simplistic. Some of these trends were undoubtedly

[2] See, for example, Jenkins, Crespin, and Carson (2005), Thorson (1998), Cox and McCubbins (2005), Krehbiel, Meirowitz, and Woon (2005), and Lawrence, Maltzman, and Smith (2006); consult Krehbiel and Woon (2005) for a thoughtful critique of this practice.

happening concurrently. Quite possibly, at various times, the arrows should be going in both directions. A more complete model would more seriously examine the intermediate steps and feedback loops.

Furthermore, as the nexus of the represented and the representatives, Congress has many influences acting upon it, including presidents, the media, and interest groups. This book has not explicitly focused on any of these external influences and their role in polarizing the parties within Congress. Although the model depicted in figure 3.2 may be incomplete, the many anecdotes, political observations, and data analysis show that it provides an accurate skeleton that needs to be fleshed out. Constituencies have become more partisan, and lawmaking has become a more procedural enterprise. Once the relationship with these core features is determined, we can work on integrating the other influences on Congress.

Is Polarization Bad?

Political scientists rarely collectively step out of their role as researchers to become advocates. The publication of the American Political Science Association's "Toward a More Responsible Two-Party System" in 1950 was one such occasion. Although not all political scientists signed on to the report, the association issued a report in hopes of gaining the "attention of everyone interested in politics" (APSA Committee on Political Parties 1950, v).[3] Weak political parties, so their argument went, made the coordination between the political institutions difficult and the passage of a comprehensive governing program almost impossible, both of which severely impaired democratic accountability.

Not only did the report outline the shortfalls of the mid-century parties, but, also, it provided a set of recommendations that would be sure to create more responsible parties. By and large, the political science community either predicted or instigated the change: "By the end of the Twentieth Century, the major party organizations have met many but not all of the recommendations of the APSA Report" (Green and Herrnson 2002, 37). True to the promise of political scientists, the parties inside Congress became more distinct.

[3] The publication of the report garnered lots of opposition. See for example Turner (1951), Ranney (1951), and Ranney and Kendall (1956).

When the report was released (the 81st Congress, 1950), the average Democrat in the House was less than 3 standard deviations away from the average Republican. In the Senate, the distance was less than 2.25 standard deviations. Little changed in the ensuing 25 years. In the 93rd Congress (1973–4), the average Democrat was separated from the average Republican by about 3 standard deviations in the House and 2.5 standard deviations in the Senate. As a result of both polarization between the parties and homogenization within the parties, by the 108th Congress (2003–4), the average party members were separated by more than 5 standard deviations in the House and almost 5 standard deviations in the Senate. In the 93rd Congress, 252 members and 40 senators were ideologically in between the most liberal Republican and the most conservative Democrat in their respective chambers. In the 108th Congress, no members and only 4 senators fell into the overlap region.

Now, political scientists, in claiming that party polarization has drastic consequences, are offering reforms to weaken the party leadership inside Congress. True, no one enjoys the "all-time low" in congressional civility or a House of Representatives that has been called a "snake pit"[4] or "plantation."[5] Although polarized parties may be ugly for the legislative process, they were the prescription for a responsible electorate. No longer are constituents forced to make the complicated vote choice between a liberal Republican and a conservative Democrat. Additionally, voters need not wonder whom to credit or blame for the way that Congress operates. I do not mean to suggest that we should embrace polarized parties, just that we should also consider their attributes before we embark on another set of reforms.

Is the Polarization Real?

If the overwhelming majority of party polarization has occurred on procedural votes, are the parties really polarized? Those answering that question affirmatively would suggest that the substantive divide between the parties is being hashed out in the beginning of the floor

[4] Quote from David Broder, November 16, 2003, "We're Losing Our Sense of Comradeship," *Bay City Times*, p. 10A.

[5] Quote from Hillary Clinton in Michael McAuliff, January 17, 2006, "Hil's King Day Shocker," *New York Daily News*, p. 4.

debate rather than in the middle or the end of the floor debate. They would suggest that if there were no real difference between the parties, the increasingly cumbersome procedures would be a waste of time.

On the other side of the debate are those who think that the parties are distinctive from one another, though not with a particularly big substantive difference. In other words, the parties are more internally homogeneous than the parties of yesterday, although the positions that they propound are more centrist than their predecessors' policy prescription. For example, the debate in trade is no longer taking place at the polar ends of isolation versus integration; rather the debate is taking place some place in the middle between free traders and fair traders.

Little of the analysis inside this book can speak to this important debate. In order to get at this question, scholars will have to dig deep inside the substance of legislation and the preferred policies of the respective parties. It is exceedingly difficult to answer the question of real versus imagined polarization with a large-N study – the analysis must be much more nuanced and qualitative.

A Theory of Polarization?

This book outlines a comprehensive argument for the polarization between the parties in the U.S. Congress during the last quarter of the twentieth century. It is likely that this explanation is restricted to this time period. It is also possible that previously polarized periods in congressional history might also have at their core the two-step processes of electoral changes followed by institutional changes. In order for this two-step process to become a theory of polarization, it must be tested across different historical periods.

Although the parties of today may be highly polarized, they are not as polarized as the parties at the turn of the last century. Following the electoral upheaval of the 1890s, the parties began a more than 50-year period of roll call voting convergence. If the two-step process of party polarization that I use to explain the current period were a time-independent theory of party polarization, it should also be able to explain the polarization of the parties in the post-Reconstruction period and the convergence of the parties in the first three-quarters of the twentieth century. I suspect that further data analysis on these lines will suggest that the current period is not nearly as exceptional as the politicians, pundits, and scholars think it is.

When Senator Pat Leahy recalled his passing of the 10,000-vote milestone in the Senate, he explained: "When somebody asked me about those votes, whether they were all important, I said: No, a lot of them were merely procedural votes that we all cast."[6] This study of party polarization in Congress suggests that Leahy is simultaneously factually correct and interpretatively wrong. True, many of those votes – in fact, an increasing number of those votes – are procedural. He is false, though, in claiming that those votes can be easily dismissed as "merely procedural." For better or worse, procedures in modern law making are increasingly frequent, increasingly polarizing, and increasingly consequential.

[6] Congress, Senate, 106th Congress, 2nd session, *Congressional Record* (29 March 2000): S1872.

Bibliography

Abramowitz, Alan, Brad Alexander, and Matthew Gunning. 2006. "Incumbency, Redistricting, and the Decline of Competition in U.S. House Elections." *Journal of Politics* 68 (Feb.): 75–88.

Abramowitz, Alan, and Kyle L. Saunders. 1998. "Ideological Realignment in the U.S. Electorate." *Journal of Politics* 60 (Aug.): 634–52.

Aldrich, John H. 1995. *Why Parties? The Origins and Transformation of Political Parties in America*. Chicago: University of Chicago Press.

Aldrich, John H., and David W. Rohde. 2001. "The Logic of Conditional Party Government: Revisiting the Electoral Connection," in *Congress Reconsidered*, 7th Edition, Lawrence C. Dodd and Bruce I. Oppenheimer, eds. Washington, D.C.: CQ Press.

American Political Science Association. 1950. "The Need for Greater Party Responsibility," *American Political Science Review* 44:15–36.

Ansolabehere, Stephen, James M. Snyder, and Charles Stewart, III. 2001. "Candidate Positioning in US House Elections." *American Journal of Political Science* 45 (Jan.): 136–59.

Arnold, R. Douglas. 1990. *The Logic of Congressional Action*. New Haven, CT: Yale University Press.

Asher, Herbert B. 1973. "The Learning of Legislative Norms." *American Political Science Review* 67 (Jun.): 499–513.

Asher, Herbert B., and Herbert F. Weisberg. 1978. "Voting Change in Congress: Some Dynamic Perspectives on an Evolutionary Process." *American Journal of Political Science* 22 (May): 391–425.

Bailey, Stephen K. 1959. *The Condition of Our National Political Parties*. New York: Fund for the Republic.

Barone, Michael, with Richard E. Cohen. 2005. *The Almanac of American Politics. The National Journal*, Washington, D.C.

Barone, Michael, Grant Ujifusa, and Douglas Matthews. 1972. *The Almanac of American Politics*. Boston: Gambit.

Bartels, Larry M. 1991. "Constituency Opinion and Congressional Policy Making: The Reagan Defense Build Up." *American Political Science Review* 85 (Jun.): 457–74.

Binder, Sarah. 1997. *Minority Rights, Majority Rule: Partisanship and the Development of Congress*. New York: Cambridge University Press.

Binder, Sarah. 2004. "The Limits of Senatorial Courtesy." *Legislative Studies Quarterly* 29 (Feb.): 5–22.

Binder, Sarah, and Steven S. Smith. 1997. *Politics or Principle? Filibustering in the United States Senate*. Washington, D.C.: Brookings Institution Press.

Bishop, Bill. 2004. "A Steady Slide Toward a More Partisan Union." *Austin American-Statesman*, May 30, A1 and A8.

Bond, Jon R., Kristin Campbell, and James B. Cottrill. 2001. "The Puzzle of Constituency Diversity Revisited: Conditional Effects of District Diversity on Competition in Congressional Elections." Paper read at Annual Meeting of the Southern Political Science Association, Atlanta.

Brady, David. 1978. "Critical Elections, Congressional Parties and Clusters of Policy Change." *British Journal of Political Science* 8: 79–99.

Brady, David W. 1991. *Critical Elections and Congressional Policy Making*. Stanford, CA: Stanford University Press.

Brady, David, and Naomi Lynn. 1973. "Switched-Seat Congressional Districts: Their Effect on Party Voting and Public Policy." *American Journal of Political Science* 17 (Aug.): 528–43.

Brady, David, and Barbara Sinclair. 1984. "Building Majorities for Policy Changes in the House of Representatives." *Journal of Politics* 46 (Nov.): 1033–60.

Brady, David W., and Craig Volden. 1998. *Revolving Gridlock: Politics and Policy from Carter to Clinton*. Boulder, CO: Westview Press.

Brady, David W., John F. Cogan, Brian Gaines, and R. Douglas Rivers. 1996. "The Perils of Presidential Support: How the Republicans Captured the House." *Political Behavior* 18 (Dec.): 345–68.

Brewer, Mark D., Mack D. Mariani, and Jeffrey M. Stonecash. 2002. "Northern Democrats and Party Polarization in the U.S. House." *Legislative Studies Quarterly* 27 (Aug.): 423–44.

Broder, David. 1972. *The Party's Over: The Failure of Politics in America*. New York: Harper and Row.

Broder, David. 2001. "Unnoticed Redistricting to Change Politics for Decade." *The Bay City Times*, October 21, p. 9A.

Burnham, Walter. 1970. *Critical Elections and the Mainspring of American Politics*. New York: W.W. Norton.

Burns, James MacGregor. 1963. *The Deadlock of Democracy*. Englewood Cliffs, NJ: Prentice-Hall.

Burstein, Paul. 1978. "A New Method for Measuring Legislative Content and Change." *Sociological Methods and Research* 6:337–65.

Burstein, Paul. 1980. "Attitudinal Demographic and Electoral Components of Legislative Change: Senate Voting on Civil Rights." *Sociology and Social Research* 64:221–35.

Cain, Bruce, John Ferejohn, and Morris Fiorina. 1987. *The Personal Vote: Constituency Service and Electoral Independence.* Cambridge, MA: Harvard University Press.

Carson, Jamie, Michael H. Crespin, Charles J. Finocchiaro, and David W. Rohde. 2007. "Redistricting and Party Polarization in the U.S. House of Representatives." American Politics Research 35 (Nov.): 878–904.

Clapp, Charles. 1963. *The Congressman: His Work As He Sees It.* Garden City, NY: Anchor Books.

Clausen, Aage R. 1973. *How Congressmen Decide: A Policy Focus.* New York: St. Martin's Press.

Coleman, John J. 1997. "The Decline and Resurgence of Congressional Party Conflict." *Journal of Politics* 59 (Feb.): 165–84.

Collie, Melissa P., and John Lyman Mason. 2000. "The Electoral Connection Between Party and Constituency Reconsidered: Evidence from the U.S. House of Representatives, 1972–1994," in David W. Brady, John F. Cogan, and Morris P. Fiorina, eds. *Continuity and Change in House Elections.* Stanford, CA: Stanford University Press.

Combs, Jerald A. 1970. *The Jay Treaty: Political Battleground of the Founding Fathers.* Berkeley: The University of California Press.

Congressional Districts in the 1990s: A Portrait of America. 1993. Washington, D.C.: Congressional Quarterly Press.

Converse, Philip. 1964. "The Nature of Belief Systems in Mass Publics," in *Ideology and Discontent*, David Apter, ed. New York: Free Press.

Cook, Charlie. May 3, 2003. "The Senate and House are a Study in Contrasts," *National Journal* 35 (18): 1406.

Cooper, Joseph, and David W. Brady. 1981. "Institutional Context and Leadership Style: The House from Cannon to Rayburn." *American Political Science Review* 75 (June): 411–25.

Cox, Gary W., and Jonathan N. Katz. 2002. *Elbridge Gerry's Salamander: The Electoral Consequences of the Reapportionment Revolution.* New York: Cambridge University Press.

Cox, Gary W., and Mathew D. McCubbins. 1993. *Legislative Leviathan: Party Government in the House.* Berkeley: The University of California Press.

Cox, Gary W., and Mathew D. McCubbins. 2005. *Setting the Agenda: Responsible Party Government in the U.S. House of Representatives.* New York: Cambridge University Press.

Cox, Gary W., and Keith T. Poole. 2002. "On Measuring Partisanship in Roll-Call Voting: The U.S. House of Representatives, 1877–1999." *American Journal of Political Science* 46 (July): 477–89.

Davidson, Roger H., Walter J. Oleszek, and Frances E. Lee. 2008. *Congress and Its Members*, 11th ed. Washington, D.C.: CQ Press.

Den Hartog, Chris, and Nathan W. Monroe. 2008. "Agenda Influence and Tabling Motions in the U.S. Senate" in Jason R. Roberts and David W. Rohde, eds., *Why Not Parties? Party Effects in the U.S. Senate.* Chicago: University of Chicago Press.

Denzau, Arthur, William Riker, and Kenneth Shepsle. 1985. "Farquharson and Fenno: Sophisticated Voting and Home Style." *American Political Science Review* 79 (Dec.): 1117–34.

DiMaggio, Paul, John Evans, and Bethany Bryson. 1996. "Have Americans' Social Attitudes Become More Polarized?" *American Journal of Sociology* 102 (Nov.): 690–755.

Dion, Douglas. 1997. *Turning the Legislative Thumbscrews: Minority Rights and Procedural Change in Legislative Politics.* Ann Arbor: University of Michigan Press.

Downs, Anthony. 1957. *An Economic Theory of Democracy.* New York: Harper and Brothers.

Duncan, Philip D., and Christine C. Lawrence. 1997. *Politics in America 1998: The 105th Congress.* Washington, D.C.: Congressional Quarterly Press.

Edwards, III, George C. and Andrew Barrett. 2000. "Presidential Agenda Setting in Congress," in *Polarized Politics: Congress and the President in a Partisan Era*, Jon R. Bond and Richard Fleisher, eds. Washington, DC: CQ Press.

Edwards III, George C., Andrew Barrett, and Jeffrey Peake. 1997. "The Legislative Impact of Divided Government." *American Journal of Political Science* 41:545–63.

Edwards, Mickey. 2003. "The American Congress." Unpublished manuscript.

Erikson, Robert S., Michael B. MacKuen, and James A. Stimson. 2002. *The Macro Polity.* New York: Cambridge University Press.

Evans, C. Lawrence, and Walter J. Oleszek. 1997. *Congress Under Fire: Reform Politics and the Republican Majority.* Boston: Houghton Mifflin Company.

Evans, C. Lawrence, and Walter J. Oleszek. 2001. "Message Politics and Senate Procedure," in Colton C. Campbell and Nicol C. Rae, eds., *The Contentious Senate: Partisanship, Ideology, and the Myth of Cool Judgment.* New York: Rowman & Littlefield.

Farquharson, Robin. 1969. *Theory of Voting.* New Haven, CT: Yale University Press.

Fenno, Richard F., Jr. 1966. *The Power of the Purse: Appropriations Politics in Congress.* Boston: Little Brown.

Ferejohn, John. 1977. "On the Decline of Competition in Congressional Elections." *American Political Science Review* 71 (Mar.): 166–76.

Fiorina, Morris P. 2006. *Culture War? The Myth of a Polarized America.* 2nd ed. New York: Pearson Longman.

Fiorina, Morris P. 1977. "The Case of the Vanishing Marginals: The Bureaucracy Did It." *American Political Science Review* 71 (Mar.): 177–81.

Fleisher, Richard, and Jon R. Bond. 2000. "Partisanship and the President's Quest for Votes on the Floor of Congress," in Jon R. Bond and Richard Fleisher, eds. *Polarized Politics: Congress and the President in a Partisan Era.* Washington, DC: CQ Press.

Fleisher, Richard, R. Bond. 2004. "The Shrinking Middle in Congress," *British Journal of Politics* 34: 429–51.

Frank, Thomas. 2004. *What's the Matter with Kansas? How Conservatives Won the Heart of America*. New York: A Metropolitan/Owl Book.

Froman, Lewis A., and Randall B. Ripley. 1965. "Conditions for Party Leadership: The Case of the House Democrats." *American Political Science Review* 59 (Mar.): 52–63.

Galston, William A., and Elaine C. Kamarck. October 2005. "The Politics of Polarization." The Third Way Middle Class Project.

Gilmour, John B. 1995. *Strategic Disagreement: Stalemate in American Politics*. Pittsburgh: University of Pittsburgh Press.

Gilmour, John B., and Paul Rothstein. 1994. "Term Limitation in a Dynamic Model of Partisan Balance." *American Journal of Political Science* 38:770–96.

Gimpel, James A., and Jason E. Schuknecht. 2003. *Patchwork Nation: Sectionalism and Political Change in American Politics*. Ann Arbor: University of Michigan Press.

Ginsberg, Benjamin. 1973. "Critical Elections and the Substance of Party Conflict: 1844–1968." *Midwest Journal of Political Science* 16:603–25.

Ginsberg, Benjamin. 1976. "Elections and Public Policy." *American Political Science Review* 70 (Mar.): 41–9.

Giroux, Gregory L. 2001. "Remaps' Clear Trend: Incumbent Protection." *CQ Weekly*, November 3, pp. 2627–32.

Giroux, Gregory L. 2005. "A Line in the Suburban Sand." *CQ Weekly*, June 27, p. 1714.

Green, John C., and Paul S. Herrnson. 2002. "Party Development in the Twentieth Century: Laying the Foundation for Responsible Party Government," in John C. Green and Paul S. Herrnson, eds., *Responsible Partisanship? The Evolution of American Political Parties Since 1950*. Lawrence: University Press of Kansas.

Groseclose, Timothy, and Nolan McCarty. 2001. "The Politics of Blame: Bargaining Before an Audience." *American Journal of Political Science* 45 (Mar.): 100–19.

Hacker, Jacob S., and Paul Pierson. 2005. *Off Center: The Republican Revolution and the Erosion of American Democracy*. New Haven, CT: Yale University Press.

Herrera, Richard. 1992. "The Understanding of Ideological Labels by Political Elites: A Research Note." *Western Political Quarterly* 45 (December): 1021–35.

Herrera, Richard, and Karen Shafer. 2003. "The Influence of Party on the Legislative Process: Constituents are Key." Paper presented at the Annual Meeting of the American Political Science Association.

Hetherington, Marc J. 2001. "Resurgent Mass Partisanship: The Role of Elite Polarization." *American Political Science Review* 95 (Sept.): 619–31.

Hetherington, Marc J. 2005. *Why Trust Matters: Declining Political Trust and the Demise of American Liberalism*. Princeton, NJ: Princeton University Press.

Hibbing, John R., and Elizabeth Theiss-Morse. 1995. *Congress as Public Enemy: Public Attitudes Toward American Political Institutions*. New York: Cambridge University Press.

Hibbing, John R., and Elizabeth Theiss-Morse. 2002. *Stealth Democracy: Americans' Beliefs about How Government Should Work*. New York: Cambridge University Press.

Highton, Benjamin, and Michael S. Rocca. 2005. "Beyond the Roll-Call Arena: The Determinants of Position Taking in Congress." *Political Research Quarterly* 58 (June): 303–16.

Hirsch, Sam. 2003. "The United States of Unrepresentatives: What Went Wrong in the Latest Round of Congressional Redistricting." *Election Law Journal* 2 (Nov.): 179–216.

Jackley, John. 1992. *Hill Rats: Blowing the Lid Off Congress*. Washington, D.C.: Regnery Publishing, Inc.

Jacobson, Gary C. 1987. "Running Scared: Elections and Congressional Politics in the 1980s," in Mathew D. McCubbins and Terry Sullivan, eds. *Congress: Structure and Policy*, pp. xx. New York: Cambridge University Press.

Jacobson, Gary C. 2000. "Party Polarization in National Politics: The Electoral Connection," in Jon R. Bond and Richard Fleisher, eds. *Polarized Politics: Congress and the President in a Partisan Era*. Washington, D.C.: CQ Press.

Jacobson. Gary C. 2004. *The Politics of Congressional Elections*. 6th ed. New York: Pearson Longman.

Jenkins, Jeffery A., Michael H. Crespin, and Jamie L. Carson. 2005. "Parties as Procedural Coalitions in Congress: An Examination of Differing Career Tracks." *Legislative Studies Quarterly* 30 (Aug.): 365–390.

Jones, Charles. 1974. "Speculative Augmentation in Federal Air Pollution Policy-Making." *Journal of Politics* 36 (May): 438–64.

Jones, Charles O. 1968. "Joseph G. Cannon and Howard W. Smith: An Essay on the Limits of Leadership in the House of Representatives." *Journal of Politics* 39 (Aug.): 617–46.

Kessler, Daniel, and Keith Krehbiel. 1996. "Dynamics of Cosponsorship." *American Political Science Review* 90 (Sept.): 555–66.

Key, V.O., Jr. 1961. *Public Opinion and American Democracy*. New York: Knopf.

King, Anthony. 1997. *Running Scared: Why America's Politicians Campaign Too Much and Govern Too Little*. Glencoe, IL: Free Press Publishers.

Kingdon, John W. 1989. *Congressmen's Voting Decisions*. Ann Arbor: University of Michigan Press.

Koger, Gregory. 2003. "Position Taking and Cosponsorship in the U.S. House." *Legislative Studies Quarterly* 28 (May): 225–46.

Krehbiel, Keith. 1995. "Cosponsors and Wafflers from A to Z." *American Journal of Political Science* 39 (Nov.): 906–23.

Krehbiel, Keith. 1998. *Pivotal Politics: A Theory of U.S. Lawmaking.* Chicago: University of Chicago Press.

Krehbiel, Keith, and Adam Meirowitz. 2002. "Minority Rights and Majority Power: Theoretical Consequences of the Motion to Recommit." *Legislative Studies Quarterly* 37 (May): 191–217.

Krehbiel, Keith, and Jonathan Woon. 2005. "Selection Criteria for Roll Call Votes." Paper presented at the Annual Meeting of the American Political Science Association.

Krehbiel, Keith, Adam Meirowitz, and Jonathan Woon. 2005. "Testing of Theories of Lawmaking," in David Austen-Smith and John Duggan, eds., *Essays in Honor of Jeffrey S. Banks*, pp. 249–68. Berlin: Springer.

Krutz, Glen S. 2005. "Issues and Institutions: 'Winnowing' in the U.S. Congress." *American Journal of Political Science* 49 (April): 313–24.

Layman, Geoffrey C., and Thomas M. Carsey. 2002. "Party Polarization and 'Conflict Extension' in the American Electorate." *American Journal of Political Science* 46 (October): 786–802.

Layman, Geoffrey C., Thomas M. Carsey, and Juliana Menasce Horowitz. 2006. "Party Polarization in American Politics: Characteristics, Causes, and Consequences." *Annual Review of Political Science* 9 (June): 83–110.

Lee, Frances. 2008. "Agreeing to Disagree: Agenda Content and Senate Partisanship, 1981–2004." *Legislative Studies Quarterly* 32 (May): 199–222.

Mann, Thomas E., and Norman J. Ornstein. 2006. *The Broken Branch: How Congress Is Failing America and How to Get It Back on Track.* New York: Oxford University Press.

Matthews, Donald. 1960. *U.S. Senators and Their World.* Chapel Hill: University of North Carolina Press.

Mayhew, David R. 1991. *Divided We Govern: Party Control, Lawmaking, and Investigations*, 1946–1990. New Haven, Connecticut: Yale University Press.

Mayhew, David R. 2005. *Divided We Govern: Party Control, Lawmaking, and Investigations*, 1946–2002, 2nd ed. New Haven, Connecticut: Yale University Press.

McCarty, Nolan, Keith Poole, and Howard Rosenthal. 2006. *Polarized America: The Dance of Ideology and Unequal Riches.* Cambridge: Massachusetts Institute of Technology Press.

McClosky, Herbert, Paul J. Hoffman, and Rosemary O'Hara. 1960. "Issue Conflict and Consensus Among Party Leaders and Followers." American Political Science Review 54: 406–427.

Miller, Warren E., and Donald E. Stokes. 1963. "Constituency Influence in Congress." *American Political Science Review* 57: 45–56.

Miller, Warren E., and M. Kent Jennings. 1986. *Parties in Transition: A Longitudinal Study of Party Elites and Party Supporters.* New York: Russell Sage Foundation.

Ornstein, Norman J. 2002. "Why Close Races Ruin Politics." *New York Times*, November 4, p. 23.

Oppenheimer, Bruce I. 2005. "Deep Red and Blue Congressional Districts" in Lawrence C. Dodd and Bruce I. Oppenheimer, eds., *Congress Reconsidered*, 8th ed. Washington, D.C.: CQ Press.

Pearson, Kathryn. 2005. "Party Discipline in the Contemporary Congress: Rewarding Loyalty in Theory and in Practice." Ph.D. diss. University of California at Berkeley.

Poole, Keith T., and Howard Rosenthal. 1984. "The Polarization of American Politics." *Journal of Politics* 46 (Nov.): 1061–79.

Poole, Keith T., and Howard Rosenthal. 1997. *Congress: A Political-Economic History of Roll Call Voting*. New York: Oxford University Press.

Rae, Nicol C., and Colton C. Campbell. 2001. "Party Politics and Ideology in the Contemporary Senate" in Colton C. Campbell and Nicol C. Rae, eds., *The Contentious Senate: Partisanship, Ideology, and the Myth of Cool Judgment*. Lanham, MD: Rowman & Littlefield Publishers, Inc.

Ranney, Austin. 1951. "Toward a More Responsible Two-Party System: A Commentary." *American Political Science Review* 44 (June): 488–99.

Ranney, Austin, and Willmoore Kendall. 1956. *Democracy and the American Party System*. New York: Harcourt Brace.

Riker, William H. 1986. *The Art of Political Manipulation*. New Haven, CT: Yale University Press.

Roberts, Jason M., and Steven S. Smith. 2003. "Procedural Contexts, Party Strategy, and Conditional Party Voting in the U.S. House of Representatives, 1971–2000." *American Journal of Political Science* 47 (Apr.): 305–17.

Rohde, David W. 1991. *Parties and Leaders in the Postreform House*. Chicago: The University of Chicago Press.

Rohde, David W., and John H. Aldrich. 2001. "The Logic of Conditional Party Government: Revisiting the Electoral Connection," in Lawrence C. Dodd and Bruce I. Oppenheimer, eds., *Congress Reconsidered*, 7th ed. Washington, D.C.: CQ Press.

Rothenberg, Stuart. 2002. "Redistricting Shortfall May Not Cost GOP House Majority." *Roll Call*, October 21, p. A-6.

Rothenberg, Stuart. 2001. "Sparing Incumbents Won't Improve Tone on Capitol Hill." *Roll Call*, November 29, p. 6.

Schickler, Eric. 2001. *Disjointed Pluralism: Institutional Innovation and the Development of the U.S. Congress*. Princeton, NJ: Princeton University Press.

Schickler, Eric, Eric McGhee, and John Sides. 2003. "Remaking the House and Senate: Personal Power, Ideology, and the 1970s Reforms." *Legislative Studies Quarterly* 28 (Aug.): 297–332.

Shepsle, Kenneth A. 1989. "The Changing Textbook Congress," in *Can the Government Govern?* John E. Chubb and Paul E. Peterson, eds. Washington, DC: The Brookings Institution.

Shepsle, Kenneth A., and Barry R. Weingast. 1987. "The Institutional Foundations of Committee Power." *American Political Science Review* 81 (Mar.): 85–104.

Shipan, Charles R., and William R. Lowry. 2001. "Environmental Policy and Party Divergence in Congress." *Political Research Quarterly* 54 (Jun.): 245–63.

Sinclair, Barbara. 1977. "Party Realignment and the Transformation of the Political Agenda: The House of Representatives, 1925–1938." *American Political Science Review* 71 (Sept.): 940–53.

Sinclair, Barbara. 1982. *Congressional Realignment* 1925–1978. Austin: University of Texas Press.

Sinclair, Barbara. 2000. *Unorthodox Lawmaking: New Legislative Processes in the U.S. Congress*, 2nd ed. Washington, D.C.: CQ Press.

Sinclair, Barbara. 2006. *Party Wars: Polarization and the Politics of National Policy Making*. Norman: University of Oklahoma Press.

Smith, Steven S. 1989. *Call to Order: Floor Politics in the House and Senate*. Washington, D.C.: The Brookings Institution.

Snyder, James M. 1992. "Artificial Extremism in Interest Group Ratings." *Legislative Studies Quarterly* 17 (Aug.): 319–45.

Stonecash, Jeffrey M., Mark D. Brewer, and Mark D. Mariani. 2003. *Diverging Parties: Social Change, Realignment, and Party Polarization*. Boulder, CO: Westview Press.

Sundquist, James. 1988. "Needed: A Political Theory for the New Era of Coalition Government in the United States." *Political Science Quarterly* 103: 613–35.

Talbert, Jeffery C., and Matthew Potoski. 2002. "Setting the Legislative Agenda: The Dimensional Structure of Bill Cosponsoring and Floor Voting." *Journal of Politics* 64 (Aug.): 864–91.

Theriault, Sean M. 2004. "Public Pressure and Punishment in the Politics of Congressional Pay Raises." *American Politics Research* 32 (Jul.): 444–64.

Theriault, Sean M. 2005. *The Power of the People: Congressional Competition, Public Attention, and Voter Retribution*. Columbus: Ohio State University Press.

Theriault, Sean M. 2006. "Party Polarization in the U.S. Congress: Member Replacement and Member Adaptation." *Party Politics* 12 (4): 483–503.

Thorson, Gregory R. 1998. "Divided Government and the Passage of Partisan Legislation, 1947–1990." *Political Research Quarterly* 51 (Sept.): 751–64.

Tufte, Edward R. 1973. "The Relationship Between Seats and Votes in Two-Party Systems." *American Political Science Review* 67 (Jun.): 540–54.

Turner, Julius. 1951. "Responsible Parties: A Dissent from the Floor." *American Political Science Revew* 45:143–52.

Turner, Julius, and Edward Schneier, Jr. 1970. *Party and Constituency: Pressures on Congress*. Rev. ed. Baltimore, Maryland: Johns Hopkins Press.

Van Houweling, Paul P. 2003. "Legislators' Personal Policy Preferences and Partisan Legislative Organization." Ph.D. diss., Harvard University.

Weingast, Barry R. 1992. "Fighting Fire with Fire," in *The Post-Reform Congress*, Roger H. Davidson, ed. New York: St. Martin's Press.

Wildavsky, Aaron. 1965. "The Goldwater Phenomenon: Jurists, Politicians, and the Future of the Two-Party System." *Review of Politics* 27 (July):386–413.

Wilson, James Q. 1962. *The Amateur Democrat.* Chicago: University of Chicago Press.

Wilson, Rick K., and Cheryl D. Young. 1997. "Cosponsorship in the U.S. Congress." *Legislative Studies Quarterly* 22:25–44.

Wilson, Woodrow. 1956 (originally published in 1885). *Congressional Government: A Study in American Politics.* New York: Meridian Books.

Wilkerson, John. 1991. *The Evolution of Strategy: A Case Study of Congressional Pay Raises.* Ph.D. diss., University of Rochester.

Wlezien, Christopher. 1995. "The Public as Thermostat: Dynamics of Preferences for Spending." *American Journal of Political Science* 39 (Nov.): 981–1000.

Zone, Rob. 2002. "Why So Many Races Lack One Thing: Competition." *The Seattle Times*, October 13, p. A1.

Index

Advance Praise for *Party Polarization in Congress*

"Sean Theriault has done something far too rare in the study of American politics: provided truly synthetic account of a vital political development, the dramatic polarization of Congres over the last generation. Mixing rigorous analysis with revealing stories and careful consideratio of alternative explanations, Theriault's book is a one-stop source for those wishing to understan why Republicans and Democrats just can't get along in the modern Congress."

– Jacob S. Hacke
University of California, Berkele

"Sean Theriault gracefully integrates the many explanations that have been offered for th increasing party polarization evident in the U.S. Congress. He compellingly argues that a congressional districts become more homogeneous, party leaders become stronger and thu better positioned to employ procedural strategies that exacerbate party polarization. All told *Party Polarization in Congress* is a creative, synthetic, and extremely valuable treatment of one o the most intensely studied topics in modern American politics."

– John R. Hibbing
University of Nebraska-Lincoln

"Probably no topic has received more attention from analysts of American politics over the last couple of decades than partisan polarization. In this book, Sean Theriault has substantially advanced our understanding of the many facets of that phenomenon. He deals with the electoral sources of polarization, including the roles of redistricting, geographic sorting, and party activists. Theriault also assesses the relationship between these electoral roots and the evolution of legislative procedures and their effect in turn on elite polarization in both the House and Senate. This is an exceptional book, valuable and accessible to congressional researchers and undergraduate students alike."

– David Rohde,
Duke University

Sean M. Theriault received his Ph.D. in political science from Stanford University in 2001. An Associate Professor at the University of Texas at Austin, he has received numerous teaching awards. His first book, *The Power of the People: Congressional Competition, Media Attention, and Public Retribution*, was published in 2005. He has published a number of articles on a variety of subjects including congressional retirement, the Louisiana Purchase, and redistricting commissions. Professor Theriault resides with his partner, Anthony Bristol, in Houston and Austin, Texas.

Cover art: © iStockphoto
Cover design by Logan Johnson